KT-463-075

DISPOSED OF
BY LIBRARY
HOUSE OF LORDS

GOVERNING WITH JUDGES:
CONSTITUTIONAL POLITICS IN EUROPE

Governing with Judges

Constitutional Politics in Europe

ALEC STONE SWEET

OXFORD

UNIVERSITY PRESS

OXFORD

UNIVERSITY PRESS

Great Clarendon Street, Oxford OX2 6DP

Oxford University Press is a department of the University of Oxford.
It furthers the University's objective of excellence in research, scholarship,
and education by publishing worldwide in

Oxford New York

Athens Auckland Bangkok Bogotá Buenos Aires Calcutta
Cape Town Chennai Dar es Salaam Delhi Florence Hong Kong Istanbul
Karachi Kuala Lumpur Madrid Melbourne Mexico City Mumbai
Nairobi Paris São Paulo Singapore Taipei Tokyo Toronto Warsaw

and associated companies in Berlin Ibadan

Oxford is a registered trade mark of Oxford University Press
in the UK and in certain other countries

Published in the United States
by Oxford University Press Inc., New York

© Alec Stone Sweet 2000

The moral rights of the author have been asserted

Database right Oxford University Press (maker)

First published 2000

All rights reserved. No part of this publication may be reproduced,
stored in a retrieval system, or transmitted, in any form or by any means,
without the prior permission in writing of Oxford University Press,
or as expressly permitted by law, or under terms agreed with the appropriate
reprographics rights organizations. Enquiries concerning reproduction
outside the scope of the above should be sent to the Rights Department,
Oxford University Press, at the address above

You must not circulate this book in any other binding or cover
and you must impose this same condition on any acquirer

British Library Cataloguing in Publication Data

Data available

Library of Congress Cataloging in Publication Data

Stone Sweet, Alec.
Governing with judges: constitutional politics in Europe / Alec Stone Sweet.
Includes bibliographical references and index.
1. Constitutional courts—Europe. 2. Judicial power—Europe.
3. Law and politics. I. Title
KJC5456.S757 2000 347.4'012—dc21 99–44358
ISBN 0–19–829730–0
ISBN 0–19–829771–8 (Pbk.)

1 3 5 7 9 10 8 6 4 2

Typeset by Hope Services (Abingdon) Ltd.
Printed in Great Britain
on acid-free paper by
Biddles Ltd.,
Guildford & King's Lynn

For Louis, Martin, and Yves,
with gratitude

PREFACE

In this book I set out to explain certain deep transformations in governance that have resulted from the establishment of enforceable constitutions in Europe. At a more abstract level, the book is about the sources and consequences of the construction of judicial power, which I see as symptomatic of even more generic social processes. Most important, third-party dispute resolution and rule-making constitutes one, often privileged, mechanism of adapting rule systems to the needs and purposes of those who live under them. I have drawn connections between my concerns and the concerns of public law and comparative political science. But the book's broader purpose is to demonstrate why dispute resolution and judicial rule-making are often basic to 'politics-within-institutions', and to more general processes of institutionalization and political change.

With strong encouragement from my editors, I have kept this book short. Although the text is now longer than we originally planned, it remains incomplete (and, to my mind, inadequate) in at least three important respects. First, there is no sustained discussion of federalism, which has always been central to constitutional politics in Germany, and is increasingly so in Spain. I focus far more attention on the adjudication of constitutional rights. Second, I relegate the European Convention of Human Rights to a sentence and a footnote, despite the Convention's growing impact on the work of the judiciary. Although social scientists have produced several books on European constitutional courts in recent years, it is unfortunate that none of these examines the Convention with any seriousness. In my case, an even cursory discussion of the regime (which, with reference to the operation of national judiciaries, raises a set of enormously complex issues) was impossible, given space limitations. Third, I do not elaborate a theory of constitutional interpretation, although the makings of such a theory are implied. Instead, I typically infer, from patterns revealed as case law accretes, what constitutional judges are doing as they resolve constitutional disputes, given the theory of constitutional politics that underlies my approach.

My editors also wanted a book that would both be scholarly and appropriate for use in classrooms at the advanced undergraduate and graduate levels. In writing the text, I assumed that the average reader would not have any special, prior knowledge of law or judging or constitutions. I know, however, that at times too much has been packed into too little space.

ACKNOWLEDGEMENTS

I am grateful to a great many people and organizations for their support.

For an American, this kind of research is massively dependent on support for travel and living in Europe. The German Marshall Fund (1991–2), the University of California Institute for Global Conflict and Cooperation (1994–5), the National Endowment for the Humanities (1995–6), the National Science Foundation (1996–8), and the US Council for European Studies (1994–6) provided such funding. In addition, Louis Favoreu and the University of Aix-en-Provence (France), Michael Pretina and the Camargo Foundation (Cassis, France), Yves Mény and the Robert Schuman Centre of the European University Institute (Florence, Italy), Sally Kenney and the Obermann Center of Advanced Studies (University of Iowa), Giuseppe di Federico and the Institute for Research on Judicial Systems (Bologna, Italy), and the Max Planck Institute for International and Comparative Law (Heidelberg, Germany) arranged or granted resident fellowships. I owe an enormous debt to William Schonfeld, the Dean of the School of Social Sciences, the University of California, Irvine. Dean Schonfeld always appears eager to approve my requests for leave, and pretends to be pleased to see me return.

The book was written in France and Italy, over a six-month period beginning in the Summer of 1998. In France, Louis and Marie-Odile Favoreu (Aix-en-Provence), Manuel and Aurélia Mestre (Paris), Joseph 'Pépino' Mignon (Roquevaire), Raphael Perez and Virginie Massoni (Cassis), and Simone Lemaire and Vlad Cargiale (Busset) all provided gracious hospitality, with space to write and gorgeous views. In Italy, I thank Yves Mény (Florence) for the same.

Finally, the theoretical materials presented in the book developed only gradually, partly as a result of doing the empirical research, and partly as a result of conversations with friends and colleagues. I have been heavily influenced by ongoing discussions with a small group of good friends about the nature and explanatory status of institutions. For these, I wish to thank, in particular, James Caporaso, Harry Eckstein, Neil Fligstein, Ron Jepperson, Paul Pierson, and Wayne Sandholtz. It has been a great advantage for me that these discussions so rarely focus on law and courts.

I am grateful to Martha Lewis, Martin Shapiro, Michel Troper, Georg Vanberg, and Mary Volcansek for reading the first draft of the manuscript. Their comments provoked many important revisions. The problems, errors, and omissions that remain are due to my own limitations and obstinance.

The book would never have been completed without the help of Rachel Cichowski, my graduate student-research assistant during this period. I have not taught her much, except by way of example. As Ms Cichowski begins work on her doctoral dissertation, she will surely avoid the many pitfalls from which she has patiently extricated me.

Last, I want to give special thanks to Louis Favoreu, Yves Mény, and Martin Shapiro, each of whom I met, at roughly the same time, as a graduate student in the latter half of the 1980s. In too many ways to detail, this book owes its existence to them.

CONTENTS

LIST OF FIGURES

LIST OF TABLES

1

Norms, Dispute Resolution, and Judicialization

Parliamentary supremacy, understood by most students of European politics to be a constitutive principle of European politics, has lost its vitality.
After a polite, nostalgic nod across the Channel to Westminster, we can
declare it dead. In contrast to central tenets of the British parliamentary
model (and of traditional Continental state theory), the 'new constitutionalism' has it that legislation must conform to the dictates of the constitution—as interpreted by constitutional courts—or be invalid. The work of
governments and parliaments is today structured by an ever-expanding
web of constitutional constraints. In a word, European policy-making has
been *judicialized*. Constitutional judges routinely intervene in legislative
processes, establishing limits on law-making behaviour, reconfiguring
policy-making environments, even drafting the precise terms of legislation.
The development of European constitutionalism has also infected the
European Union. The European Court of Justice, the constitutional court
of the Union, has fashioned a kind of supranational constitution, and this
law binds governments and the parliaments they control.

   Constitutional judges also participate in the work of the judiciary. As
they have consolidated their role as authoritative interpreters of the constitution, their capacity to shape the greater legal system has been revealed.
European judiciaries now must take into account the dictates of constitutional 'jurisprudence'—the corpus of case law produced by the constitutional court—which is formally binding upon them as higher law. As this
case law has expanded in scope and content, once relatively autonomous
legal domains (such as penal, administrative, and contract law) have been
gradually but meaningfully placed under the tutelage and supervision of
constitutional judges. Consequently, judicial processes and litigation
strategies, but also the teaching of law and legal scholarship, are being
transformed. In short, the process of *constitutionalizing* European law has
not only begun, it is irreversible.

This book provides an account of the impact of constitutional courts on law and politics in France, Germany, Italy, Spain, and the European Union. A number of introductory remarks will make clearer what this book is and what it is not.

INTRODUCTION

Until recently, little social science research on European constitutions or courts had been produced. The reasons for this neglect have been discussed elsewhere (Stone 1992*a*: introduction; Shapiro and Stone 1994*b*). In the past decade, comparative political science has been in the process of rediscovering law and courts, and especially constitutional judicial review. *Comparative Political Studies* (Shapiro and Stone *eds.* 1994*a*), *Policy Studies Journal* (Jackson and Tate *eds.* 1990), and *West European Politics* (Volcansek *ed.* 1992) have each published special issues comparative judicial and constitutional politics; and books on the 'global expansion of judicial power' (Tate and Vallinder *eds.* 1995), and on the constitutional courts of France (Stone 1992*a*), Germany (Kommers 1989, 1997), and Italy (Volcansek in press) have appeared.

Social scientists working in this field face a general problem that I will address in three ways. First, no coherent body of theorizing on these institutions exists. The central conceptual frameworks that structure this book are of my own design. These frameworks appear in relatively general and abstract forms, disguising the fact that they were developed only gradually, from the interpretation of accumulated data.

Second, the comparative study of judicial politics is hampered by powerful, but arcane and unproductive, interdisciplinary boundaries. Public law political scientists are overwhelmingly Americanists, who rarely do comparative research. Comparative politics scholars, even in their studies of government institutions and policy-making, mostly ignore law and courts. The field of international relations has all but banished international law from its midst. In Europe, political scientists leave research on law and courts to law professors, while legal scholars have organized themselves into insular domains (e.g. civil, penal, administrative, constitutional, European, international), and manifest a common resistance to perspectives 'external' to the law.

This project, however, is inherently interdisciplinary. The subject matter *per force* spills across the normal boundaries that divide scholarly disciplines and subfields. The concerns of comparative politics, public law, democratic political theory, international relations, and international law are all implicated, and these concerns inform and are addressed by this research. Still, the book cannot provide a comprehensive treatment of all of the topics raised: European legal and political systems, public policy, jurisprudence, intrajudicial interaction, regional integration, legal scholarship, constitutional political economy, and so forth. Nonetheless, I do provide a theory of constitutional politics, and attempt to map, as systematically as is now possible, how the activities of constitutional courts impinge on these topics.

Third, European constitutional politics—the reciprocal impact of constitutional rule-making, legislating, and judging—constitute a multidimensional phenomenon that often escapes easy characterization in terms commonly employed by political scientists and legal scholars. The normal distinctions between judicial interpretation and legislating, for example, or the work of the constitutional judge and that of the ordinary judge, obscure more than they clarify. To take just one example, one inevitable result of the constitutional politics theorized and described in this book is that constitutional judges will increasingly behave as sophisticated legislators, and that legislators will act as constitutional judges do.

In the rest of the chapter, I lay out the approach that underlies this book. I then survey several perspectives on the politics of constitutional law that are employed or addressed, at various points, in subsequent chapters. I am aware that much more could have been written about the nature of norms, dispute resolution, and judicial rule-making, and about the relationship between rules and strategic behaviour, and that what is presented here will strike some as inadequate or idiosyncratic.

RULES, DISPUTE RESOLUTION, STRATEGIC BEHAVIOUR

Under certain conditions, the continuous settlement of disputes by a third-party dispute resolver will construct, and then manage over time, specific causal linkages between the strategic behaviour of individuals and the development of rule systems. To the extent that individuals, interacting in any given social setting, regularly refer the conflicts that arise among them to a third party for resolution, and to the extent that the dispute resolver effectively resolves these conflicts while giving reasons for decisions taken, society will gradually be placed under the authority of the dispute resolver or, more precisely, under the authority of an evolving set of behavioural norms, as managed by the third party.

These statements probably do more to confuse than to instruct at this point, since they are presented abstractly, without reference to constitutional law and politics *per se*, or to hypotheses about outcomes in any specific social setting. To make sense, the statements also depend on common understandings of rather complex concepts and ideas, yet the words used to convey these ideas are often employed in different ways by social scientists.

By 'strategic behaviour', I mean how individual actors pursue their own self-interest, by way of decisions and other actions that they take, in a social context. The conception adopted is broadly congruent with basic precepts of rational choice approaches to politics, namely, that people tend to choose those courses of conduct that will best enhance their well-being, given their own established preferences and the nature of the social constraints that they face. 'Rule system' refers in part to these social constraints and, more broadly, to the institutional—or normative—structure in place in any given social setting. Such structures embody those behavioural norms that enable individuals to interact with one another. Rule systems sustain the richness of human interaction in society, and human interaction powerfully tends to reproduce rule systems (Jepperson 1991; March and Olsen 1989; North 1990).

Human beings possess an extraordinary capacity not only to construct rules, but to learn, use, and thrive under, diverse sets of them. Consider a student who drives to school in the morning, attends classes and prepares for examinations until lunch, plays basketball in the afternoon and guitar in a rock band in the evening. In doing so, she has mastered, and regularly enacts, multiple sets of general, relatively formal, *rules*: of the road, an educational institution, a sport, and a specific musical grammar that sets her preferred genre of music apart from others. Further, general rules tend to beget more specific, relatively informal, *behaviours* which, once scripted as regular practices, may come to be accepted to those involved as 'normal', perhaps even enactments of rules. Thus: the student shoots more when she plays with some of her team-mates, and passes more when she plays with others; she studies harder as examination time approaches.

Although rules and behaviour are often tightly interdependent, social scientists often separate them for analytical purposes. One simple way of doing so, is to conceive of each as a *level of analysis*, or domain of inquiry, that is relatively autonomous from the other. For our purposes, the behaviour of individuals can be said to constitute the *micro-level* of analysis. In focusing on this level, we observe people making decisions, acting purposively, interacting with one another, and so on. The social structure in which this behaviour takes place constitutes the *macro-level* of analysis. When we pay attention to this level, we observe the normative systems that give meaning to human action. Simplifying, most social scientists give priority to one level or the other. Some look at the world from the 'bottom-up', noting that individuals, in egoistically pursuing their own interests, produce and provoke change in their institutional environment (the normative structure). Others take a 'top-down' view, seeing that rule systems condition how individuals conceive of themselves in society, allowing them, among other things, to form and pursue their interests. Neither perspective, on its own, can provide a very satisfactory picture of what is happening, which is why, in actual research, some blending of perspectives almost always occurs.

I will presently try to show how third-party dispute resolution can effectively bind together rules and behaviour into a system of reciprocal influence. Beforehand, we need to bring politics—a concern for authority relations and power—into the mix.

Norms, Interests, Power

Norms, what I will also call rules, are the basic building blocks of society. Legal norms are a subset of social norms, but let's begin by examining norms that are not formally produced and applied by the political and legal system. The word, 'norm', has two common meanings. First, the word refers to stable patterns of behaviour, as in phrases that begin: 'it is the norm that . . .'. The statements—'the Franklin children go to bed at 8:00 p.m.,' 'students study harder as examination day approaches', and 'the English shake hands when they meet, the Japanese bow'—are *normative*, to the extent that they are accurate renderings of what most often occurs in these particular contexts (i.e. what is *normal*). Second, the word refers to principled human behaviour, that is, to the kinds of behaviour either encouraged or discouraged in a community. The statements—'do unto others as you would have them do unto you', 'come to class on time, prepared to discuss the readings', and 'do not eat meat on Friday' (or 'never eat pork')—are *normative* not because they depict how one behaves (as in the first meaning of the word), but how one ought to, or must, behave. We can call the first class of normative statements 'descriptive', because they describe actual behaviour, and the second class 'prescriptive', because they prescribe behaviour.

On closer examination, one notices that the two meanings are often knotted together, and nearly impossible to unravel. The relationship can be expressed in this way: to the extent that an individual or community generally complies with prescriptive norms, we can rephrase the statement in descriptive terms. If my students generally do come to class on time, prepared to discuss the readings, and if Jews and Muslims generally do respect the prohibition against eating pork, then we can easily shift from a statement of *what ought to be* to *what is*. Further, as a matter of causality, the prescription may have had something to do with producing, and reproducing over time, the pattern of actual behaviour observed. The fact that the Franklins go to bed early may be related to their belief in the legitimacy (or inherent goodness) of the prescription, 'early to bed, early to rise, makes a person healthy, wealthy, and wise'. And ritualistic handshaking and bowing is part of a complex system of courtesy with ancient roots. Social norms assign meanings to behaviour, providing us with guidance about how one ought to behave in a particular context, and generating expectations about how others will behave.

Normative structures underpin all established social settings and human communities. Indeed, from a 'top down', macro-level perspective, society and rule systems appear to be organically linked, even one and the same thing. Human relationships evolve as the structure of rules that helps individuals determine how they should behave evolves. Although important disagreements divide them, cultural theorists (Eckstein 1988; Wildavsky 1987), institutionalists and organizational sociologists (March and Olsen 1989; Powell and Dimaggio *eds.* 1991), social constructivists (Giddens 1984; Onuf 1989), and social psychologists (Rosenberg 1995) all take the next step, arguing that our very identities—who we are, and how we comprehend our goals and express ourselves—are socially constituted. If they are right, then the study of norms and their development is the study of social power, and thus the study of 'politics', in a very broad and profound sense.

The causal arrows may also point in the other direction. Rational choice and game theoretic approaches to politics typically imagine hypothetical, pre-normative human beings, thus denying the naturalness and ubiquity of rule systems, and then seek to uncover the conditions under which people are likely to create society. Individuals are conceived primarily as bearers of interests or preferences; in interactions with others, they behave 'rationally' to the extent that they pursue—relentlessly and egoistically— those outcomes that best substantiate their interests. Politics, whether conflictual or cooperative, are constituted by the interactions of human beings pursuing different goals, given their own capacities and resources. Norms, stable systems of rules, can emerge from these interactions, but these structures tend to reflect how interests and resources in any group of human beings are organized.

In order to understand how normative order is produced in the first place, rationalists argue, we will have to take into account factors that are outside normative structures *per se*, namely, the distribution of preferences and relatively capacities among a given set of individual actors. If students actually do come to class on time, prepared to discuss the readings, it may be because they believe the rule to be a good one. But it also may be that I, in my role as professor: (1) have declared my interest in this outcome, by announcing a rule; and (2) possess the (institutional) power to penalize students who do not conform to it. In seeking to avoid punishment, students act in accordance with my preferences. The Franklin children may go to bed early because their parents command this behaviour and have the resources to punish non-compliance. Religious injunctions and requirements of 'common courtesy', too, can be analysed as mechanisms of establishing social power and control. Viewed in this way, the rule systems that underpin social settings appear as artefacts—they are revelatory—of power relations. Rarely 'neutral', they serve the interests of some at the expense of others.

Many of the most important debates concerning the nature of the relationship between law and politics are arguments about the extent to which macro-structures, such as the law, are autonomous from an underlying social structure of power and interests, the micro setting of politics (Smith 1988; Stumph *et al.* 1983; Burgess 1993). In my opinion, these arguments are irresolvable. Empirically, the causal arrows point in both directions. Individuals and groups compete, in part, to be positioned to establish normative structures, and norms underpin social power relations. At the same time, once established, normative structures develop in ways that can neither be predicted by initial determinations, nor deduced by aggregating individual preferences at any given moment; further, normative evolution clearly shapes how interests are formed and power operates. Reflecting further on the origin and maintenance of norms, we see that the perspectives of rationalists and social constructivists not only rest on different conceptions of human nature but explain different, if interrelated, aspects of the relationship between rules and power.

Norms and Cooperation

The social logic of norms is straightforward. Rules resolve collective action problems—in plain language, they help us get along together—hence their legitimacy. Indeed, most social settings are hardly anything but a set of particular normative resolutions to a cluster of particular collective action problems. The micro-foundation of norms—how and why they emerge, develop, or die out within any group—is problematic, and remains somewhat mysterious. This is largely because the process by which a norm is established, or maintained, constitutes itself a potentially irresolvable collective action problem.

The rationalist assumes that people are selfish (rational) and will relentlessly pursue self-interest unless the costs associated with such pursuit outweigh potential benefits. If we further assume that, within a community, no single individual or group is powerful enough to impose a social system by coercion, we notice that even when two or more people share common goals and know that in cooperating with one another each would be better off, the incentives may be such that non-cooperative behaviour is more rational than cooperation. This is the famous prisoner's dilemma. A central puzzle is therefore: why do people *ever* cooperate or get along?

Rationalists have formulated two general responses to this question. First, the more individuals interact with each other on a regular basis, the greater the possibility that some individuals will develop a reputation for trustworthiness. Within this core group, cooperative behaviour becomes 'normal', and non-cooperative behaviour is punished. As others see the advantages of cooperation, trust will diffuse, and with trust, cooperation will disseminate.[1] For example, individuals know that they can make themselves better off by trading (engaging in interactions) with one other. At the same time, each trader recognises that cheating a trading partner can be advantageous if that partner abides by the contract made (the prisoner's dilemma). On the other hand, some may choose not to cheat, but not just because of the prescription, 'promises must be kept'. Instead, some may deduce that cheating today will likely make it more difficult to find trading partners tomorrow. Cheating damages one's reputation for trustworthiness. Once any group of traders establish trustworthy reputations with

---

[1] I have adapted the finding, of game theory, that iterated play and communication facilitates cooperation. Rationalists, however, have not explained in any generally compelling way how cooperation (and norms) emerge and evolve. When two individuals interact with each other over an indefinite period, it is possible that cooperation may arise between them. Yet it is equally possible that they will fail to cooperate at all, or that they will find themselves in a situation where one gains more than the other from the relationship, leading it to break down. At the moment, rationalists have no convincing means of predicting when cooperation will arise, or when it will not, unless they assume pre-existing norms and institutions. Last, the outcome discussed in this paragraph heavily depends on rules (e.g. 'don't trade with those who cheat': see note 2).

each other, they will only trade among themselves. And traders that fail to establish good reputations will be punished by being excluded from the trade regime (or community).[2]

A second means of achieving better cooperation is to impose rules, by developing and enforcing them. Let us assume that a group of individuals adopts the rule, 'one must not cheat', to govern certain interactions. For any individual in that group, the 'one must not cheat' norm constitutes a constraint on behaviour in the service of what I will now call 'the social interest' (since it furthers the interests of the group as a whole, over longer rather than shorter time horizons). Like all norms, this rule generates common expectations, and facilitates the monitoring of behaviour and the punishment of those who fail to abide by the rule. However, the establishment of the social interest, being itself an act of cooperation, is subject to the same potentially insurmountable obstacles all such efforts face (the prisoner's dilemma again). Further, once this or any rule has been established, these problems do not go away. The critical test of a norm's robustness, or legitimacy, occurs when the social interest comes into evident conflict with the self-interest, or interest-driven objectives, of any given individual. In such a case, an individual may well choose to behave in contravention of a norm, especially if the probable outcome of conforming to it would be to leave that individual worse off. So, even after norms have been created, the linked problems of how to ensure compliance and to punish non-compliance persist. Of course, if we assume that the social interest has been clearly expressed, that some mechanism of letting everyone know who is and who is not a cheater has been put into place, and that everyone is rational (and thus will eschew trading with cheaters), cooperation will be the outcome, but assuming such things does not explain them.

Culturalists and social constructivists begin with very different assumptions about human nature, and arrive at very different conclusions about the origin and nature of norms. Human beings may be selfish, but they are not only selfish. They are also born morally reflective, that is, they use their reasoning abilities to interrogate the social consequences of their own behaviour. Further, because human beings are communicative, because they possess language, moral reflection is a social activity. In short, norms

---

[2] Because the ability to communicate, and the concepts of trust and reputation, are deeply embedded within normative constructs, this kind of process and outcome can only be explained by taking for granted the pre-existence of norms. Some rationalists admit that they can not explain how cooperation results from purely 'selfishly rational' behaviour, unless rules are somehow brought in (e.g. Elster 1989: 37–44). Others disagree (e.g. Greif 1989).

are the natural product of our propensity for moral reflection, and rule systems are sustained by an ongoing, collective conversation about how society ought to be ordered. In contrast to rationalists, the emergence of cooperation and norms is not problematic; rather, it is central to our nature as human beings. Once in place, rule systems organize ongoing normative deliberations that seek to define and redefine the nature of the community. This latter function is one of the core subjects of this book.

These distinctions can be drawn out further. For rationalists, the legitimacy of a social norm is proportionate to the extent to which that norm constrains and facilitates punishment. As Deakin, Lane, and Wilkinson put it: 'The fundamental function of the social norm . . . is to ensure cheaters are punished' (1994: 336). For constructivists, norms do indeed constrain behaviour and facilitate punishment, not least, because individuals may internalize norms as self-controls and admonish others who violate them. But a norm's capacity to control and sanction is hardly its only, or even its most important, social function. The legitimacy of normative constructs is better measured, not by the extent to which contraventions are punished, but by the extent to which these constructs meaningfully influence how individuals conceive of themselves as part of a community, and how, in communication with others, individuals deliberate and make principled choices.[3]

Three summary points deserve emphasis. First, rationalists and constructivists conceptualize power quite differently. For rationalists, power is a commodity, possessed in relative amounts by individuals, to be used *instrumentally*, as means to ends, in collusion or competition with other individuals. Norms, because they condition the strategic use of power (i.e. politics), must also be understood instrumentally. Constructivists tend to conceive of power *constructively*, as a dynamic field that enables individuals to define themselves, existentially and in community with others. Normative systems constitute and animate these fields, and therefore also constitute and animate individuals as political actors. Second, norm-driven behaviour is not always rationality in disguise, nor can rationality always be reduced to normativity. At different moments in the same field or political process, either may be paramount. Further, norms may at times work along with self-interest to produce behaviour. That is, individuals may well choose a course of action with reference to both. Third, notwithstanding these huge differences, rationalists and constructivists agree that

---

[3] In this formulation, both the individual and individual choice neither disappear nor are made into 'objects' of a determinative normative construct.

a social science that fails to notice how rules are produced and disseminated is an incomplete social science. Normative constructs (partly) determine how people behave, and therefore (partly) determine political outcomes. That is more than enough reason to take them seriously.

Law

In the world of formal systems of governance, we find a common solution to the problem of cooperation and social control: human beings establish institutions to generate, monitor, and punish non-compliance with rules. This is the logic of government. Legal norms are a subset of social norms, and this subset is distinguished not in kind, but by their higher degree of clarity, formalization, and binding authority.[4] I do not mean that we all agree on the nature, content, and application of legal norms. There would not be lawyers or judges in the world if this were so. But legal norms have a more formal source than do most other social norms (compare a criminal code with table manners, for example), and compliance with them is usually obligatory. Formalization and clarity reduce our uncertainty about whether a given norm exists and what human interactions the norm was meant to govern; they therefore facilitate the monitoring of compliance and the punishment of contravention.

Law is the fetishization of normative clarity. Law formalizes, by making explicit, the rights and obligations of individuals or groups to act in a particular way, in a given social setting. We know that individuals and groups often expend enormous resources to alter existing, or to put into place new, legal provisions. At the same time, legal norms derive much of their force from the perception that they represent an expression of the social interest, one that is fundamentally superior to the expression of the interests of one person or just a few people. Law codifies, for entire populations, just how duty pre-empts choice. Where the social interest has been established, the

---

[4] Elster disagrees. Legal norms, according to Elster, differ from social norms in that: (1) they are explicitly deterrent; (2) rest on formal rather than informal punishment; and (3) are enforced by officials who are professionally obligated to apply sanctions. In contrast to social norms, the argument goes, the effectiveness or agency of legal norms is more a matter of rational calculus than 'the voice of conscience' (Elster 1989: 101). This distinction can not be sustained. Social norms also deter; many legal norms are not designed to punish (or event to be enforced), but to express a society's morality or collective 'voice of conscience'; and the obligation to enforce legal norms is often the obligation to engage in moral reflection (e.g. the adjudication of human rights). In either case, the various functions of legal and social norms remain linked, if not identical. In my mind, the distinction is one of degree (of formalization), not kind.

contravention of a norm constitutes an injury against the group as a whole. Legal norms thus establish binding, reciprocal relationships among individuals. Because of this, legal norms have the capacity to constitute, or otherwise define, a political community.

Norms and Dispute Resolution

Rule systems perform a crucial social function not yet discussed: they facilitate the peaceful resolution of disputes. Rules do so on at least three dimensions. First, the existence of a norm may prevent conflicts from arising in the first place. Many rules are expressly designed to obviate conflict, or emerged themselves as solutions to prior conflicts.[5] Second, when conflict between two people does arise, normative structures provide the disputants with the materials for settling it on their own, 'dyadically', among themselves. Rules constitute standards for evaluating both the disputed behaviour and potential solutions to the problem. The authority of these standards is often reinforced by the fact that they have autonomous existence, being external to, and pre-dating, the dispute. Third, when people are unable to resolve their conflicts dyadically, they may seek the help of a third party. When they do so, the disputants construct a new social institution, a 'triad', which is comprised of the two parties to the conflict and the dispute resolver. Although more will be said about the subject in the next section, normative structures facilitate the third party's task, to the extent that they supply ready-made, principled standards of behaviour that the triadic entity can invoke to decide the case, or to bolster the authority, or legitimacy, of the decision taken.

Courts are but one form of triadic dispute resolution (TDR).

THE CONSTRUCTION OF JUDICIAL POWER

In this section, I present a theory of the 'judicialization' of social life. The theory, like any model, does some violence to reality, in that it assumes a purely consensual world. In this world, individuals are free to choose the rules under which they interact with others, but are not able, unilaterally, to impose a solution to any conflict which arises under these rules, or to force those with whom they dispute to move from two-party to third-party

---

[5] Consider rules that co-ordinate, such as the rule that we drive on the right (or the left) side of the road only, or the scheduling of classrooms.

dispute resolution. I begin with a consensual, rather than a coercive, model of governance in order to focus attention on outcomes that result exclusively from the internal logic of rules, dyads, and triads. Put differently, mine is a theory of ideational and normative, rather than physical or material, power (influence). The theory, elaborated more formally elsewhere (Stone Sweet 1999), organizes the book, and is specifically adapted to European constitutional politics as the concluding chapter.

Judicialization is the process through which: (1) a TDR mechanism develops authority over the normative structure in place in any given community; and (2) the third party's decisions—what I will call triadic rule-making—come to shape how individuals interact with one another. Because judicialization entails observable, and therefore measurable, changes in individual behaviour and in the nature of the rule systems under which individuals live, the theory must give 'micro-foundations' to the macro-changes predicted, and 'macro-foundations' to the micro-changes predicted.

As depicted in Fig. 1.1, the model breaks down the judicialization process into four stages, each a chronological shift along a circular path,

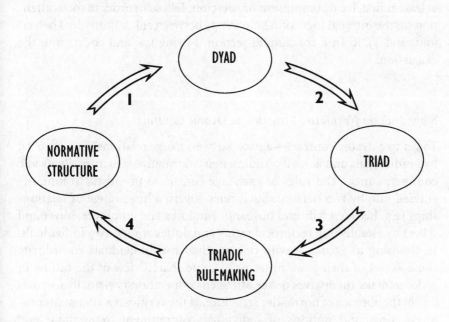

FIG. 1.1. *The Judicialization of Society*

moving clockwise. I have labelled the right hemisphere of the circle, stages 2 and 3, the micro-level, and the left hemisphere, stages 4 and 1, the macro-level. The micro-level is animated by the behaviour of individual actors, including potential third-party dispute resolvers. The dyad refers to any two people in society who may choose to enter into a rule-governed relationship with one another. The triad refers to the situation that results when both members of a particular dyad choose to ask a third party to help them settle a dispute about the terms of their relationship. The macro-level is constituted by the normative structure underlying social relationships, and by those processes that serve to give social agency to rules. Triadic rule-making bridges the micro and the macro in important ways.

Movement around the circle is driven by the mixture of harmony and tension that inheres in the relationship between rules and individual decision-making. Although what happens at any given stage partly depends on what has happened in prior stages, the discussion focuses on what is analytically distinct about each shift. I make several assumptions. First, I assume that individuals (the dyad and the dispute resolver), behave in purely self-interested ways, that is, they are 'rational actors'. Second, I assume a world wherein both the construction of dyadic relationships and the move to the triad issues from the free consent of individuals. I exclude, at least at first, legal compulsion or coercion. I do so in order to focus attention on the internal logic of relationships between rules, individual behaviour, and TDR. In a concluding section, I bring law and courts into the discussion.

Stage 1: From Normative Structure to Dyadic Contract

To get to a dyadic contract—a two-party exchange relationship—we need two individuals and at least a rudimentary normative structure. By dyadic contract, I mean the rules of exchange (or, those promises) voluntarily entered into by two persons. Such rules govern a huge range of relationships (e.g. between wife and husband, employer and employee, buyer and seller) by establishing reciprocal rights and duties among two individuals. In choosing to exchange with one another, two individuals co-ordinate some aspect of their lives, in terms of some shared view of the future, in order to make themselves better off. Such cooperation is virtually impossible in the absence of normative structure, at the very least a system of communication, and notions of individual commitment, reputation, and responsibility.

Stage 2: From Dyad to Triad

The legitimacy of the dyadic relationship is rooted in the self-interest of the contracting parties. For each party, the benefits of constructing the dyad outweigh the costs, and that the benefits of a particular exchange relationship outweigh the benefits of going it alone. Rules (the set of promises made) partly organize how the relationship is understood, over time, helping both to monitor compliance and to identify problems. Conflict is always possible, perhaps inevitable. As circumstances change, for example, the meanings attached to the same set of rules may diverge. Or the perceived value of the dyadic relationship may decline for one party. Or one party may choose not to fulfil obligations, in order to exploit the other. In any case, dyadic relationships generate a massive social demand for dispute resolution.

If the disputing parties fail to settle their conflict on their own, they may choose to delegate the matter to a third party, thus constituting the triad. This act of delegation can be understood as a simple, universal act of 'common sense', as Shapiro does (1980: 1). It can also be understood in utilitarian terms. Delegation is likely when, for each disputant, going to a third party is less costly, or more likely to yield a desired outcome, than breaking the contract and going it alone. Nevertheless, the move to TDR entails potential costs, the most important of which is that the dispute may be resolved in unfavourable ways. In the long run, however, the more two disputants interact with one other—the more a relationship is perceived as beneficial by both—the less that risk matters. Other things being equal, each contracting party may expect to win some disputes and to lose others, over time, against a backdrop of absolute benefit. The social logic of delegation, like that of the dyadic contract, is one of long-range utility: each party must believe that it is better off resolving disputes than dissolving the relationship altogether.

The delegation of conflicts to a third party is the fuel that drives judicialization. If disputes were always able to be resolved dyadically, or if one of the disputants was always able to impose a solution on the other, then judicialization could not proceed.

Stage 3: The Crisis of Triadic Legitimacy

The triadic dispute resolver faces a potentially intractable dilemma (Shapiro 1980: ch. 1; Kratochwil 1994: 478–9). On the one hand, the third party's reputation for neutrality is crucial to the social legitimacy of the triad itself. There would be no move from dyad to triad if either of the disputants believed that the third party was biased or unfair. Yet in resolving disputes, the third party may well compromise her reputation for neutrality by declaring one party the loser. That is, after all, what each of the disputants probably hopes. Thus, the dispute resolver's basic interest is to resolve conflicts effectively while maintaining the social legitimacy of the triad. In pursuit of this objective, she deploys two main tactics.

First, the dispute resolver seeks to secure legitimacy by defending her behaviour normatively, as meaningfully enabled and constrained by the rules embedded in normative structure. As noted above, norms provide ready-made standards of appropriate behaviour, and therefore constitute a template for resolving dyadic conflict. Simplifying a complex phenomenon, dispute resolvers tend, first, to consider the dispute as a conflict about the meaning and applicability of norms, and, second, to present their decisions as the result of normative reasoning—one in which the appropriate rules to govern a particular situation are determined. In doing so, they show that they have taken seriously the arguments of each party, and have recast these arguments as the best possible normative ones, and they obscure, behind their own normative position, whatever influence personal preferences may have played in their decision. The triadic figure would have the disputants believe that the decision was generated, or even preordained, by the structure of the rules relevant to the conflict. The appeal to norms is an appeal to objectivity.

Second, the dispute resolver anticipates the disputants'—and the community's—reactions to her decision, since she hopes to gain compliance with her decision. Figure 1.2 depicts this calculus. Position A.1 represents the substantive outcome desired by disputant A, and position B.1 represents the substantive outcome preferred by disputant B. Outcomes situated between positions A.1 and A.2 (or substitute B.1–B.2 for B) represent outcomes that the dispute resolver believes will not provoke A to refuse compliance. The space between B.2 and A.2 constitutes the dispute resolver's assessment of the range of decision-making outcomes that will lead to the resolution of the dispute, to compliance, and (much the same thing) to the re-establishment of a disputed rule. The calculus also helps her to fashion

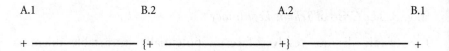

| A.1 | B.2 | A.2 | B.1 |

FIG. 1.2. *The dispute resolver's calculus.*

settlements that avoid the declaration of a clear winner or loser: in the area between B.2 and A.2, each disputant achieves a partial victory. For some disputes, the positions of A and B are more polarized, and no B.2–A.2 space exists; in such cases, the dispute resolver is unable to deploy the tactic (she has an interest in creating such a space by, for example, mediating between the parties). These are 'hard cases', ones in which the dispute resolver can expect that any decision taken is likely to result in protests or even non-compliance. If she does attempt to resolve the dispute by rendering a decision, her legitimacy will rest all the more on the persuasiveness of normative justifications.

Stage 4: Triadic Rule-making

In taking a decision and justifying it normatively, the triadic entity makes rules. First, she has made rules that are concrete, particular, and retrospective, that is, she has resolved a pre-existing dispute between two specific parties about the terms of one dyadic contract. Second, in justifying her decision—in telling us why, normatively, a given act should or should not be permitted—she has made rules of an abstract, general, and prospective nature. This is so to the extent that her decision has clarified or altered rules that comprise the normative structure.

This latter form of triadic rule-making constitutes a predictable response to the crisis dispute resolvers face (see first tactic, above). Yet it raises a delicate, second order legitimacy issue. From the point of view of the disputing parties, it makes evident that the exact content of the rules governing the dispute could not have been ascertained at the time the dispute erupted. The perception of the dispute resolver's neutrality erodes as her capacity to make rules is revealed. The dispute resolver can never permanently resolve this problem. The best she can hope to do is to persuade others that her decision is the inevitable result of an exhaustive, inherently normative, deliberation. Triadic rule-making can then be portrayed as a by-product of dispute resolution, rather than an outcome desired in and of itself.

By-product or not, triadic rule-making constitutes a discourse about how people ought to behave. Because rules, reasoning about rules, and the application of particular rules to particular conflicts constitute the core of this discourse, precedent follows naturally. Precedent helps to legitimize TDR by acknowledging rule-making behaviour, while constraining that same behaviour with a rule: that like cases shall be settled likewise. In encapsulating this sequence—*dyadic rules* → *conflict* → *triadic rule-making* → *precedent*— TDR organizes (a potentially expansive) conversation about a community's normative structure. In doing so, it performs a profoundly governmental function to the extent that individuals are drawn into this conversation and help to perpetuate it.

Shift 1 (again): (Re)Constructing the Dyad

In moving through shifts 1–4, we see that the triad occupies a pivotal position between the dyad (a community) and normative structure, bridging the two. TDR tends to knot rules and strategic behaviour together. Thus: a dyadic dispute erupts; the disputants delegate the matter to a dispute resolver; the dispute resolver resolves the conflict in a process involving normative reasoning, revising (at least subtly) normative structure. In returning to shift 1, the impact of structure on strategic behaviour, we come full circle, to our initial starting point. But we find ourselves in a rather different world this time: the individuals comprising the dyad have learned something about the nature of their relationship (the rules governing their exchange) and about the environment (the normative structure) which sustains it.

Put simply, dispute resolution has reconsecrated the contract and re-enacted the normative structure. The dispute resolver may have done so in a relatively conservative manner, fashioning a partial victory for each disputant and appealing to rules whose prior existence is relatively unquestioned. In so doing, she has reinforced existing structure while clarifying its domain of relevance and application. The dispute resolver may have done so in a relatively progressive manner, declaring a clear winner and loser while revising an existing rule or crafting a new one. In so doing, she has reshaped normative structure, expanding its domain.

Given two conditions, such rule-making is likely to generate powerful pedagogical (or positive feedback) effects, to be registered on subsequent exchange and dispute resolution. First, contractants must perceive that they are better off in a world with TDR than they are in a world without TDR. If they are rational actors, then they will evaluate the rulefulness of any potential action and anticipate the probable outcome issuing from TDR. That is, they will become active participants in the discourse about rules organized by the dispute resolver's decisions. Second, the dispute resolver must understand that her decisions have some authoritative (i.e. precedential) value.

If these conditions are met, TDR will inexorably become a mechanism of social change, more precisely, it will serve to gradually adapt rules to the needs of those who live under them, and dyadic exchange will inevitably be placed in the 'shadow' of triadic rule-making. As we move around the circle a second time, and then again and again, this shadow will deepen and expand, covering more and more forms of human interaction. A virtuous circle is thereby constructed: to the extent that TDR is effective, it encourages cooperation (dyadic exchange); as cooperation increase in number and in scope, so does the demand for the authoritative interpretation of rules; as TDR is exercised, the body of rules that constitutes normative structure steadily expands, becoming more elaborate and differentiated; these rules then will feedback onto dyadic relationships, structuring future interactions, conflict, and dispute resolution.

Law, Courts, and Judicialization

Triadic dispute resolution is found in virtually all human communities, in a variety of forms that can be arrayed on a spectrum. On one pole of the continuum, we find mediation, which proceeds from the mutual consent of the disputants. The mediator seeks to help the disputants resolve their conflict, but she may not impose solutions against the will of either party. On the other pole, we find adjudication, which is compulsory for at least one of the disputants, and proceeds on the basis of jurisdiction. In adjudicating a conflict, the judge possesses the authority to impose a solution on the parties. Courts are adjudicators whose authority to resolve legal disputes (jurisdiction) is constituted under law.

In the consensual world of my model, judicialization can be thwarted, or stifled, at different points: individuals may choose not to refer their conflicts to the third party for settlement; the third party may make capricious decisions or choose not to give normative justifications for her decisions at all; future contractants may choose to ignore rule innovation issuing from triadic decision-making, and so on. Law, rules of standing (who may sue whom and under what conditions), and jurisdiction function to enhance the linkages between rules systems and strategic behaviour discussed; these rules facilitate judicialization, by reducing, or eliminating altogether, the power of any individual to block movement around the circle. Typically, the referral of a conflict to a judge for adjudication may be effected by either one of the parties, without the other's consent. The judge may be required, by law or precedent, to give a justification for his decision. The decision has the effect of law, binding on the parties to the dispute, but also may have precedential value to the extent that the decision serves to clarify the rules relevant to particular behaviours or relations.

In taking decisions, judges, too, make rules. Judicial law-making tends to undermine judicial legitimacy in the same ways that triadic rule-making undermines TDR more generally. But because courts are governmental institutions that interact with other governmental institutions, the legitimacy problem not only concerns individual litigants; it is also partly intragovernmental in nature. Judicial law-making tends to pose a *separation of powers* problem, to the extent that in any given polity one expects some institutions to make law (the legislature), and some institutions to apply the legislature's law to resolve legal disputes (the judiciary). Separation of powers doctrines are constitutive principles of governance found in a polity's constitutional law.

CONSTITUTIONALISM AND POLITICS

Constitutionalism refers to the commitment, more or less operative in any polity, to the idea that the interactions that take place within it are to be governed by a set of authoritative rules—the constitutional law. A constitution is a body of rules that specifies how all other legal rules are to be produced, applied, and interpreted. Constitutional norms are not only higher order rules; they are prior, organic rules: they constitute a given political community. To the extent that constitutional rules are expected to be long-lived, or quasi-permanent, their establishment is an attempt at institutionalizing the social interest in the form of a political regime. In liberal democracies, constitutions establish the institutions of the state, and distribute governmental authority to act among them. State institutions exist to assert or ensure, in an ongoing manner, the superiority of the social interest over contrary self or group interests, as when a legislature passes a statute, an agency applies an administrative rule, a policeman makes an arrest, or a court settles a dispute.

Two ideal types of liberal-democratic constitutions are relevant for our purposes. In the first type, the legislative supremacy model, the constitution establishes a set of electoral rules, and distributes capacities and functions among governmental institutions. To the extent that all other official acts are produced or taken according to the procedures laid down by the constitution, these acts are lawful and therefore binding. Elections legitimize legislative authority, and legislative majorities legitimize statutory authority. Once promulgated, statutes are commands (until abrogated by subsequent commands), binding on the polity. The British parliamentary system and the French Third (1875–1940) and Fourth (1946–58) Republics are examples. In these polities, the constitutional law enshrines legislative supremacy. Simply put, parliament can do no (legal) wrong because the people have elected it.

The second type, the higher law constitutionalism model, shares with the first a common attribute: constitutional rules establish governmental institutions and link these institutions to society, via elections. In this second type, however, a layer of substantive constraints on the uses of public authority is added, and a triadic mechanism of enforcing them established. These substantive constraints—the most important of which are rights— give to non-state actors enforceable claims against the state. These claims come in the form of arguments that state acts are invalid (illegitimate) to the extent that they violate individual rights. In such polities, the production of lower order legal norms, like legislation, is relatively more participatory. The legislative process, for example, does not end on promulgation of legislation, but is lengthened by judicial politics, and opened up to include litigants and judges. Examples of such polities are Canada, the United States, and—with the establishment of constitutional rights and constitutional courts to protect those rights—the regimes in now place in France, Germany, Italy, Spain, and in many more countries across Europe.

Constitutional Review

Constitutional review is the authority of an institution to invalidate the acts of government—such as legislation, administrative decisions, and judicial rulings—on the grounds that these acts have violated constitutional rules, including rights. It is a distinguishing feature of higher law constitutionalism. In exercising review, the judge interprets and applies (enforces) the constitutional law, which is normatively superior to all other legal norms. As will be discussed in the next chapter, judicial review of the American kind is but one form, a subclass, of constitutional review. European constitutional review is performed by judges sitting on special tribunals called constitutional courts. As discussed in subsequent chapters, other, non-constitutional (or 'ordinary') judges today also apply the constitutional law to resolve disputes among private individuals.

Constitutional Politics

Constitutional politics comprises the relationship, as mediated by the rule-making of constitutional judges, between constitutional rules (the macro-level) and the decision-making of public officials and other individuals (the micro-level). The theory of judicialization suggests that, under certain conditions, constitutional judges will (re)make these rules and, in so doing, construct a discourse, a set of dialogues and collective conversations, about the capacities and limits of the use of state power. Given certain conditions, we can expect to find that other public officials—such as ministers of government, parliamentarians, administrators, and ordinary judges—will be drawn into this discourse, and help to perpetuate it. And we can expect that they will at times be persuaded or cajoled to alter their behaviour in order to conform to constitutional rules.

UNDERSTANDING CONSTITUTIONAL POLITICS

In this section, I survey a variety of perspectives on European constitutional politics. Each focuses attention on some aspects of the phenomenon, while neglecting others. As the book proceeds, these perspective are employed to help explain different aspects of European constitutional politics.

Constitutional Politics as Contracting and Delegation Politics

Rational choice scholars tend to conceptualize constitutions as contracts. The perspective makes sense where two or more parties, or social groups, negotiate the constitution as a means of fixing authoritative rules to govern their interactions over time. In fact, nearly all contemporary European constitutions have issued from negotiations among representatives of political parties, followed by ratification by popular referenda. The nature and content of these contracts are the topics of the next chapter. For now, let us focus on more general contracting and delegation problems as they relate to constitutions and courts.

Recall that, for rationalists, the establishment and maintenance of rule systems can be problematic. Even if all parties to the contract know that they will be better off cooperating with one another in a joint venture, they may still fail to overcome two obstacles: (1) the difficulty of agreeing on the specific rules that will govern their mutual relations in the first place; and (2) the difficulty of maintaining the contract over time, to the extent that differences in rule interpretation will arise as unforeseen circumstances arise. Further, since each party may have good reason to doubt that the other(s) will abide by promises made over the life of the contract, each may be unwilling to compromise enough to achieve the best possible agreement, or any agreement at all. In practice, the existence of a law of contracts and of courts to enforce this law is one way of resolving these difficulties. Contracts are codified promises, and adjudication serves to guarantee that such promises will be kept.

Constitution-making often multiplies contracting problems. Its higher law status, and its expected permanence, raise the stakes for negotiating parties enormously. The establishment of a constitutional court to settle disputes that arise under the constitution can be read as a response to these difficulties. A system of constitutional adjudication will enhance the capacity of the contracting parties to monitor compliance and punish contraventions. But delegating the power of constitutional review to judges is not without costs.

Principal–agent Issues

Costs of delegation inhere in what theorists of delegation call 'principal–agent' relationships. 'Principals' are the rulers, those in positions of authority at a given moment of delegation; 'agents' are those on whom the political rulers have conferred the power to govern, some meaningful decision-making authority in order to perform services desired by the principals. The problem, as Hechter puts it (1987: 130), is that 'agents [being rational] will not always act in the best interest of the principal[s] but in their own best interests instead'. Social scientists have explored the problem in some depth, notably in studies of American and European bureaucracies (e.g. Moe 1987; Pollack 1998), of state formation and tax collection (e.g. Levi 1988), and more recently, of courts (e.g. Garrett 1992; Stone Sweet and Caporaso 1998; Shapiro 1988 is a compatible analysis).

For our purposes, the principal–agent (P–A) construct provides a framework for understanding: (1) why political rulers establish courts; and (2) why rulers tolerate a certain amount of judicial autonomy. Judges (the agents) are delegated some amount of governmental authority in order to perform the linked function of dispute resolution and law application. The legitimacy of the judiciary partly flows from this delegation. Although the principals recognize that a certain degree of discretion is necessary for the satisfactory performance of this service, judicial discretion constitutes the power to make law. From a P–A perspective, judicial rule-making is an omnipresent agency problem since, as discussed, dispute resolution and rule-making go hand-in-hand.

Just how much judicial rule-making the principals will tolerate is the crucial question. Let us assume that such tolerance is conditioned by rationality: rulers will permit delegated power to operate only as long as the benefits of such delegation outweigh the costs. When the costs of delegation come to outweigh the benefits (i.e. when agents begin to govern in the place of the rulers), the principals will rein in their agents. Principals do so by reversing the agents' decisions, restricting or abolishing their powers, or reducing their available resources.

According to traditional separation of doctrines in Europe, the principals are comprised of the members of parliament, and the normative instrument parliament controls—statute, or legislation—is supreme. Judges are agents whose purpose it is to enforce parliament's laws. We know that, as often as not, European judiciaries engage in such extensive interpretation of the various legal codes that these statutes mean only what the courts say they mean. Nevertheless, the principals remain in charge. At any point, parliament can change its law, if the members notice that a judge has applied a statutory provision in a way that they did not intend or do not like. Thus, to the extent that the agency problem can be identified, it can be corrected: the principals can overturn judicial decisions by reworking the normative instrument that they themselves directly control, that is, they can amend the relevant legislation to specifically preclude the offending judicial interpretation. Other things equal, the decision rule governing the P–A relationship—a majority vote of the parliament—favours relatively tight control by the principals.

The agency problem that develops as a result of constitutional review is far more acute than the one just described. This difference can be expressed in three ways. First, in ordinary adjudication, the judiciary is asked by the rulers (the political parties in parliament) to help regulate the conduct of the ruled (individuals). In constitutional adjudication, the service being rendered is, often enough to matter a great deal, the regulation of the actions of the political parties themselves. Second, the exercise of constitutional review authority by constitutional judges regularly results in the nullification of the normative instrument that law-makers control: the statute. Depending on the relevant constitutional rules in place, the political parties may be able to overturn constitutional jurisprudence, or restrict the constitutional court's powers, but only by reconstituting themselves as a constituent (constitution-making) assembly and then amending the constitutional law. Put differently, political parties as legislators are not, *per se*, principals at all, at least not in their relationship to constitutional judges. Instead, they are subject to the authority of constitutional judges, since the normative instrument the judges control, the constitutional law, is superior to statute. Further, the decision rules governing constitutional revision processes are more restrictive than those governing the revision of legislation; it is normally harder for the political parties to change the constitution than it is to change a law. These decision rules heavily favour the continuous dominance of constitutional judges over the interpretation of the constitutional law.

Constitutional Politics as Legislative Politics

In a classic approach developed by Martin Shapiro (1965), political scientists take the existence of the constitutional law and of constitutional review as given, and then go on to document and assess the impact of review on political outcomes (policy). The approach views courts as policy-making institutions, litigation activity as a form of policy input, and the resulting case law as a form of policy output. On the input, or demand, side, constitutional politics are legislative politics to the extent that people go to the courts to obtain policy change. Legislation supported by a stable legislative majority, for example, can only be nullified by convincing a judge to declare it unconstitutional, hence the utility of litigation. Since judges do not activate themselves, they rely on litigants, whose behaviour judges partly structure by their own rule-making, for caseload and influence over policy outcomes. On the output, or supply, side, constitutional politics are legislative politics to the extent that judges use the opportunities afforded by litigation to make policy by way of judicial rule-making.

The self-interested behaviour of litigators and judges is considered to drive the judicial process, and in this sense, it is broadly congruent with rationalist theories of politics. The flip side of the coin is the denial that judging is a purely normative exercise. The analyst assumes that judicial decision-making is at least partly indeterminate. That is, no single judicial theory, philosophy of jurisprudence, or process of normative reflection can yield one 'right' answer to any complicated legal question, not least, because the most important questions are so complicated that there can be no one 'right' answer. The approach focuses attention on how courts interact with other political actors in providing answers to these questions (i.e. in making of public policy).

Stated in this very general way, the constitutional politics as legislative politics formulation actually lumps together a wide variety of research traditions in public law political science. In studies of American constitutional law, it developed under the 'political jurisprudence' banner in the early 1960s, and it quickly became dominant (see Stumph *et al.* 1983). The seminal and best of this work, did not banish normative concerns altogether;

Shapiro, for example, always took case law seriously, if only as the medium through which legal problems were communicated to, and resolved by, judges. Within the Critical Legal Studies movement, many share the basic 'constitutional politics as legislative politics' orientation, while remaining hostile to rationalist theories of politics generally (Tushnet 1986, 1988). My previous work on the judicialization of European constitutional politics (Stone 1989, 1992*a*, *b*, 1994*a*, 1996) is yet another version. As elaborated in this book, this version integrates rationalist and more constructivist components.

Constitutional Politics as Judicial Decision-making

In this approach, political scientists study judges just as they have other policy-makers—as groups of individual decisionmakers. The approach privileges the micro-level, focusing on individual judges in interaction with other judges on the court. The central thrust of this work has been to show that US Supreme Court justices, like presidents and congressional representatives, make policy choices according to their own policy preferences, given institutional constraints.[6] Thus, proponents of the approach declare that 'the justices make decisions by considering the facts of the case in light of their attitudes and values' (Segal and Spaeth 1993: 73), and 'when they make decisions they want the outcomes to approximate as nearly as possible those policy preferences' (Rohde and Spaeth 1976: 72). Because the American Court is composed of nine justices, each pursuing his or her own preferences, the Court's decision-making is modelled as a bargaining and coalition building process. The power of the law itself, or of normative reasoning, to influence judicial decision-making is downplayed or denied altogether.

In this book, I raise these issues but, at least implicitly, reject the method. The law, and normative reasoning itself, is assumed to be at least partly autonomous from personal preferences, except in so far as a judge's preferences include her desire to legitimize her decisions by appealing to norms.

Conceptualizing Legal Normative Autonomy

Judicial autonomy can be defined and measured variously. One common mode goes as follows: within the political system, the judiciary is more or less autonomous to the extent that it is capable of (re)constructing pre-

[6] The judges' preferences are presumed to have prior existence (i.e. they are exogenous to any given judicial process underway).

existing legal rules and generating new ones. In this version, autonomy is evaluated in terms of separation of powers doctrines, as judicial law-making or empowerment, or as a principal–agent pathology.

A second, very different, mode of conceptualizing autonomy is based on a distinction between behaviour that is purely self-interested in the rationalist sense, and behaviour that is generated by normative deliberation, to the extent that the latter is not entirely reducible to the former. Law is a normative construct; judges face normative problems which they must resolve normatively—with reference to the law. Thus: within the political system, the judiciary behaves relatively autonomously to the extent that it succeeds in resolving legal problems through a process of reasoning about the nature, content, and applicability of legal rules. If, in judging, judges are simply implementing their own policy preferences, we need to know a great deal about the judges' preferences, but little about the law. But if judging is fundamentally (or at least meaningfully) a normative activity, we need to know much more about how judges reason about rules, and how normative reasoning affects judicial outcomes.

Scholars argue endlessly about whether judges strive first to make principled decisions, according to the law, or whether judges decide on the basis of their own preferences, and then use the law to justify these decisions. The debate is a version of the one that I argued is ultimately irresolvable: is it self-interest or a normative construct that has motivated the behaviour? To make matters more complicated, these two modes of conceptualizing autonomy often overlap, as they do in arguments about the legitimacy of constitutional law-making. Constitutional law scholars constantly invoke the second mode of conceptualizing autonomy in order to legitimize the law-making that the first mode inevitably reveals. Judges make law, legitimacy issues are raised, but the legitimacy of constitutional law-making is bolstered to the extent that such law-making can be portrayed as an inherently meaningful, exercise in normative deliberation (e.g. Ely 1982, Perry 1982; Tribe 1985).

In a broader sense, quite apart from arguments about legitimacy, what is being conceptualized as autonomous in the second mode can be thought of as the product of *legal discourse* or *legal consciousness*. A growing judicial politics literature does just that (e.g. Carter 1991; Gordon 1984; Shapiro and Stone *eds.* 1994*a*; Smith 1988; Stone 1992*a*). The central claim is that legal actors—judges, lawyers, and law professors—think and talk differently than do actors outside of the legal world, and that these differences matter to politics. Just how autonomous the legal system is, and exactly how much this autonomy impacts on political outcomes, remains a mystery. Many, myself included, think of autonomy in *relative* terms. Legal discourse is insular and self-referential, driven by its own concerns, but it is not completely divorced from socio-political contexts. Put differently, judges participate in the work of government, they make policy, but this policy-making is nevertheless partly an exercise in normative reasoning. Others view autonomy as quasi-absolute, entirely insular and entirely self-referential (King 1993; Teubner and Febbrajo 1992).

How and why I think students of comparative politics and of judicial politics should attend to the autonomy of the law is addressed directly in Chapter 5, and indirectly in the two sections that follow.

Constitutional Politics as the Defence of the Hierarchy of Norms

In Europe, judges and legal scholars rarely acknowledge judicial law-making or engage in systematic study of it. By training and inclination, they are concerned above all else with the structure, development, and coherence of the law as a system of norms (Merryman 1985). I have portrayed judges as official dispute resolvers, noting that in resolving disputes judges apply but also make breathe life into the law, by progressively developing it. But the judicial function can also be characterized as the responsibility, the mission, of judges to defend 'legality', that is, to ensure the integrity of the system of legal norms.

The commitment to safeguarding legality goes under a number of labels which, while not being perfectly equivalent, are roughly so: rule of law (Britain), *état de droit* (France) and its variants (Italy, Spain), and *Rechtsstaat* (Germany). These phrases refer to two linked principles: (1) that public authority can only be legitimately exercised in conformity with higher order, enabling legal rules; and (2) that these rules bind all members of the polity—including public officials. In traditional Continental state theory, safeguarding 'legality' meant conforming to statute, because the statute (legislation) occupied the highest rung of a hierarchy of laws that was capable of being judicially enforced. All other acts of government (e.g. administrative decrees, arrests and detentions, tax collecting, etc.) derived their legal authority from statute. In Europe, extensive administrative court systems exist to defend this hierarchy, by ensuring that public officials act within the authority delegated to them by statute. The defence of this legal hierarchy is called administrative judicial review. In such review processes, an act of a public official found to be in violation of a governing statute is voided (annulled). In polities where constitutional courts have been established, a new top rung on the normative hierarchy has been established, the constitution. The mission of constitutional courts is to defend the superior status of the higher law, by ensuring that all lower order norms, including statute, conform to it. Thus, the *Rechtsstaat* is today the constitutional *Rechtsstaat*, and the *état de droit* has been constitutionalized.

Constitutional judging involves the resolution of constitutional disputes and the enforcement of the constitution as higher law. Because 'legality' flows from the highest rung of legal norms, the constitution, to the lower rungs, the integrity of the entire legal system ultimately depends upon it. As we will see, the task is often an extremely difficult one, since some constitutional provisions are often vague and may appear, in any particular case, to contradict one other. Judges must decide what the constitution means, which of its provisions are most relevant to a particular dispute, and how intraconstitutional normative conflicts are to be resolved. Such decision-making is itself partly governed by the techniques and rules of legal reasoning. Constitutional decisions, and the commentaries on them by law professors, provide a written record—and defence—of the judges' reasoning process. As time passes, the constitution will become heavily supplemented by the jurisprudential corpus, which itself comes to look increasingly like a theory—or set of theories—about the constitution.

Considered in this way, constitutional politics generate the ongoing construction, or development, of the normative basis of the state itself. Social scientists ought to take this theorizing seriously to the extent that it meaningfully impacts the behaviour of specific institutions, such as legislatures and courts.

Constitutional Politics as Constitutional Justice

As discussed in the next chapter, the inclusion of constitutional rights provisions in modern European constitutions radically transformed the nature of European judging. The protection of human rights is a central purpose of modern European constitutionalism, and constitutional judges are the agents of that purpose. The great majority of the most important decisions rendered by constitutional courts are settlements of disputes about the meaning of rights. This task is, again, normatively difficult because, in any constitutional dispute before a constitutional judge, a rights provision at issue may conflict with another right provision, or with non-rights provisions. In settling such matters, constitutional courts come to construct theories of constitutional rights, or constitutional justice, developing hierarchies of norms and values within the constitution itself. Conceived as politics, such theories yield commands, of more or less precision, about how constitutional rights must be protected by legislators, administrators, and the courts. They are thus instruments of governance.

CONSTITUTIONAL POLITICS IN WESTERN EUROPE

The book will proceed as follows. In Chapter 2, I contrast the American and European models of constitutional review, provide an overview of the structure and function of European constitutional courts, and then discuss the main determinants of European constitutional politics. In Chapter 3, constitutional politics are examined as the interactions, or constitutional dialogues, between law-makers and judges within policy processes. Chapter 4 focuses on constitutional politics as a set of constitutional dialogues—between law-makers, constitutional judges, and judiciaries—about how best to protect human rights. In Chapter 5, I examine how the democratic legitimacy of constitutional review is most commonly debated in Europe, and argue for the need to reconceptualize traditional separation of powers, doctrines, and other legitimating devices. Chapter 6 traces the development of constitutional politics in the European Community, focusing on the European Court of Justice and its interactions with national constitutional courts and judiciaries. In the final chapter, I elaborate a theory of constitutional politics in Europe, summarizing the major findings of the book.

2

Constitutional Adjudication and Parliamentary Democracy

In pre-World War II Europe, democratic constitutions could typically be revised at the discretion of the legislature; they prohibited review of the legality of statutes by the judiciary; and they did not contain substantive constraints, such as rights, on legislative authority. The rule of legislative supremacy meant that conflicts between a statute and a constitutional norm were to be either ignored by judges, or resolved in favour of the former. Since the end of World War II, a 'new constitutionalism' has emerged and widely diffused (Shapiro and Stone 1994*b*). Human rights have been codified and given a privileged place in the constitutional law; and quasi-judicial organs called constitutional courts have been charged with ensuring the normative superiority of the constitution. Such courts have been established in Austria (1945), Italy (1948), the Federal Republic of Germany (1949), France (1958), Portugal (1976), Spain (1978), Belgium (1985) and, after 1989, in the post-Communist Czech Republic, Hungary, Poland, Romania, Russia, Slovakia, the Baltics, and in several states of the former Yugoslavia.[1]

This chapter examines how constitutional politics are organized in France, Germany, Italy, and Spain,[2] focusing on how parliamentary systems of governance have accommodated constitutional adjudication. I begin by introducing the European model of constitutional review, contrasting it to the American model. I then provide an overview of the main structural features of 'the new constitutionalism'. I end with a discussion of the most important factors that determine the nature, scope, and intensity of constitutional politics.

---

[1] Austria, Germany, Spain, and the communist states of Eastern Europe had possessed constitutional courts, of varying ineffectiveness, in the interwar years.

[2] Because nearly all important structural variations are present in at least one of these four cases, the analysis is relevant to constitutional politics across Europe.

THE EUROPEAN MODEL OF CONSTITUTIONAL REVIEW

European constitutional courts comprise an institutional 'family' to the extent that they share important features that distinguish them from institutions that exercise constitutional review elsewhere. Contrasting the European and American 'models' of review is a common starting point (Favoreu 1990, 1996).

The European Model v. the American Model

In American judicial review, 'any judge of any court, in any case, at any time, at the behest of any litigating party, has the power to declare a law unconstitutional' (Shapiro and Stone 1994*b*: 400). Although formulated broadly, the power is in practice conditioned by a number of doctrines designed to distinguish 'the judicial function'—*the settlement of legal disputes*—from 'the political function'—*legislating*. Most important, judicial review powers are said to be exercised only to the extent that they are necessary to settle what the American constitution calls a 'case or controversy', a legal dispute involving two litigants who have an opposed interest in the outcome of the case. It can then be claimed that the power of judicial review is not desired, in and of itself, but at times must be exercised in order to resolve a conflict involving the constitutional law. American separation of powers notions—which rest on the formal equality of the executive, legislative, and judicial branches of government—both enable and restrict the exercise of judicial review. Courts are responsible for defending the constitution as higher law; advisory opinions on constitutionality are precluded, as potential usurpations of the legislative function; and judges may choose to curtail their review authority, deferring to the 'political' branches (e.g. by invoking doctrines such as act of state and political questions).

In contrast, the subordination of the work of the judiciary to that of the legislature is a foundational principle of civil law systems, and therefore of Continental constitutional law. As in the United States, the function of the European judiciary is to settle legal conflicts according to the applicable law. But European judges may not invalidate or refuse to apply a statute (legislation) as unconstitutional. From 1780 in Germanic states and from 1791 in France, for example, the prohibition of judicial review has been proclaimed in written constitutions, and the penal codes established penalties for any transgression. The paradigmatic statement of this prohibition is the French law of 16 August 1790, which remains in force today, and which has never been violated

Courts cannot interfere with the exercising of legislative powers or suspend the application of the laws.

This constitutional orthodoxy spread across Europe during the 19th century. According to this orthodoxy, American-style judicial review, rather than corresponding to a separation of powers, actually establishes a permanent *confusion* of powers, because it enables the judiciary to participate in the legislative function. In European parlance, to the extent that courts interfere with the legislative function, a 'government of judges' emerges. The fear of creating a government of judges has been at the heart of European animosities to American judicial review since the French revolution (Davis 1987).

American judges are responsible for defending the integrity of a hierarchy of legal norms, the apex of which is the constitution; and, because legislative norms are juridically inferior to constitutional norms, constitutional provisions must prevail in any legal conflict with statutory provisions. This is the logic of judicial review and the Supreme Court's famous opinion in *Marbury* v. *Madison*. European judges are also charged with defending a normative hierarchy, the apex of which is the statute: legislative norms (as in the United States) trump conflicting, inferior norms (regulations, decrees, local rules, and so on). But European judiciaries do not possess jurisdiction over the constitution. The constitutional law is formally detached from the hierarchy of laws which European judges are otherwise responsible for applying and defending.

A problem is posed: who will defend the constitution law, arguably the law most in need of protecting, if not the judiciary? The invention of a new institution, the constitutional court, provided the solution.

We can break down the European model of constitutional review into four constituent components. First, constitutional courts enjoy exclusive and final constitutional jurisdiction. Constitutional judges possess a monopoly on the exercise of constitutional review, while the judiciary remains precluded from engaging in review, and no appeal of a constitutional decision is possible. Second, terms of jurisdiction restrict constitutional courts to the settling of constitutional disputes. Unlike the US Supreme Court, constitutional courts do not preside over judicial disputes or litigation, which remain the function of judges sitting on the 'ordinary courts' (all courts with the exception of the constitutional court).[3] Instead, constitutional judges answer *constitutional questions* referred to them. Third, constitutional courts have links with, but are formally detached from, the judiciary and legislature. They occupy their own 'constitutional' space, a space neither clearly 'judicial' nor 'political'. Fourth, some constitutional courts are empowered to review legislation before it has effected anyone negatively, as a means of eliminating unconstitutional legislation and practices *before* they can do harm. Thus, in the European model, the judges that staff the ordinary courts remain bound by the supremacy of statute, while constitutional judges are charged with preserving the supremacy of the constitution.

The Kelsenian Constitutional Court

The European model of constitutional review has a seminal antecedent: the constitutional court of the Austrian Second Republic (1920–34).[4] The Austrian court was the brainchild of Hans Kelsen, an influential legal scholar who also drafted the constitution of 1920, founding the Second Republic. In 1928, he (1928) wrote a widely translated article elaborating and defending the European model of review. Kelsen argued that the integrity of the legal system, which he conceived as a kind of central nervous system for the state, would only be assured if the superior status of the constitution law, atop a hierarchically ordered system of legal norms, could be guaranteed by a 'jurisdiction', or 'court-like' body. Because Kelsen foresaw nearly all of the variations on the model now in place, and because Kelsen's constitutional theory is the standard reference for debates about the legitimacy of European constitutional review even today, it is worth examining these arguments closely (see also Chapter 5).

In his article, Kelsen provided an institutional template, or 'tool kit', for constructing systems of constitutional justice in Europe.[5] Kelsen faced two hostile camps: politicians suspicious of the judiciary and judicial power;

---

[3] For convenience sake, European legal scholars commonly distinguish between the constitutional court and constitutional judges on the one hand, and the ordinary courts and ordinary judges on the other. By ordinary courts, they mean the judiciary; and by ordinary judges, they mean those judicial officials charged with handling litigation and judicial appeals. By convention, the category of 'ordinary courts' includes, but only for purposes of discussing the specificities of constitutional adjudication, the 'specialized' courts (e.g. French and Italian administrative courts). In this book, I use the phrase 'the ordinary courts' to denote all courts except the constitutional court.

[4] A full discussion of the politico-historical origins of European constitutional courts is beyond the scope of this book, but see von Beyme (1989), Kommers (1997: chs 1–2), Stone (1990, 1992a: chs 1, 2, 9), and Volcansek (in press: ch. 2).

[5] This section is based on Stone (1992a: ch. 9).

and a pan-European movement of prominent legal scholars who favoured installing American judicial review on the Continent (Stone 1992*a*: ch. 1; Neumann 1964: ch. 2). Kelsen understood that the political elites would not accept the establishment of judicial review in Europe. Nevertheless, he believed that a constitutional court, if granted carefully prescribed powers, would not arouse their hostility. The trick would be to show that such a system could provide the benefits of constitutional review, without turning into a government of judges.

Kelsen (1928: 221–41) engaged both fronts at once. First, he distinguished the work of legislators, which he characterized as 'creative' and 'positive', from the work of constitutional judges, which he characterized as 'negative'. Legislators make law freely, limited only by procedural constitutional law (which distributes governing authority among institutions and levels of government and establishes the rules of the legislative process). Kelsen acknowledged that the authority to declare legislation unconstitutional is also a law-making, and therefore political, authority:

To annul a law is to assert a general [legislative] norm, because the annulment of a law has the same character as its elaboration—only with a negative sign attached. . . . A tribunal which has the power to annul a law is, as a result, an organ of legislative power.

But if constitutional judges make law, they do not do so freely, since the judges' decision-making is 'absolutely determined by the constitution'. A constitutional court is therefore only 'a negative legislator'.

Kelsen's distinction between the positive and negative legislator relies almost entirely on the absence, within the constitutional law, of a judicially enforceable charter of rights. Here, we encounter another feature of Kelsen's thought, a conception of the law and of the proper role of courts that goes under the label, 'legal positivism'. Grossly simplifying, for positivists, the law is the corpus of prescriptions that some person or group (a law-maker) has made, that are enforceable by courts and other state institutions, and that are meant to apply authoritatively to specific situations.[6] Kelsen's conception of the unity of the legal system (a hierarchical system of interdependent rules) rested on the fundamental *positive* nature of the constitution. Positivism is often juxtaposed to 'natural law' theories, which generally assert that human will, however organized in any given society, is neither the only, nor the ultimate source of law. Instead, some foundational principles of law (such as human rights) transcend time and place, and therefore are (or ought to be) directly applicable in every legal system, even

---

[6] For a contemporary discussion of the relevance of legal positivism, see George *ed.* (1996).

when they have not been explictly proclaimed by a law-maker. In the positivist legal order, judges apply the law-maker's law; in the natural law legal
order, judges seek to 'discover' and then apply principles that have an
existence which is prior and independent of the law-maker's law. Kelsen
believed that constitutions should not contain human rights, which he
associated with natural law, because of their open-ended nature.
Adjudicating rights claims would inevitably weaken positivism's hold on
judges, thereby undermining the legitimacy of the judiciary itself, since
judges would become the law-makers. Thus, he wrote

Sometimes constitutions themselves may refer to [natural law] principles, which
invoke the ideals of equity, justice, liberty, equality, morality, etc., without in the
least defining [precisely] what are meant by these terms. . . . But with respect to
constitutional justice, these principles can play an extremely dangerous role. A
court could interpret these constitutional provisions, which invite the legislator to
honor the principles of justice, equity, equality . . . as positive requirements for the
contents of laws.

To the extent that constitutional judges would actually invoke natural law,
Kelsen believed, they would become positive legislators, a government of
judges would ensue, and a political backlash against constitutional review
would be the likely outcome.

Second, Kelsen argued that the constitutional court should be able to
review the constitutionality of legislation before its enforcement in the
public realm, thus preserving the sovereign character of statute within the
legal system afterwards. Elected politicians, within parliaments, or in subnational governments (within federal systems), would be able to initiate
such review.

Third, Kelsen argued that constitutional courts should look as much as
possible like other courts. He insisted that professional judges and law professors be recruited to the court, and emphasized that 'members of parliament or of the government' be excluded (on the other hand, he insisted
that, because the court would play a legislative role, elected officials should
appoint the court's members). He also proposed that the court might be
given jurisdiction over constitutional controversies originating in the
courts, as a means of securing the superiority of constitutional law, but also
in order to link the court's work with formally judicial processes. Finally,
individuals and/or a special constitutional ombudsmen might be given the
authority to refer matters to the constitutional court.

With the exception of Austria, Kelsen's ideas about constitutional justice
were ignored or dismissed during the interwar period. Traditionalists, like

the German theoretician, Carl Schmitt (e.g. 1958: 77–90), argued that Kelsen's court would not function as a court at all, but would instead become a kind of supralegislature (see Zanon 1991). Proponents of American-style review regarded Kelsen's ideas as heresy, a brief for 'political' rather than 'judicial' review (Stone 1992a: ch. 1). Most important, across Europe the major political parties remained hostile to the establishment of review of any kind. Legislation must respect constitutional principles, the argument went, but only legislators should possess the authority to assure that respect. Last, the experience of American judicial review, which had decisively blocked social reform in the decades leading up to the New Deal, was widely discussed (by way of Lambert 1921); many assumed that a move to establish constitutional review would engender a similar, European, 'government of judges'.

The New Constitutionalism

The awesome destruction of World War II made possible the diffusion of the Kelsenian court. The bitter experience of fascism in Italy and Germany before the war, and the massive American presence in both countries after it, conspired to undermine fatally deeply entrenched ideologies that emphasized the state's omnipotent nature. Taming the state—constraining government in a system of democratic controls, recognizing the liberties of individuals, and embedding states in pan-European structures (like NATO and the emerging European Communities)—was suddenly at the very top of the European agenda. As democratic reconstruction proceeded, higher law constitutionalism became the new orthodoxy. The precepts of this new constitutionalism can be simply listed: (1) state institutions are established by, and derive their authority exclusively from, a written constitution; (2) this constitution assigns ultimate power to the people by way of elections; (3) the use of public authority, including legislative authority, is lawful only insofar as it conforms with the constitutional law; (4) that law will include rights and a system of justice to defend those rights. As an overarching political ideology, or theory of the state, the new constitutionalism faces no serious rival today.

The European model of review proved popular because—unlike American judicial review—it could be easily attached to the parliamentary-based architecture of the state. Nevertheless, Kelsen's institutional blueprint had to be modified in one crucial respect. Kelsen had argued that constitutional courts should be denied jurisdiction over constitutional rights, in order to ensure that judicial and legislative functions remain as separate as possible. Since World War II, Europe has experienced a rights revolution, a hugely important movement to codify human rights at both the national and supranational levels. The burden of protecting these rights has fallen on modern Kelsenian courts.

CONSTITUTIONAL CONTRACTING

New constitutional forms emerge only under extraordinary historical conditions, moments when pre-existing political, economic, and social structures have been weakened, delegitimized, or swept away by deep crisis or war. Such was the case in Germany and Italy after World War II, in France at the height of the Algerian crisis in 1958, in Greece, Portugal, and Spain with the erosion of fascist-military rule in the 1970s, and in Central and Eastern Europe with the demise of communism after 1989. A new constitution promises a new beginning, the birth of a new polity (see Ackerman 1997).

Although consensus on the ideals of democratic constitutionalism facilitated the drafting of new constitutions in Germany, Italy, and Spain, this drafting process was in fact full of hard-nosed politics. Although I have characterized the new constitutionalism in terms of a new hierarchy of norms, or a new state theory, constitutions may also be seen as contracts—a set of nested bargains—among those who negotiate them. Most post-World War II European constitutions were in fact produced by intense, often conflictual negotiations among the main, national political parties. Each party, of group of parties, arrayed or clustered on the left, right or in the centre of the ideological spectrum, brought to the bargaining table there own constitutional preferences, ideas about how the new polity was to be constructed. Each party or grouping fought to enshrine these ideas as constitutional provisions. This bargaining was structured partly by the relative power of the participants in the constitutional convention, partly by the extent to which constitutional preferences either converged or diverged.

Constitutional Bargains

Parties contract with each other in order to achieve joint purposes (i.e. in order to provide benefits they could not expect to realize on their own). In the case of political parties, such benefits include the potential to rule, to direct the polity. Of course, in establishing parliamentary democracy, each political party knows that its capacity to determine events will ebb and flow depending on its relative electoral fortunes. Each party hopes to see its policy preferences substantiated as law, through legislation. Yet the parties also know that the construction of stable rules for competition among them is a necessary first step to governing. Constitutional contracting—the choice of rules governing the interactions of policy-makers—is often easier than choosing among those policy alternatives that are possible within the rules (Brennan and Buchanan 1985). Given the consensus in favour of parliamentarianism, the parties were able to come to agreement on the basic rules, not least, since each could see itself, over time, benefiting from them.

In Germany, Italy, and Spain, negotiations produced four main outcomes. First, the contracting parties established parliamentary systems of government. Such systems are based on the principle that the winners of parliamentary elections legislate and govern as they see fit. The people elect legislators (members of parliament); legislators elect the head of government (prime minister) and elect or approve the prime minister's government (cabinet); and the government directs the activities of the parliament, while remaining 'responsible' to it.

The other three outcomes ran counter to these centralizing tendencies. The bargaining over the distribution of powers between the national and subnational levels of government were rancorous and often paralyzing, but in the end the German, Italian, and Spanish constitutions, in varying degrees, provided for federalism (Germany) or strong regionalism (Italy and Spain).

The third outcome, the codification of an enforceable body of fundamental rights and liberties, proved to be the most difficult to achieve. Elster has argued (1989: 215, 244–7), that 'norm-free bargaining'—where 'the only thing at stake is self-interest'—is most likely to result in a settlement, whereas 'norm conflicts' frequently lead to 'bargaining impasse' since the parties bargain from the standpoint of radically opposed social values. Arguments about rights are inherently arguments about social values (and therefore policy alternatives). Indeed, the general problem of determining the exact content of rights provisions proved to be the most difficult aspect of constitutional negotiations in all countries. Simplifying what were enormously complex politics, impasses were broken in a similar way: each party was allowed to enshrine its own preferred set of rights, usually watered down somewhat by the 'horse-trading', thus giving partial victories to everyone.

Despite these disagreements, new European constitutions bestow a privileged status on rights provisions. In Germany, Italy, and Spain, constitutions announce rights before state institutions are established and governmental functions distributed. Partly in consequence, academic lawyers and some judges consider rights to possess supraconstitutional status (see Chapter 4). As will be discussed below, this privileged status is reinforced by rules governing constitutional amendment, which tend to treat non-rights provisions as more flexible, and rights provisions as more rigid and immutable. Thus, although the constitutional law is viewed as positive law in these countries, parts of that law—rights—express (or codify) natural law.

Table 2.1 lists those constitutional rights and duties expressly contained in the German, Italian, and Spanish constitutions, and in texts incorporated into the French constitution by the French constitutional court, the Constitutional Council. The scope of these texts is far more extensive than the American bill of rights. European charters typically include the traditional 'liberal', or 'negative', rights and freedoms of speech, assembly, religion, equality before the law, and due process. But they also enshrine newer, more 'collective', or 'positive', rights, to education, employment, trade union activity, healthcare, the development of 'personality', and leisure. And they also enumerate the responsibilities of citizens to their state, and of the state to the citizenry.

The fourth outcome was the adoption of the Kelsenian court.

Constitutional Courts

The normative logic of a constitutionalism that limits legislative sovereignty by recognizing the rights of individuals and the prerogatives of subnational government all but necessitates the establishment of a means of enforcing these rules. In occupied Germany and Italy, the Americans insisted that new constitutions include a charter of rights and a means of protecting them. American-style judicial review was nonetheless rejected in these states, and across Europe thereafter, for diverse reasons. Most important, a majority of political élites remained hostile to sharing policy-making authority with judiciaries; left-wing parties, especially, fiercely opposed judicial review, seeing in it the spectre of the dreaded 'government of judges'. Kelsenian constitutional review provides a means of defending constitutional law as higher law, while retaining the general prohibition on judicial review. Kelsenian review, it was also thought, could also be more easily controlled than American judicial review, since review authority is concentrated in a single body. Constitutional courts diffused even more widely during the second and third waves of post-war Continental democratization and constitution-making (the 1970s in southern Europe, and the 1990s in the post-Communist East). The Spanish Constituent Assembly, which modelled the Spanish constitutional review system on the German, never seriously considered *not* establishing a Kelsenian court. In the debates, only the Spanish Communists argued against establishing a system of constitutional review.

I have left France out of the discussion so far because the new constitutionalism emerged there by a different, far more circuitous, route (Stone 1992*a*). Unlike Germany and Italy, France was not occupied by the Americans. Other logics favouring constitutional review are weak or nonexistent. The state is unitary not federal, with a tradition of weak regional and local government. The two post-war constitutions (1946, 1958) did not establish enforceable rights, indeed, statutory supremacy remained unquestioned dogma. The constitution of the Fifth Republic was not so much the product of inter-party bargaining, but rather the choice of one political force, the entourage of General de Gaulle, acting almost unchecked. The entire Left—Socialists and Communists—voted against the new constitution in parliament, but the Right majority prevailed.

The Gaullists replaced France's traditional, British-style, parliamentary system with a 'mixed presidential–parliamentary' one, strengthening the executive. The constitution established a Constitutional Council, but its purpose was to guarantee the dominance of the executive (the government) over a weak parliament. Beginning in 1971, however, the Council began to assert its independence. In that year, for the first time, it declared a government-sponsored law unconstitutional on the grounds that the law violated constitutional rights (Council 1971). This decision paved the way for the incorporation of a charter of rights into the 1958 constitution, a charter that the Council has taken upon itself to enforce.[7] Thus, for the first time, and against the wishes of de Gaulle, his agents, and the other political parties in 1958, France has both an effective bill of rights and an effective constitutional court.

Constitutional Courts and the 'Relational' Contract

Constitutional contracting itself produces a demand for the establishment of something like a constitutional court. Generally, contracts can be said to be 'incomplete' to the extent that there exists meaningful uncertainty as to the precise nature of the commitments made. Due to the insurmoutable

---

[7] This charter is composed of rights texts mentioned or contained in the preamble to the 1946 constitution, which itself is mentioned in the preamble to the 1958 constitution.

TABLE 2.1. Rights and responsibilities in European constitutions

	France	Germany	Italy	Spain
Right or freedom				
Human dignity		x		
Life		x		x
Equality before the law	x	x	x	x
Equal rights for men and women	x	x	x	x
Religion	x	x	x	x
Conscientious objection to military service		x		x
Security	x		x	x
Privacy	Y	x	x	x
Personal honour		x		x
Inviolability of home and person	Y	x	x	x
Movement and travel	Y	x	x	x
Spoken and written expression	x	x	x	x
Marriage and family	Y	x	x	x
Freely develop one's personality	x	x		x
Asylum for persecuted non-nationals	x	x	x	
Adequate health care	x		x	
Concerning association and political participation				
Political participation	x	x	x	x
Vote and run for elected office	x	x	x	x
Petition		x	x	x
Personal beliefs, ideology	x	x	x	x
Resist political oppression	x	x		
Assembly	x	x	x	x
Association	x	x	x	x
Concerning the economic system				
Private property	x	x	x	x
Inheritance		x	x	x
Private enterprise	Y	x	x	x
Work	x	x	x	x
Choose occupation		x	x	x
Adequate pay			x	x
Adequate housing			x	x
Equal pay for men and women			x	
Form and join unions	x	x	x	x
Worker's participation in management	x		x	
Strike	x	x	x	x
Unemployment compensation	x		x	x
Old age pensions	x		x	x
Vocational training			x	x
Leisure and vacations	x		x	x
Concerning the educational system				
Public education	x	x	x	x
Religious education	Y	x		x
Participate in school management				x

	France	Germany	Italy	Spain
Teaching and research	Y	X	X	X
Private schooling	Y	X	X	
Concerning the judicial and penal system				
Access to the courts and judicial protection	Y	X	X	X
Remedies for judicial malfeasance			X	X
Legal defence	Y		X	X
Public trial				X
Speedy trial				X
Refusal to self-incriminate				X
Immunity from retroactive application of the law	X	X	X	X
Habeas corpus		X		X
Presumption of innocence	X		X	X
Immunity from double jeopardy		X		
Rehabilitation while incarcerated			X	X
Social security benefits while incarcerated				X
(Death penalty constitutionally abolished)		X	X	X
Duties				
Of citizens				
Military service		X	X	X
Pay taxes	X		X	X
Work			X	X
Financially support, educate their children			X	X
Vote			X	
Of the state				
Guarantee media pluralism	X	Y	Y	X
Protect the family and children	X	X	X	X
Facilitate social and economic progress			X	X
Regulates property rights in public good			X	
Provide equitable distribution of resources				X
Provide public health care	X		X	X
Pursue full employment				X
Provide unemployment compensation	X		X	X
Guarantee safety of working conditions			X	X
Protect public health	X		X	X
Guarantee leisure or vacation time	X		X	X
Promote culture and science	X		X	X
Protect the environment			X	X
Provide old age pensions	X		X	X
Protect handcapped			X	X
Protect consumers				X
Protect linguistic minorities			X	
Provide public education	X	X	X	X
Nationalize industries	X			

* *Note:* x denotes that the right, freedom, or duty is expressly provided for by one or more constitutional provisions. y denotes that the right, freedom, or duty exists by virtue of a decision of the constitutional court. Where neither x nor y appear in cells, that country's constitutional law does not provide for the corresponding right, freedom, or duty.

difficulties associated with negotiating rules for all possible contingencies, and given that, as time passes, conditions will change and the interests of the parties to the agreement will evolve, all contracts are incomplete in some significant way.[8] Most agreements of any complexity are generated by what organizational economists call 'relational contracting'. The parties to an agreement seek to 'frame' broadly their relationship, by agreeing on a set of basic 'goals and objectives', fixing outer limits on acceptable behaviour, and establishing procedures for completing the contract over time (Milgrom and Roberts 1992: 127–33; see also Majone 1996).

Modern European constitutions—complex instruments of governance designed to last indefinitely, if not forever—are paradigmatic examples of relational contracts. Much is left general, even ill-defined and vague, as in the case of rights. Generalities and vagueness may facilitate agreement at the *ex ante*, constitutional moment. But vagueness, by definition, is normative uncertainty, and normative uncertainty threatens to undermine rationales for contracting in the first place. The establishment of constitutional review can be understood as an institutional response to the incomplete contract, the linked problems of uncertainty and enforcement. Each party to it has an interest in seeing that other parties obeys their obligations, and will reprimanded when failing to do so. Review functions to clarify, over time, the meaning of the contract, and to monitor compliance.

The constitution itself, through rules of jurisdiction, delegates authority to constitutional judges, determining how they are to exercise review.[9]

Jurisdiction

Table 2.2 summarizes (and simplifies) the constitutional review mechanisms established in France, Germany, Italy, and Spain. There are three basic types of review jurisdiction: abstract review, concrete review, and the individual constitutional complaint procedure.[10] Abstract review is

---

[8] A 'complete' contract, in Milgrom and Roberts' terms (1992: 127), 'would specify precisely what each party is to do in every possible circumstance and arrange the distribution of realized costs and benefits in each contingency so that each party individually finds it optimal to abide by the contract's terms'.

[9] Although important rules of jurisdiction are constitutional in nature, some jurisdictional details are regulated by statutes called organic laws. The distinction is not of great importance here, but see Ch. 3.

[10] I have simplified the language commonly used to distinguish different modes of constitutional control, and aggregated similar modes into larger categories. For more nuanced discussions, see Weber (1987), Rubio Llorente (1988a), and the Seventh Conference of Constitutional Courts (1989). Constitutional courts may also perform other functions not discussed here, including: reviewing the constitutionality of international agreements (see

'abstract' because the review of legislation takes place in the absence of lit-igation, in American parlance, in the absence of a concrete case or contro-versy. Concrete review is 'concrete' because the review of legislation, or other public act, constitutes a separate stage in an ongoing judicial process (litigation in the ordinary courts). In individual complaints, a private indi-vidual alleges the violation of a constitutional right by a public act or gov-ernmental official, and requests redress from the court for this violation.

Abstract review processes result in decisions on the constitutionality of legislation that has been adopted by parliament but has not yet entered into force (France), or that has been adopted and promulgated, but not yet applied (Germany, Italy, Spain). As Table 2.2 shows, abstract review is ini-tiated by specifically designated, elected politicians. Executives and legisla-tors (France, Germany, Spain), federated member states or regional governments (Germany, Italy, Spain), or an ombudsman (the Defender of the People in Spain) may, within prescribed time limits, attack legislation as unconstitutional before the constitutional court. These attacks are made in writing, in documents known as referrals or petitions. In practice, nearly all such referrals are made by members of opposition parties, against legis-lation proposed by the majority, or governing, party or parties. Referrals usually suspend the legal force of the referred law (France, Germany, Italy) pending a ruling, but in Spain the law may be applied until a ruling, which must take place within prescribed time limits (Spain).[11] Abstract review processes serve to organize a constitutional dialogue between elected politicians and constitutional judges in the making of legislation and the meaning of the constitution.

Concrete review processes organize constitutional dialogues between constitutional judges and the judiciary in the defence of the supremacy of the constitution, the administration of justice, and the protection of human rights. Concrete review is initiated by the judiciary (Germany, Italy, Spain) in the course of litigation in the courts. Judicial officials are autho-rized to refer constitutional questions—is a given law, legal rule, judicial decision, or administrative act constitutional?—to constitutional judges. The general rule is that a presiding judge will go to the constitutional court if two conditions are met: (1) that the constitutional question is material to litigation at bar (i.e. who wins and who loses depends on the answer to the question); and (2) there is reasonable doubt in the judge's mind about the constitutionality of the act or rule in question. Referrals suspend

Ch. 6), verifying the compliance of political parties with electoral laws, presiding over impeachment proceedings, and so on.

[11] The time limits binding the Spanish court are rarely respected.

proceedings pending a review by the constitutional court. Once rendered, the constitutional court's judgment is sent back to the referring judge, who then decides the case with the help of the ruling. Constitutional decisions are binding on the judiciary. Ordinary judges are not permitted, at least in theory, to determine the constitutionality of public acts on their own (but see Chapters 4 and 5).

Individual complaints (a *Verfassungsbeschwerde* in German, an *amparo* in Spanish) bring private actors into the mix (Sánchez Morón 1986; Singer 1982). Once judicial remedies have been exhausted, individuals (Germany, Spain), and an ombudsman (Spain) have the right to go to directly to constitutional judges. In Spain, individuals may attack the act of any public official that they think has violated their constitutional rights, with one important exception. Technically, the *amparo* may not be used to attack a statute, although this occurs under certain conditions (Guasch 1994). In Germany, persons who believe that they have suffered as a result of a specific infringement of the constitutional law, by a public official, may file a complaint.[12] A statute may be targeted, as long as the complainant's rights have been abridged in some 'personal' and 'direct' way (Schenke 1986). In both countries, appeals of judicial decisions (on the grounds that due process has been denied) comprise, by far, the largest class of complaints.

Once constitutional review processes have been activated, constitutional judges are legally obligated to render a decision. The law further requires judges to justify their rulings in written, 'reasoned' decisions.

Composition

Table 2.3 compares rules governing the recruitment of constitutional judges in France, Germany, Italy, and Spain. Two modes of appointment exist—nomination and election. Where nomination procedures are used, the appointing authority simply names a judge or a slate of judges; no countervailing confirmation or veto procedures exist. Such is the case of France, where all constitutional judges are named by political authorities. Italy and Spain have mixed nomination and election systems. Where election systems are used, a qualified, or super, majority (a 2/3 or 3/5 vote) within a parliamentary body is necessary for appointment. Because the German, Italian, and Spanish polities are multi-party systems, and because no single party has ever possessed a super-majority on its own, the

---

[12] In Germany, local officials can also file complaints if they believe that the constitutional prerogatives of local government have been abridged by the public actions of another level of government.

TABLE 2.2. Jurisdiction of European constitutional courts

	France (1959)	Germany (1951)	Italy (1948)	Spain (1978)
Constitutional Court	Constitutional Council (Council)	Federal Constitutional Court (GFCC)	Italian Constitutional Court (ICC)	Spanish Constitutional Tribunal (SCT)
Year created/ began operations	1958/1959	1949, 1951	1948, 1956	1978, 1981
Abstract review Authority to initiate abstract review of legislation	Yes President Pres. Assembly Pres. Senate *Since 1974:* 60 Assembly deputies 60 Senators	Yes Federal govt *Länder* govts 1/3 Bundestag	Yes National govt (against regional laws) Regional govts (against national laws)	Yes Prime Minister Pres. of Parliament 50 Deputies 50 Senators Executives of autonomous regions Ombudsman ('Defender of the People')
Laws referred	National legislation	Federal and *Länder* (federated member state) legislation	National and regional legislation	National and regional legislation
Laws must be referred	Within 15 days following adoption by parliament	Within 30 days following adoption by federal or *Länder* parliament	Within 30 days following adoption by regional or national govt	Within 90 days following adoption by parliament or regional govt
Effect of referral	Suspends promulgation pending a ruling. Council must rule within 30-day limit	Suspends application of the law pending ruling	Suspends application of the law pending ruling	Referral has no legal effect on the law. STC must rule within 30-day limit
Concrete review Authority to initiate concrete review of legislation	No	Yes Judiciary Individuals (after judicial remedies exhausted)	Yes Judiciary	Yes Judiciary Ombudsman Individuals (after judicial remedies exhausted)

qualified majority requirement effectively necessitates the parties to negotiate with each other in order to achieve consensus on a slate of candidates.
This bargaining process occurs in intense, behind-closed-doors negotiations. In practice, these negotiations determine which party will fill
vacancies on the court, with allocations usually roughly proportionate to
relative parliamentary strength.

Table 2.3 also indicates who may serve as a constitutional judge. All
German, Italian, and Spanish judges must have had advanced legal training, as well as professional experience in some domain of law. The constitution may also contain precise quotas, guaranteeing a minimal number of
professional judges drawn from the ordinary courts. In Germany, the
sixteen-member court must always contain at least six federal judges; in
Italy, representatives of the judiciary control the appointment of 5/15 seats;
and in Spain, they control 2/12. In France, no legal training is required.
Perhaps in consequence, a majority of the French Council has always been
made up of former ministers and parliamentarians, although many of
these have studied or practised some law. Several influential law professors
and a few former ordinary judges have served on the French Council, but
far fewer than in the other countries. In Germany, Italy, and Spain, law professors make up the largest group of appointees, followed by former ordinary judges and lawyers. Only in Italy does the number of politicians
appointed approach that of France: of the judges elected by parliament
through 1988, 15/20 had been at one time parliamentarians; but factoring
in double careers, the great majority of all appointees have also been either
law professors (28/64) or former ordinary judges (26/64).[13]

In the introductory chapter, I surveyed a number of approaches to constitutional politics typically employed by political scientists. One of these,
the judicial decision-making approach, is not easily exported to Europe.
The data commonly used by scholars, voting records and anecdotal evidence about internal decision-making, are simply unavailable in much of
Europe. In France and Italy, decisions are presented as unanimous, and
publication of votes and dissents is prohibited by law. In Germany and
Spain, dissents are permitted but rare. In all cases, internal deliberations
are, by law, secret. We know that those who possess the power to name or
elect constitutional judges do so with an eye to the political advantage of
this or that appointment. But we cannot study systematically the extent to
which these appointments alter the court's production. The absence of
dependable data on the internal politics of courts, however, cannot mean

[13] The best source for such information is the symposium on judicial recruitment to
constitutional courts (Table Ronde 1990).

TABLE 2.3. Recruitment and composition of European constitutional courts

	France	Germany	Italy	Spain
Number of members	9	16	15	12
Recruiting authorities	*Named by:* President (3) Pres. Assembly (3) Pres. Senate (3)	*Elected by:* Bundestag (8) Bundesrat (8) (by 2/3 majority)	*Named by:* National Govt (5) Judiciary (5) *Elected by:* Parliament (5) (2/3 majority of joint session)	*Named by:* National Govt (2) Judiciary (2) *Elected by:* Congress (4) Senate (4) (by 3/5 majority)
Length of term	9 years	12 years	9 years	9 years
Age limit	None	40 year min. 68 year max.	None	None
Requisite qualifications	None	6/16 must be federal judges; all must be qualified to be federal judges	All must be judges with 20 years in practice, or tenured law professors	May be judges, law professors, lawyers, or civil servants, with at least 15 years of experience, and whose 'judicial competence' is well known

that such politics are absent or unimportant (see Chapter 5). None the less, a social science of the political behaviour of European constitutional courts must be constructed on other bases. In this book, one such basis is the impact of constitutional courts on the decision-making of other legislative and judicial actors.

PARLIAMENTARY GOVERNMENT AND CONSTITUTIONAL REVIEW

Prior to the appearance of Kelsen's court, it was widely assumed that constitutional review was incompatible with parliamentary governance. The parliamentary system owes its popularity to its capacity to combine centralized political authority with representative democracy. The system privileges the ideology of majority rule, what the French call 'the general will'. Constitutional review, by contrast, was thought to 'fit' only in polities where unfettered majority rule had been rejected. The democratic legitimacy of constitutional review rests on the ideology of higher law constitutionalism, which subordinates the exercise of all governmental authority, even that which is made according to the general will, to the law of the constitution. The new constitutionalism assumes that parliament can do wrong, and that some wrongs must be corrected. As constitutional review has evolved in Europe, traditional notions of parliamentary supremacy have had to be adjusted. This adjustment process has been partly driven by interactions between constitutional judges and legislators, and partly by interactions between constitutional courts and judiciaries.

I now discuss, in a relatively abstract manner, the main structural factors that condition these interactions.

Constitutional Politics and the Legislature

Two factors: (1) the mode(s) of review exercised by a constitutional court, and (2) the extent to which parliamentary majorities seek to enact radical reform legislation, broadly determine the nature, scope, and intensity of the interactions between legislators and constitutional judges. A third factor, the stage of development of those constitutional rules relevant to the decision-making of law-makers and judges, is a product of constitutional politics itself, and thus must be treated somewhat differently. Put in terms of the theory presented in Chapter 1, these three factors explain variation in the extent of the 'judicialization' of parliamentary governance in Europe.

Jurisdiction, or Mode of Review

The first factor is jurisdiction. Figure 2.1 depicts two stylized legislative processes, one incorporating *abstract*, and the other *concrete*, review procedures. Government ministers draft virtually every important legislative proposal. Once approved, the government sends the bill to parliament. Parliamentarians, working in committees and in plenary sessions, either (1) adopt, (2) amend and adopt, or (3) reject the bill, in a series of 'readings'. Abstract review referrals lengthen the legislative process, by adding another stage to it: a final, 'constitutional reading' of the law by constitutional judges, after final adoption by parliament. Referrals are almost always made by members of the opposition parties (members of the governing majority have no incentive to refer their own bills for review). In abstract review processes, legislators and constitutional judges interact with each other directly. Parliamentary petitions make up the French Council's entire caseload, and a portion of the German and Spanish courts' docket. Italian parliamentarians do not possess the power to refer legislation they oppose to their court.[14]

Other things being equal, systems that contain abstract review ought to experience more judicialization than systems that do not. Abstract review harnesses the (virtually continuous) struggle between parliamentary majority and opposition over policy outcomes to a particular end: the progressive development of constitutional constraints on law-making.

As Fig. 2.1 shows, concrete review jurisdiction, too, may enable constitutional judges to participate in the activity of the legislature. But in concrete review processes, law-makers and constitutional judges interact only indirectly, through the medium of litigation in the ordinary courts. Compared with abstract review, concrete review is a more costly way of undermining a law: it may take years and several decisions by ordinary judges before the constitutional court decides. Normally, concrete review is also less politically provocative. By the time the constitutional court renders a decision on a given law, whatever partisan bickering had taken place at the time of its adoption may have calmed or disappeared altogether. Still,

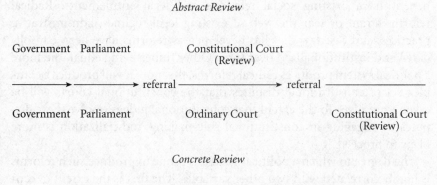

FIG. 2.1. *Constitutional review and the legislative process.*

---

[14] The Italian constitutional convention debated the relative merits of abstract review and American-style judicial review. The present system—concrete review by a specialized constitutional court, but abstract review of centre-periphery disputes—was the product of a complex set of compromises (Pizzorusso, Vigoriti, and Certoma 1984).

because concrete review can result in constitutional rule-making, judicialization can proceed. In polities that have both concrete and abstract review, the latter tends to accentuate the judicializing effects of constitutional rule-making produced by the former (see Chapters 3 and 4).

Jurisidiction over disputes about federalism or regionalism also generates constitutional caseload and influence on law-making. In Germany and Spain, and to a far lesser extent in Italy, a proportion of the decisions rendered by constitutional courts concern the delimitation of competences among national and subnational levels of governance. Disputes about competence may nevertheless have national political implications. In Germany and Spain, for example, the subnational wings of national opposition parties in control of state level or regional governments regularly use their abstract review powers to refer national legislation touching on the competences of the federated states or autonomous regions to their respective constitutional courts.

Reform and the Status Quo

The more radical the legislation adopted by parliament, the more likely that the law will be referred to the constitutional court. A legislative reform is 'radical' the more it moves from the status quo (the initial situation governed by legislation then in place). By its very nature, a radical reform provokes resistance because its implementation will be costly to those who benefit from existing social relations and legal entitlements. Radical reforms strain or tear the web of existing legal regimes, administrative practices, and case law that has developed as reforms have been consolidated and institutionalized over time. Other things being equal, the more a political system produces radical reforms, the more it will produce a complex set of constitutional disputes that the constitutional courts will be asked to resolve. To the extent that constitutional judges resolve these disputes by engaging in constitutional rule-making, judicialization is more likely to proceed.

The degree to which a political system is prone to produce such reforms is highly correlated with two other variables. The first is the extent of centralized control over the legislative process. Compared with presidential systems (like the American), the degree of centralized control in European parliamentary systems is generally quite high. The rise of prime ministerial (or cabinet) government—reinforced by relatively strict party discipline within parliament, and anchored by relatively stable party systems outside it—has come at the expense of the legislature (Blondel 1973). Polsby's transformative–arena dichotomy is helpful in this regard. *Transformative* legislatures are those which 'possess the independent capacity, frequently exercised, to mold and transform proposals from whatever source [including itself] into laws'. The US Congress is the prototype of the transformative legislature. *Arena* legislatures are formal 'settings' for the ratification and legitimation of policy made elsewhere (Polsby 1975), that is, by the government (the executive). The French, German, Italian, and Spanish parliaments are all arena legislatures of varying degree.

Cross-national variance in the degree of centralized control is best understood in the light of relevant 'veto points' in the legislative process. A veto point is a formally organized opportunity for opponents of the governing majority to block legislative provisions they do not like from becoming law. Abstract review comprises one such veto point: oppositions can refer legislation to constitutional judges; neither the government nor the parliamentary majority can block this referral; and the constitutional court can veto the bill as unconstitutional.

Before a bill can become law, the lower house of parliament must give its assent but, with some important exceptions, parliamentary stages of the process are relatively veto-free. The French process is the most centralized: the government controls the National Assembly's timetable; deputies are not allowed to propose bills or amendments that would have the effect of raising or spending money; and only those laws or amendments which the government supports may be adopted. The Spanish system is similarly organized. Members of the German and the Italian lower houses possess more law-making autonomy than do their French and Spanish counterparts, and because of fragmented executives, they exercise it more. But all legislative questions are ultimately decided by majority votes, and if the executive is always supported by a majority, the executive will always get its way.

Whether or not the upper house can veto the decisions of the lower house may be a matter of great importance if the partisan make-up of the two chambers differ. The French and Spanish Senates possess only suspensive vetoes, that is, the government can, by obtaining a simple majority vote of the lower house, overturn the veto. The German Bundesrat, a body comprised of government ministers of the federated states (the *Länder*), possesses an absolute veto over bills that fall within a shared area of competence of the member states of the German federation. In practice, this amounts to well over 50 per cent of all legislation adopted. The Italian Senate, which possesses virtually the same powers as the lower house, must give its consent for any bill to become law. Thus, the upper houses in Italy and German constitute veto points.

Finally, the size of the share of seats in the lower house controlled by the party, or parties, of government can also make a difference. Other things being equal, coalition and minority governments tend to produce less audacious legislation than do governments supported by a single-party majority. In a coalition government, the senior partner may be forced to compromise aspects of its preferred legislative agenda, to the extent that the junior partner may demand such compromises as a condition for its continued support. Minority governments depend on the support of parliamentary parties not represented in the government to stay in power; in consequence, they are often forced to compromise with those parties on the terms of legislation. These outcomes are correlated with the type of electoral system used to elect the lower house. Proportional representation systems (Germany, Italy), tend to produce multi-party governments; single district, plurality systems (France, Spain) tend to produce single-party governments.

The degree of centralized control over the policy process impacts the conduct and intensity of constitutional politics on a number of dimensions. Where abstract review constitutes the only veto opportunity available, one would expect oppositions to make the most use of petitions to the constitutional court (France and Spain). Where the court is only the second, or even the third, filter of legislative ambition, the opposition might well be able to achieve its objectives without making use of the abstract review referral (Germany, Italy). Given the logic of radical versus status quo legislation, referrals are most likely where the government and majority have been able to resist compromise .

Now, let us put these elements together. Assume that governments always seek to translate their policy preferences into law with as little compromise with the opposition as possible, and that oppositions always seek to block or dilute the government's legislative initiative as much as possible (that is the opposition prefers the status quo). Other things being equal, legislative processes that are less centralized and more veto-laden will produce fewer politically controversial bills, compared with systems where the process is more centralized and relatively veto-free. On one pole is Italy, where we find both unstable coalition governments and a strong upper house—but no abstract review. In Germany, the combination of coalition government and the Bundesrat's veto tends to filter out the most audacious legislative reforms. France and Spain constitute the other pole, where permissive legislative processes tend to encourage governments to push for relatively radical reform.

Finally, alternations in power—from a Left majority to a Right majority, or vice versa—are important to the conduct of constitutional politics, for two reasons. First, the longer a political party (or coalition of parties) has been in the minority, the more that party is likely to seek radical legislative reforms, and the more the outgoing majority will seek to defend the status quo (its legacy). Constitutional judges would then face a relatively more difficult and politically sensitive caseload. Second, given the rules governing recruitment to the court, we have good reason to think that the longer a single governing majority political maintains dominance, the more a court's membership will reflect that majority's values. If this majority loses an election and is replaced by a new majority, a compositional disjuncture occurs to the extent that the majority of the court has been named by members of the outgoing majority. Thus, other things being equal, we can expect that abstract review referrals will rise after an election yielding an alternation in power from Left to Right and vice versa. And we can expect that public confrontations between legislators and constitutional judges will occur more often when alternations in power create disjunctures between the composition of parliament and the court. Although these propositions have not been the subject of systematic empirical study, the evidence appears to support them (see Stone 1992*a*: ch. 9; Stone 1994*a*).

Constitutional Rule-making

A third factor, the relative development of the constitutional law through constitutional rule-making (case law), is endogenous to the politics I am describing, to the extent that constitutional rule-making 'feeds back' onto the legislature reinforcing the same behaviours that provoked constitutional review in the first place. Put somewhat crudely, constitutional courts and oppositions are connected to one another by a kind of judicializing transmission belt. Oppositions judicialize legislative processes in order to win what they would otherwise lose in 'normal', unjudicialized processes (they would be outvoted). Abstract review petitions enable constitutional courts to construct the constitutional law, to extend techniques of control over law-making activities, and (the same thing) to make policy. As the constitutional law expands to more and more policy areas, and as it becomes 'thicker' in each domain (more dense, technical, and differentiated), so do the grounds for judicialized debate. The process powerfully tends to reproduce itself, and in so doing, judicialization is provoked and reinforced. At any given moment, therefore, the judicialization of parliamentary governance varies across policy sectors, as a function of the relative intensity of the interactions between law-makers and constitutional judges, and the relative scope of constitutional rule-making.

Summary and Assessment

Three factors explain most of the variance in the judicialization of law-making in Europe, both at the aggregate, cross-national level, and across policy domains within any given polity. We will find more judicialization in those systems that: (1) possess abstract review; and (2) produce radical reforms (exhibit relatively more centralized control over the policy process). In emphasizing the third factor—constitutional rule-making—I do not mean to imply that constitutional judges necessarily wish to impose their policy preferences on law-makers. I take no position on that question here. Instead, let us assume that constitutional judges do their jobs in a responsible (rather than fraudulent or corrupt) manner, and that they actually employ the two legitimation techniques I described in chapter 1. My thesis is that the more constitutional judges: (1) have a caseload; (2) resolve disputes by (at least periodically) 'splitting the difference' between the parties to the dispute, and thus sometimes annul legislation; and (3) justify their decisions normatively, and in a way that implies that their decisions constitute authoritative interpretations of the law,[15] judicialization will proceed. The first two variables largely determine variance in caseload. The third variable both reflects how judicialization has evolved, and conditions how it will develop in the future.

Constitutional Politics and the Judiciary

Although traditional separation of powers doctrines in parliamentary systems preclude judicial review of legislative acts, the new constitutionalism enables review by Kelsenian courts, and organizes a set of interactions between the judiciary[16] and constitutional judges. Concrete review

---

[15] All four constitutions provide that the constitutional court is the authoritative interpreter of the constitution whose decisions are binding on all public authorities. Recall that constitutional courts are obliged, either by constitutional provisions or by the laws that established them (organic laws), to give reasons for decisions taken, in published rulings.

[16] Due to length considerations, I assume a basic knowledge of how European judiciaries are organized here and in Chs 4 and 5. I am aware that this is a heroic assumption. Simplifying, the French, German, Italian, and Spanish legal systems share certain common attributes. In contrast to most American judicial institutions, European courts are organized by function. In Germany, five court systems (administrative, tax, labour, social security, and civil–criminal) coexist, each of which is capped by a supreme court, and each supreme court is autonomous from the others. France and Italy have two autonomous supreme courts, one to take appeals from criminal and civil courts (Court of Cassation), the other to take appeals from the administrative courts (Council of State). The Spanish Supreme Court is the final court of appeal for the civil, criminal, administrative, and social

processes require ordinary judges to participate in the scrutiny of legislation, weakening (at least formally) the domination of the codes over judicial work. In addition to this legal requirement, judicial officials have an interest in activating constitutional review to the extent that they wish: (1) to participate in the construction of the constitutional law; and (2) to remove unconstitutional (and perhaps unwanted) laws. Both are new powers for them. The constitutional court also benefits from the system. Concrete review enlists potential litigants and the judiciary in a general, relatively decentralized effort to detect violations of the constitution; judicial officials provide the constitutional court with a caseload; and the rules governing the process generally favour the constitutional court's control over outcomes.

Given this mix of formal rules and corporate interests, we can only expect that concrete review will undermine the dogma of the juridical supremacy of legislative acts even further, subverting traditional separation of powers schemes. Just how much subversion has actually occurred is explored in Chapters 4 and 5.

Principal–Agent Issues

As discussed in Chapter 1, delegation theories of governance organize the world into two sets of actors: (1) rulers, or 'principals'; and (2) 'agents', to whom the principals have delegated some meaningful authority to take authoritative decisions. In our four cases, the principals are the people, and they delegate power to governmental institutions through the constitution:

1. Germany (article 20.2): 'All governmental authority emanates from the People. It shall be exercised by the People by means of elections and voting, and by specific legislative, executive, and judicial organs'.
2. France (article 3): 'Sovereignty resides in the Nation. No body, no individual, may exercise authority which has not been expressly granted'.
3. Italy (article 1): 'Sovereignty belongs to the People, who exercise it in the manner and within the limits laid down by the Constitution'.
4. Spain (article 1.2): 'National sovereignty belongs to the Spanish People, from whom all powers of state emanate'.

court systems, each of which is otherwise autonomous; the Spanish Supreme Court also functions as a high military court. Overviews in English include: Bell, Boyron, and Whitaker (1998); Certoma (1985); Dadomo and Farran (1993); Foster (1993); Heyde (1994); Merino-Blanco (1996); and Watkin (1997). In Germany, Italy, and Spain, judges sitting on all of these courts possess the authority to make concrete review referrals. Neither the civil nor the administrative courts in France have any formal links with the Constitutional Council.

In practice, the political parties perform or otherwise participate in the control functions usually associated with principals, since they appoint judges to the courts, and they can initiate revision of the constitution in order to void the consequences of constitutional rule-making on the part of the judges. None the less, the political parties, in establishing review and specific procedures for constitutional revision, relinquished their monopoly over constitutional development. If they sometimes operate as principals, they are more often merely 'players' within the rule structures that are provided by the constitution, electoral laws, and parliamentary bodies. They compete with each other in order to be in the position to govern, most importantly, to legislate.

Constitutional adjudication, however, is implicated in the exercise of legislative power. If in exercising review authority, the judges simply controlled the integrity of parliamentary procedures, and not the substance of legislation, the judges would be relatively minor policy-makers (akin to Kelsen's 'negative legislator'). But the judges possess jurisdiction over rights which are, by definition, substantive constraints on law-making powers. The political parties thus transferred their own entirely unresolved problem—what is the nature and purpose of any given rights provision, and what is the normative relationship of that provision to the rest of the constitutional text?—to judges. This transfer constitutes a massive, virtually open-ended delegation of policy-making authority. Similarly, review jurisdiction organizes the elaboration of higher law rules governing federalism and regional autonomy in Germany (see Blair 1981; Kommers 1997: ch. 3; Laufer 1991), Italy (Volcansek in press), and Spain (García de Enterría 1993).

To the extent that it is costly or difficult to activate constitutional review of legislation, the importance of review within policy processes, and the authority of judges over outcomes, would be mitigated. But initiating abstract review is virtually without cost for oppositions; concrete review procedures entails delays for the litigants, but other costs are essentially borne by the state; and individual complaints can be scribbled by anyone on notebook paper. If it were relatively easy for the governing majority to overturn the case law of the court, or to curb the judges' powers, the court's authority over the legislature might be fleeting. What kinds of control mechanisms are available to the political parties is therefore relevant to predictions about how much policy autonomy judges will wield.

We can divide control mechanisms into two broad categories: direct and indirect. Direct controls are formal (they are established by explicit rules) and negative (they annul or authoritatively revise the court's decisions, or curb the court's powers). For our purposes here, the principal is that entity (or entities) which has the authority to revise the constitution in order to overturn a decision of the agent, the Court. To exercise control by direct means, the principal must succeed in revising the constitution.

The rules governing constitutional amendment are more or less permissive of agent autonomy. Most of the German constitution can be revised by a two-thirds majority vote of the Bundestag and the Bundesrat; however, the Basic Law explicitly precludes amending provisions that establish rights (and federalism). Thus, rulings interpreting rights provisions can never be overturned. In Spain, constitutional revision is normally accomplished by a 3/5 vote of the Cortes and the Senate, on initiation by either chamber or the government. But when a proposed amendment concerns a rights provision, a 2/3 majority in each chamber is required; and if this 2/3 majority is achieved, then parliament is dissolved, and the proposed amendment is submitted to the people for ratification by referendum. The 'diabolical complexity' of this process makes it 'practically impossible' to amend the constitution (Rubio Llorente 1995: 75). The Italian constitution can be amended by majority vote of the lower and upper houses, deliberating separately; but unless a 2/3 majority vote of both is secured, a ratification referendum is required if 1/5 of either house, or five regional councils, or 500,000 voters, so request. In Spain (Rubio Llorente 1995: 79) and Italy (Pizzorusso and Rossi 1995), core rights provisions are considered by legal scholars to be immune to revision. As in Germany, such provisions are consider to be possessed of 'supraconstitutional' status, a natural law position. In fact, no rights provision has been changed in Spain or Italy. In France, the revision process is the most permissive for political parties, since the parties can transform themselves into principals on their own:[17] once both parliamentary chambers have adopted the text of a constitutional amendment, a constitutional congress is organized, wherein deputies and senators, sitting together, revise the constitution by a 3/5 vote. Further, the French Council is the only one of the four constitutional courts to have determined that rights provisions are not privileged constitutional norms; every part of the constitution is open to revision as long as prescribed procedures are followed (see Favoreu 1994).

Indirect controls are informal and indirect. These mechanisms are effective only inasmuch as the agent internalizes the principal's interests, or takes cues from the revealed preferences of the latter, and acts accordingly.

---

[17] Recall that the constitution of the Fifth Republic did not originally contain a charter of rights.

It is generally assumed that the extent to which the agent does so is commensurate to the credibility of the threat that its principal will activate direct controls. Indirect controls operate according to the logic of deterrence: the more credible the threat of punishment, the more the agent will constrain itself by behaving as in the principal's interests were its own. This control is registered as an anticipatory reaction operating as a constraint on the court's behaviour.

The question of just how effective these controls have actually been is evaluated in Chapter 3.

CONCLUSION

In this chapter, I have discussed the institutional basis of European constitutional politics, focusing on how parliamentary systems of governance have accommodated constitutional review. The new constitutionalism presupposes review, for a number of important reasons. Most important, constitutional review was viewed as necessary to defend human rights. Review also can be understood as a means of 'completing' the constitution, a relational contract, over time. I then discussed the most important determinants of relations between constitutional judges, legislators, and the judiciary. In the next chapter, we focus on these relations in more detail, examining the reciprocal impact of law-making and constitutional adjudication.

3

Legislating

Legislative processes are sites of constitutional politics to the extent that they organise interactions between legislators and constitutional judges. As these interactions have grown over time, law-making and the construction of the constitutional law have tended to bind together, each process becoming at least partly constitutive of the other. This chapter explores this growing interdependence in France, Germany, Italy, and Spain.

I proceed from the view that constitutional courts ought to be conceptualized as specialized legislative organs, and constitutional review ought to be understood as one stage in the elaboration of statutes. Adopting this perspective facilitates observing and evaluating the complex relationship between constitutional adjudication and law-making. After examining how often, and with what techniques, constitutional courts intervene in legislative processes, I turn to the judicialization of parliamentary governance, focusing on the capacity of constitutional rule-making to structure ongoing legislative behaviour. Case studies illustrate my main points. Finally, I address some of the principal–agent issues raised in the previous chapters, in the light of empirical evidence presented here.

CONSTITUTIONAL COURTS AS SPECIALIZED
LEGISLATIVE CHAMBERS

One simple way of focusing attention on the policy impact of constitutional adjudication is to conceptualize the constitutional court as one kind of law-making body which interacts with other kinds of law-making bodies, within legislative processes (defended at length in Stone 1992*a*: chs 8, 9, and Stone 1994*a*). The legislative authority of constitutional judges is specialized, in that it is restricted to judging the constitutionality of statutes previously adopted by parliament. In European parliamentary systems, most of the nitty-gritty, technical legislative work is done by specialized parliamentary committees. Normally, the budget committee is far more sensitive to the fiscal consequences of proposed legislation than is the legislature as a whole; and the agricultural committee will be more competent to evaluate the likely consequences of certain proposals on farming and farmers than will the legislature as a whole. If the constitutional court were simply a specialized committee of the legislature, composed of regular members of the lower house of parliament (rather than having its own peculiar institutional separation from the legislature), it would be far more sensitive to issues of constitutionality than the chamber as a whole (Shapiro 1991). But the constitutional court has powers that are independent of those of the other two houses of parliament. When it exercises abstract review authority it operates as a separate, but specialized, legislative chamber. The opposition's referral triggers a final, constitutional 'reading' of the statute to parliamentary procedures (see Fig. 2.1 and related discussion). And constitutional rule-making can provoke, or require, new legislative processes, as when parliament must act in order to comply with the dictates of case law.

Accepting the 'constitutional court as legislative chamber' formulation does not entail ignoring obvious institutional distinctions between parliaments and constitutional courts. Two such distinctions deserve emphasis at this point, because we can expect them to condition behaviours relevant to policy-making. First, government ministers and parliamentarians are relatively self-activating law-makers, in that they are capable of deciding when and how to legislate, on their own, within limits imposed by the constitution. Until a case law relevant to a given legal domain has developed, constitutional judges act in a context that has been constructed by others (e.g. elected politicians and ordinary judges). Second, constitutional judges must, by law, give legal reasons for their decisions in writing. Elected politicians, in contrast, can take decisions on the basis of their own partisan interest, or ideology, without going further. They presume, after all, that they were elected to do so.

One purpose of this chapter is to demonstrate the extent to which the judicialization of the legislative process can blur these distinctions, even to the point of irrelevance. As constitutional rule-making proceeds in any given policy domain, governments and parliaments may find themselves operating in contexts that have been meaningfully constructed by constitutional judges. Elected officials may find that giving constitutional reasons for their behaviour cannot be avoided, and that surviving policy interests can only be effectively pursued in the language of the constitutional law. Judicialization produces constitutional constraints on law-makers. But, as important, it engenders new modes of legislative discourse and practice.

The legislative impact of constitutional courts will be assessed on two dimensions: (1) the immediate, direct, or formal effects of particular decisions on specific policy outcomes; and (2) the pedagogical, indirect, or feedback effects of constitutional rule-making on subsequent legislative processes and outcomes. We begin with first dimension effects.

The Formal Impact of Constitutional Decisions on Legislative Outcomes

Once petitioned to control the constitutionality of a statute, the constitutional court must take a decision and, in taking such decisions, it engages in behaviour whose effects are partly legislative. In annulling a legislative provision, for example, constitutional judges exercise their veto authority, an authority that inheres in constitutional review. When they announce legally binding interpretations of statutory provisions, they rewrite or amend legislation, to the extent that the court's interpretation meaningfully differs from that of the government and parliament.

Statistical summaries of the activities of constitutional courts provide some indication of the presence of constitutional courts in law-making processes, and their impact on outcomes. In France, the 1971 decision incorporating a bill of rights and the 1974 amendment authorizing parliamentarians to petition the Council (both discussed in Chapter 2) combined to expand radically the system's capacity to generate review. After 1974, all budget bills and nearly every important piece of legislation has been the subject of referral by the parliamentary opposition. The number of referrals grew dramatically again after 1981, and has since stabilized. In the 1974–80 period, the Giscard d'Estaing presidency, 46 laws were referred to the Council, 6.6 laws per year; in the 1981–7 period, the first Mitterrand presidency, 92 laws were referred, or 13.1 laws per year. The average number of laws referred has remained above 10 per year since 1987. Expressed in different terms, since 1981, about 1/3 of all legislation adopted has been referred, an extraordinary ratio given the fact that most legislation passed is politically uncontroversial. The figures also indicate why referrals are so popular with the opposition, and why the government and its parliamentary majority must take seriously the opposition's threats to go to the Council. Since 1981, more than half (54 per cent) of all referrals ended in some form of annulment by the Council. In France, where abstract review is the only type of review possible, the Council's intervention in the policy-making process can be characterized as systematic.

Compared with the French case, the importance of abstract review to German policy-making appears, at least at first glance, to be more limited.

Through 1994, the Federal Constitutional Court (GFCC) has received 119 referrals, or about 3 per year. Through 1991, these referrals led to definitive decisions on 43 laws, 23 (or 53 per cent) of which were declared to be at least partly unconstitutional.[1] These numbers underestimate the actual impact of abstract review, and in two crucial ways. First, to be discussed below, the very threat of referral—whether or not such referrals are eventually made—can profoundly alter outcomes. Second, the German policy-making process is relatively veto-ridden (see Chapter 2). The demands of coalition government (in practice, the Free Democrats have effectively reoriented reform-minded governments of both the Left and Right to the pragmatic centre), cooperative federalism (the necessity of co-ordinating national and member state policies), and the existence of a strong second chamber (the Bundesrat) possessed of substantial veto authority, combine to encourage intragovernmental and interparty compromises, and to filter out controversial legislative initiatives. In France, the Council is the only policy-making institution which can impose its will on the government and its majority, accounting for its popularity with the opposition. In Germany, the GFCC has spent most of its first four decades processing concrete review referrals (more than 3,000) and individual complaints (more than 85,000). Taking its constitutional review activities as a whole, the GFCC (through 1991) has invalidated some 200 laws, and another 223 administrative and other legal rules. Expressed in percentage terms, the Court has reviewed 20 per cent of all federal laws adopted, annulling 4.6 per cent of them (statistics in Kommers 1994; Landfried 1992; Stone 1994a). Individual complaints have a success rate of slightly less than 3 per cent (Rivers 1994).

In Spain, instances of abstract review exceed those of concrete review. During its first decade in operation, 1981–90, the Spanish Constitutional Tribunal (SCT) received 143 abstract review referrals, leading to the review of 101 laws. Of these, 53 were declared in whole or in part unconstitutionality, a success rate for petitioners of 52 per cent. Since 1986, the rhythm of such referrals has quickened, surpassing French levels. Of the 143 referrals received during the SCT's first decade, 103 (or 72 per cent) were made during the 1986–90 period, leading to 63 decisions and 37 rulings of unconstitutionality (70 per cent of all such invalidations). Spanish—like German—abstract review implicates the constitutional court not only in partisan disputes over national legislation, but also in the ongoing construction of what must now be considered a federal state (Agranoff 1993,

---

[1] The discrepancy in these figures is due to multiple referrals of the same law, withdrawals of referred laws by governments, and GFCC delay in deciding cases.

1996). Of the 143 abstract review referrals to the SCT, 33 (23 per cent) were made by parliamentary oppositions; 44 (31 per cent) by the federal government, usually against legislation passed by the autonomous regions; 60 (42 per cent) by the autonomous regions attacking national legislation; and 6 (4 per cent) by the Ombudsman. During the 1981–90 period, the SCT has also received 83 concrete review referrals—resulting in 32 invalidations of statutes for unconstitutionality—and 1,300 individual complaints.[2]

Because Italian parliamentarians do not possess the power of abstract review, constitutional dialogues between the Italian Constitutional Court (ICC) and elected politicians are mediated by concrete review processes. Most existing research on the political role and functioning of the ICC have emphasized that Italian constitutional judges have been conscientiously passive in their relations with sitting legislators (Furlong 1988; Volcansek 1994). The Court has clearly been more assertive when confronting the work of legislators past and gone, gradually but systematically 'dismantling', for instance, much of the 'offensive legislation from the fascist regime' (Volcansek 1994). The ICC also exploited delays inherent in concrete review processes to remain in the shadows. Until recently, the Court successfully 'encouraged the judiciary to refer the maximum number of constitutional questions' to it (Escarras 1987: 520–1), questions it was in fact totally incapable of processing in an efficient manner. In the 1976–85 decade, for example, the ICC rendered over 1,200 decisions. But the backlog of cases facing the judges rose, during this same period, from 1,138 to 2,748 (a backlog then representing about three years of full-time work!). About 85 per cent of these pending cases were concrete review referrals (Escarras 1987: 550).[3] Today, the ICC regularly receives more than 1,000 cases per year, and generates nearly 250 formal judgments.

There are some extremely important indications that the policy-making role of the Italian court is in the process of being transformed, to a more present and visible one, in line with that of other constitutional courts. In 1988, the ICC announced that it would process all concrete review referrals within six months, and it has since begun to keep that promise. If sustained, this change will partially reduce Italian exceptionalism, to the extent that a law is immediately attacked before a judicial body, and then passed on to the constitutional court for an immediate ruling. Since 1988, and for the first time in its history, the ICC has begun to confront

[2] Statistics provided by the STC and compiled by the author.
[3] Unlike its counterparts, the ICC does not collect and analyse basic information on many of the most important aspects of its own activities. Volcansek (in press) provides the best information currently available on the ICC's caseload and decision-making activity.

legislation adopted by a sitting parliament. In 1990, 60 per cent of all constitutional review cases involved legal texts adopted during the 1980–90 period, and over 30 per cent were laws passed in the 1988–90 period. Of the 65 texts annulled as unconstitutional in 1990, 23 were promulgated in the 1980s, and 10 in the 1988–90 period (statistics in Di Manno 1992). This development has been the source of anxiety among leading professors of constitutional law, who worry about judges making 'political choices', about the potential for 'the constitutional review process to become a continuation of the politico-party debate' in parliament, and about the ICC coming to resemble the French Constitutional Council—more a 'third chamber', and a 'political counsellor', than a 'constitutional judge' (Di Manno 1992: 793–94).

Annulments

Decisions that invalidate entire laws as unconstitutional, or 'total annulments', are rare but politically explosive. In 1975, the Court (GFCC 1975) annulled an attempt on the part of the Social–Liberal (SPD–FDP) coalition to decriminalize abortion, declaring that the foetus possessed constitutional rights, including the 'right to life' mentioned in article 2 of the German constitution. A 1985 attempt to decriminalize abortion in Spain by the Socialist-Worker's government met with a similar fate (SCT 1985a). In France, the Constitutional Council annulled the 1982 nationalization law, on the grounds that the law did not provide for adequate compensation to stockholders of companies to be nationalized (Council 1982a). In these cases, constitutional courts not only invalidated these reforms, but went on to tell legislatures exactly how legislators could 'correct' the censored texts to make them constitutional.

France: Nationalizing the Economy (1981–2)

In January 1982, the French Council rendered what is arguably its most important decision ever, a ruling on the very centrepiece of the new Socialist government's legislative programme: a bill to nationalize the five largest industrial conglomerates in France, every major bank (36 of them), and the two dominant financial investment companies (based on Stone 1992a: ch. 6). The bill was adopted after three months of tortuous constitutional debate in parliament. On three occasions, the Senate (then controlled by opposition parties of the Right) rejected the bill as unconstitutional, a violation of the 'sacred right of property'. The government and its large majority in the National Assembly refused to compromise with the opposition, overrode the Senate's vetoes, and finally passed the bill without amending it in any important way.

The bill had nevertheless been scrutinized in minute constitutional detail well before parliamentary deliberations had begun. The government had commissioned two widely respected law professors (one former and one future member of the constitutional court) to examine the bill, and they produced a long brief in favour of the bill's constitutionality. The brief was made public, and widely debated in the press. Opponents of the bill had commissioned three other law professors, who arrived at the opposite conclusion. Last, the government's official legal adviser, the Council of State, had examined the bill, and had successfully pressed for an important change in the way that stockholders to be expropriated would be compensated, substantially raising the costs of nationalizing.

The fate of the legislation was tied to the resolution of the central controversy of French constitutional law, the nature of the relationship between three seemingly contradictory texts: article 34 of the 1958 constitution, the 1789 declaration of the rights of man, and the 1946 social and economic principles. Article 34 grants to parliament the authority to legislate in certain enumerated subject matters, a grant that includes the power to nationalize companies and to privatize them. In French legislative discourse, appeals to the sanctity of article 34 are appeals to majority rule and parliamentary sovereignty. The 1789 declaration, however, lists constraints on law-making, article 17 declaring that 'property being inviolable and sacred, no one can be deprived of it in the absence of public necessity, legally declared, obviously warranted, and without just and prior compensation'. Finally, line 9 of the 1946 principles, originally intended to supersede the 1789 text, proclaim an obligation to nationalize in certain circumstances: 'Every asset, every enterprise, whose exploitation is or has acquired the character of a national public service or of *de facto* monopoly, must become the property of the collective'. In the absence of constitutional review and of an enforceable preamble, these contradictions, like so many others in French constitutional history, would have remained purely academic. Article 34 would simply have triumphed without a fight, and nationalizations would have gone ahead as the Socialists saw fit.

The Council (1982a) ruled that nationalizations were constitutional in principle, under article 34, but that the authority to nationalize could only be exercised in accordance with 'principles and rules possessed of constitutional status', that is, those dwelling within the charter of rights that the Council had begun incorporating into the constitution in 1971. The judges nevertheless vetoed the legislation on the grounds, among others, that the compensation formula did not meet constitutional requirements derivable from article 17 (1789); they all but ignored line 9 (1946), except to limit its application. The Council then went on to state in precise detail how the Socialists should have handled payment in the first place, in effect, elaborating a new compensation formula. Deciding against escalating to constitutional crisis,[4] the government drafted a second bill, writing into the new draft the Council's preferred compensation policy. This 'corrected' bill, which raised the costs of nationalization by a full 25 per cent, was approved by the Council, after the opposition had referred the matter a second time.

The decision deserves to be evaluated in terms of its impact on legislative process and outcomes, and in terms of its impact on the development of the constitutional law. The Council's decision generated a second legislative process that served, among other things, to pay stockholders more money. 'Instead of stating the law, the Council has stated the price', Michel Rocard complained. In this case, to determine the law is to fix the price. Once the Council had held article 17 (1789) to be controlling, and line 9 (1946) to be irrelevant, it had to move on to evaluate constitutionality in terms of standards for compensation contained in the former. Second, as a matter of constitutional rule-making, the decision harmonized the discordant terms of the rights texts at play. The Council ruled that the 1946 principles could never contradict or limit the enjoyment of a right contained in the 1789 declaration, now and in the future, thereby constructing a hierarchical relationship among the respective norms that comprise France's charter of rights. Thus, the annulment constituted rule-making that operates at different levels of generality and prospectivity at once.

Spain: Liberalizing Abortion (1983–5)

During the 1982 parliamentary elections in Spain, the Socialist Worker's party promised that, if it were to take power, it would move to decriminalize abortion. On winning a majority of seats in the Cortes, the party proceeded to make good on its promise, despite resistance from several fronts. The new rightwing opposition, supported by the Catholic Church and by forces nostalgic for the 'moral order' allegedly maintained by the fascist regime of General Franco, pledged all-out opposition (Bon 1988).

For most of the 20th century, the Spanish penal code has defined voluntary termination of pregnancy to be a crime, punishable by imprisonment.

---

[4] Some Socialists threatened to take the matter to the people, in referendum, and others proposed abolishing the Council by constitutional amendment.

In the years preceding the reform, it was estimated that, each year, more than 300,000 Spanish women traveled to neighbouring countries to obtain abortions (*El Pais* 12 April 1985). Of course, many poorer women could not afford this luxury, and either sought dangerous and illegal abortions, or took their pregnancies to term. In 1983, the highest appellate jurisdiction of the ordinary judiciary, the Spanish Supreme Court, upheld a judicial decision sentencing a woman to a month and a day in prison for having obtained an abortion in Britain. The Supreme Court reasoned, in effect, that the foetus constituted a life form covered by article 15 of the constitution, which proclaims that 'all possess the right to life'; and it asserted jurisdiction on the basis of a provision of the 'Organic Law establishing Judicial Authority' that grants to the courts the authority to punish crimes committed by one Spaniard (in this case, the pregnant woman) against another (the embryo) while abroad. Having lost her case, the woman filed a constitutional complaint (an *amparo*) with the constitutional court. The SCT annulled the Supreme Court's verdict (SCT 1984). The Tribunal declared that because the codes do not specifically prohibit women from obtaining abortions outside of Spain, punishing them for doing so abridges rights contained in article 25.1 of the constitution, which provides that 'no one can be . . . punished for an act . . . which, at the time it occurred, did not constitute a crime'. The constitutional judges, however, did not address the issue of whether, and how much, art. 15 protected the foetus.

While this abortion dispute was being decided by judges, parliament was heatedly debating the government's proposed reform of articles 411–417 of the penal code. The Socialists agreed with the opposition that the constitution required the protection of embryonic life, but disagreed that article 15 therefore absolutely prohibited abortions. Instead, the government claimed to have balanced the right to life provision with a woman's freedom to control her reproductive life. This freedom was derived from constitutional rights to 'personal dignity' (article 10), the 'free development of personality' (article 10), and 'personal and familial honour and privacy' (article 18).

The government sought to decriminalize abortion in three contexts: (1) when 'it is necessary to avoid serious danger to the life and health of the pregnant woman'; (2) when 'the pregnancy is the result of a rape'; and (3) when 'it is probable that the foetus will be born with serious physical or mental defects'. The Socialists had proceeded cautiously, deciding not to include a fourth—in fact, the most common—context in which abortions are sought: when having a baby might cause 'social hardship', including financial, to a woman and her family. Despite the modesty of the proposal, the opposition objected, and threatened to refer it to the Constitutional Tribunal. In December 1983, immediately after parliament had adopted the bill, the reform was sent to the Constitutional Tribunal.

Deeply divided internally, the SCT took eighteen months to produce its decision (ignoring rules requiring a decision within one month). Like the French Council's decision in the nationalization case, the SCT's judgment took the form of an annulment with draft legislation attached (SCT 1985*a*). Although the Tribunal agreed that a balance must be struck between the rights of the foetus and those of pregnant women, but annulled the bill on the grounds that article 15 required enhanced protection of the foetus, which it called 'a constitutionally protected legal good' (see Stith 1987). The judgment detailed how the legislature would have to protect this good if it wished to save the reform. Court-mandated changes included the following: that the agreement of a second doctor is necessary before an abortion can be performed in the first and third situations; that all medical consultations must take place in public health centres (or private centres licensed by the state); and that, in the case of rape, the woman must have filed a complaint on the offence before the abortion could be performed. Six of the twelve judges dissented, in five different opinions.[5] Dissenters accused the court of exceeding its powers, and of behaving more like a 'chamber of parliament' than a constitutional court, prescribing legislative outcomes (the positive legislator) rather than determining limits on what could be done (the negative legislator).

The decision was celebrated by the opposition as an important victory, and virulently criticized by the Socialists. The majority seriously considered adding a fourth, 'social abortion' exception in the corrected bill (*El Pais* 12, 13, 18 April 1985); in the end, however, the government chose to redraft the bill in strict conformity with the SCT's ruling, and to leave out the social hardship exception, probably to avoid more controversy and a second round of review.[6]

---

[5] The tie was broken by the president of the court, who voted for a decision of unconstitutionality (Bon 1988: 122).

[6] Although the number of abortions in Spain has steadily increased [from less than 2 in 1,000 women aged 15–44 (1980) to nearly 5 in 1,000 (by 1989)], the push for more liberalization has continued. In January 1991, the Supreme Court dismissed criminal proceedings against a couple who had demonstrated that they could not afford another child, although the Court upheld the conviction of the physician who performed the operation. In 1994, the Socialists drafted a bill that would have permitted abortion on request, in private clinics, after a short waiting period, but the bill was not pushed through parliament (United Nations 1995: 98–101; Boland 1994).

Partial Annulments

The great majority of all invalidations are 'partial annulments', that is, the constitutional court 'deletes' from the referred law those provisions judged to be unconstitutional, and allows the provisions that have escaped censure to enter into force. Partial annulments are a relatively more flexible means of controlling legislative outcomes. They allow the judges to, in American parlance, 'prune' bad branches, rather than chop down the whole tree (Tribe 1988: 1027–33). European legal scholars commonly use a medical analogy: judges 'amputate' those provisions judged to be 'contaminated' by unconstitutionality, thus saving the law. Partial annulments split the difference between the parties, allowing governments and their legislative majorities to claim at least some absolution. Some partial annulments have nevertheless had spectacular policy effects, obstructing central legislative priorities (see the French media pluralism cases below).

Most partial annulments are less dramatic but can, over time, add up to the virtual 'constitutionalization' of rules binding law-makers in any given sector. Probably the best cross-national example of this phenomenon is the constitutionalization of the penal law, the codes specifying crimes and the penalties for committing them, and the codes governing judicial procedures (see Greer 1994; McGee 1987; Philip 1985; Stone 1992*b*, 1996; van Zyl Smit 1992). In Italy, since the adoption of a new code of criminal procedure in 1989 (Fabri 1994; Fassler 1991; Volcansek 1990), the ICC has rendered more than 200 annulments, forcing the legislature to revise the code on dozens of occasions (documented in *Il Sole 24 Ore* 1994). In all four countries, constitutional judges have generated detailed rules meant to govern how these codes must, or must not be, revised in the future. In consequence, law-makers must now be sure to maintain, and sometimes even extend, standards of due process, habeas corpus, non-retroactivity, proportionality, equality before the law, and so on. These standards have been constructed by constitutional judges, from constitutional rights texts, in interaction with legislators and judges.

Binding Interpretations and Constitutional Surveillance

Constitutional courts have also developed a wealth of techniques designed to control the constitutionality of a law without invalidating it.[7] Most place

[7] I do not survey all such techniques, and have simplified those that are discussed. For more technical explanations, see: Volcansek (in press: ch. 2) for Italy; Kommers (1997: 52–5) and Zeidler (1987) for Germany; Di Manno (1998) for France and Italy; and Ezquiaga Ganuzas (1991) for Spain.

legislators, ordinary judges, and other public officials under some mode of constitutional surveillance: public authorities must behave in a certain way, with respect to a particular set of legislative norms, or suffer constitutional censure. As Landfried (1992) has noted with respect to the German case, these techniques give constitutional judges 'pre-eminence' over policy outcomes, not by 'invalidating' rules but by 'prescribing' them.

One set of such techniques places legislators under surveillance. In Germany, the GFCC may rule that a law is 'not compatible' with the constitution (as opposed to strictly unconstitutional), a decision that permits the law to remain in force but only for a specified period of time, pending the law's revision by the legislature. Such decisions, of which there have been 151 through 1991, constitute constitutional commands, issued by the GFCC to the government and parliament, to (re-)legislate in a given area. The Italian court employs a similar technique when it declares that a legislative provision will be struck down as unconstitutional in a future case, if the legislature does not alter it beforehand.

A second set of techniques enables constitutional judges to control how laws are to be applied by other public authorities. All four constitutional courts regularly issue, if in a variety of different forms, decisions that contain what I will simply call 'binding interpretations'. Such rulings are formal, legally binding declarations stating that a legislative provision is to be considered constitutional if and only if that provision is interpreted exactly as the constitutional court does. Put differently, the judges rule that only one interpretation of a given legislative text, the one announced by the court, saves that text from being judged unconstitutional. Constitutional courts have produced a rising tide of such declarations. In France, for example, the percentage of decisions containing binding interpretations has risen from 11 per cent (1959–74), to 14.5 per cent (1974–81), to 19.5 per cent (1981–5); in 1986, 56 per cent (9/16) of the decisions the Council rendered contained them (Stone 1992*a*: 135). In Italy, the same percentage rose from 15 per cent during the 1980s, to 25 per cent since 1990. Perhaps revelatory of the ICC's new, more policy-relevant role, more than 2/3 of the decisions rendered by the ICC on legal texts promulgated during the 1987–90 period announced binding interpretations (Di Manno 1992).

Such decisions authoritatively rewrite the legislative provisions in question, thus amending them, in that they authoritatively state exactly what the law means, and how it must be applied by judges, regardless of how legislators intended it to be applied. Binding interpretations place judicial authorities under surveillance (see Chapter 4): judicial failure to comply with such interpretations can be grounds for judicial appeals and concrete review petitions (Germany, Italy, Spain), as well as grounds for individual complaints (Germany, Spain).

LAW-MAKERS AS CONSTITUTIONAL JUDGES

The authority to veto legislation as unconstitutional is only one dimension—*immediate, direct,* and *negative*—of the policy impact of constitutional courts. We must also account for a second dimension—*prospective, indirect,* and *creative.* When government ministers and parliamentarians write, revise, and repeal statutes in order to: (1) comply with relevant case law; or (2) anticipate the direction of future constitutional decision-making, legislators ratify the pedagogical authority of constitutional rule-making over their own activities. In France, Germany, and Spain, the emergence and consolidation of this authority has been accompanied by the institutionalization of a new form of legislative politics. In these politics, legislators engage in structured deliberations of the constitutionality of legislative proposals. These debates can alter legislative outcomes, sometimes profoundly. In Italy, a recognizable form of such politics exists, although it has developed more slowly, due to the absence of abstract review.

Constitutional Deliberations and the Legislative Process

When legislators engage in constitutional deliberations, they behave much as constitutional judges do, in that they evaluate the formal, normative relationship between the statute in question and pertinent provisions of the constitution law, and they take decisions to harmonize, or at least reduce tensions between, the terms of the former and the latter. Two factors combine to generate this behaviour (see also Chapter 4). The first is the existence of a case law relevant to legislation being debated in the government or parliament. To be relevant, the court must have specified—by announcing new or clarifying existing—constitutional rules governing law-making in a given domain. Rightly or wrongly, governments and parliamentarians pay relatively more attention to annulments. Although no systematic research on the question exists, it appears that constitutional judges engage in more elaborate rule-making when they annul a legislative provision compared to when they declare a law to be 'not contrary to', or 'in conformity with', the constitution. Judges know that their best defence against charges of usurpation is to convince their most important and attentive audiences—legislators and judges—that the annulment is inescapably required by the constitutional law. Almost by definition, the more detailed the reasons a judge gives to defend a ruling, the more rule-making has occurred. Constitutional rule-making pushes legislators to employ similar modes of reasoning when they find themselves in future, more or less analogous, situations. In this way, the constitutional court's pedagogical authority over how governments and parliaments evaluate their own law-making behaviour is enhanced.

It is important to emphasize, however, that it is often impossible for law-makers, within a given legislative process and in advance of relevant case law, to discern the exact nature of the constitutional constraints that con-front them. Constitutional rule-making has the effect of (at least partly) codifying, these constraints. A succession of decisions on legislative initi-atives within the same policy domain can, as with the example of the new Code of Criminal Procedure in Italy, lead to the virtual 'constitutionaliza-tion' of that sector. In this way, normative uncertainty is replaced by constitutional obligation, and legislative initiative is pre-empted. Other important examples of pre-emption include nationalization and privatiza-tion policy in France, campaign finance in Germany, language rights in Spain, and—in all four countries—components of legal regimes governing broadcasting, electoral law, labor relations, and taxation.

The second factor is the extent to which parliamentary oppositions and subnational governments have access to, and then exploit, review processes in pursuit of their own policy objectives. The assumption that opposition politicians will use referrals liberally is a reasonable one. Referrals cost the parliamentary minority virtually nothing; governments cannot avoid hav-ing their legislative texts referred to constitutional courts; and the court's decisions bind legislative majority without the possibility of appeal. Abstract review petitions are not only potentially powerful weapons of opposition, they work: in France, Germany, and Spain, over half of all leg-islation reviewed pursuant to abstract review referrals decisions has been (at least partially) annulled.

In principle, abstract review politics facilitate judicialization. In refer-ring a statute to constitutional judges for review, the opposition obliges the court to intervene in the legislative processes, and provides the judges with opportunities for constitutional rule-making. Judges have seized these opportunities, if only to defend their own institutional legitimacy, produc-ing an increasingly dense, inherently expansionary, case law. This case law constitutes a continuously fed wellspring for arguments from which the opposition can draw to organize constitutional debate within parliament, and to obtain concessions from the government and its majority. If such concessions are not forthcoming, the opposition will produce new referrals, thus providing new opportunities for more constitutional rule-making. This sequence constitutes the feedback loop, a mechanism of institutionalization, that produces judicialization.

Judicialization makes observable the second dimension effects of constitutional rule-making on legislative process. For the most part, these effects are anticipatory reactions structured by constitutional rule-making. Translated into a simple, power-centred vocabulary, Dahl's classic formula (1957)—A has power over B to the extent that A can make B do what B would not otherwise do—can be altered to explicitly account for anticipatory reactions (by way of Friedrich 1946). Thus, A—*the constitutional court*—has power over B—*the government and its parliamentary majority*—to the extent that B *anticipates* A's interest and constrains its behaviour accordingly. As constitutional rule-making has proceeded, A's interest is articulated in a growing corpus of policy-relevant, constitutional rules binding on legislators; and B's interest in conforming to A's interest has, in turn, been made more compelling. Further, abstract review systems harness partisan competition in ways that reinforce the influence of constitutional courts on parliamentary governance. A vigilant opposition will actively monitor the governing majority's compliance with the constitutional law. It will also provoke anticipatory reactions by developing credible arguments to the effect that a legislative proposal is unconstitutional, and threatening referrals to the court if the majority does not sufficiently amend its proposal. It is then up to the governing majority to determine how it will respond to such threats.

'Autolimitation'

Autolimitation, one kind of anticipatory reaction, refers to the exercise of self-restraint on the part of the government and its parliamentary majority in anticipation of an annulment by the constitutional court.[8] More precisely, we observe autolimitation when the governing majority takes decisions, during the legislative process, that: (1) sacrifice initially held policy objectives; in order to (2) reduce the probability that a bill will either be referred to the court, or be judged unconstitutional. We can generalize about such decision-making by making certain reasonable assumptions

---

[8] The term was coined by Favoreu (1982); in Germany, the phenomenon has been studied extensively by Landfried (1984, 1992).

about the governing majority's interests, and drawing out the likely consequences of efforts by the opposition to judicialize debate.

Assume that the government and its supporters believe that their success
in fulfilling their electoral promises will partly determine their ability to
win the next election. If so, party leaders will diligently work to translate
these promises into legislative proposals, which they will work to have
adopted by parliament. In any given legislative process, the governing
majority is unlikely to compromise important policy objectives except in
so far as such self-restraint is necessary to secure a bill's entry into force as
law. Now let us bring constitutional politics into the mix. To the extent that
the majority perceives the threat of constitutional annulment as credible, it
will have an interest in policy compromise, but only enough to escape censure and secure promulgation.

Although the logic of this calculus is relatively straightforward, in practice such decision-making is fiercely complex and difficult to model (see
Stone Sweet 1998*a*; Vanberg 1998*a*, *b*). The first complexity is normative
uncertainty. In any judicialized legislative process, the most successful
actors will be those who are best able to anticipate, or guess, what the constitutional court's ruling on a given bill would be, if that bill were to be subject to review. In order to achieve its policy objectives, a 'rational' majority
will pay close attention to the constitutional law relevant to a particular bill,
and adapt its legislative action accordingly. But what should a majority do
when it finds itself in situations in which there is little or no relevant case
law? Under conditions of high normative uncertainty, it is difficult or
impossible for actors to formulate strategies that, in hindsight (after the
decision by the court) are optimal. Instead, majorities work to adopt, as far
as possible, the law they would have drafted in the absence of a threat of
constitutional review and censure. They do so, again, because they believe
it will help them get re-elected. In the French nationalization and the
Spanish abortion cases, governing majorities knew that oppositions would
attack their reforms. In both cases, majorities faced high normative uncertainty, which they responded to in two ways. First, they refused to compromise, on the grounds that the bills constituted core elements of their
legislative agendas. Second, they developed detailed and sophisticated
arguments supporting the constitutionality of the bills in questions. In
such cases, majority and opposition will work hard to convince constitutional judges to develop the constitutional law in one direction rather than
another, knowing full well that the other side will do the same. These
arguments will be transferred to constitutional judges, who will respond by
generating elaborate rules to govern policy-making in the two sectors.

The second complexity concerns how to evaluate the multidimensional, strategic opportunities that these constitutional politics provide. For the governing majority, the greater the intensity of its commitment to a specific outcome embodied in a draft statute, the less we can expect it to engage in autolimitation. If the majority compromises too much, it risks alienating party faithful, reneging on electoral promises, and handing the opposition a victory. Yet in refusing to compromise, it risks having cherished reforms blocked altogether, and the attendant development of a case law that will favour the opposition over the long run. However, normative uncertainty plays a role here too: unless the majority knows precisely how the court will rule, accurately calculation of the relative costs of available strategies is all but impossible.

To make matters more complicated, consider the following situations, all of which have occurred in various countries and contexts. The governing majority may choose to compromise, using the constitutional court as a convenient scapegoat for having been 'forced' to sacrifice a cherished policy objective. This situation is the reverse image of the one wherein the majority refuses to compromise even though it may expect the court to annul a bill; when the annulment comes, the government attacks the court for blocking the will of the electorate, and takes credit, *vis-à-vis* its own supporters, for having done all it could do to make good on its promises. In the language of game theory, these are almost always solutions to 'nested games' (Stone Sweet 1998*a*; Tsebelis 1990). A senior partner of a German coalition government may choose to compromise its own policy goals in order to placate its junior partner, thus accessing benefits that are situated on a different strategic dimension. In this example, a 'constitutional politics' game and a 'coalition politics' game are 'nested', that is, the majority plays them simultaneously.

Autolimitation effects can be registered at any stage of the legislative process, beginning with the drafting of a bill by government ministers. Intragovernmental deliberations are formally secret, but we do know that in France, Germany, and Spain, legal experts attached to cabinets evaluate the possibility of the law being referred to the court and invalidated as unconstitutional. In Spain, the government has even submitted bills to the Ombudsman for an advisory opinion. While difficult to verify, constitutional considerations have led governments to alter legislative provisions, and even suppress entire bills. In France, the Socialists radically altered the compensation formula contained in their nationalization proposal, on the advice of the Council of State (its official legal adviser), raising the cost of nationalizing by some 20 per cent (Stone 1992*a*: 150). The

Constitutional Council would later invalidate the formula as insufficient. In 1986, the rightwing, Chirac government (1986–7) undertook a revision of the laws governing French nationality and citizenship, and proposed to privatize the prison system. Both reforms were dropped, due in part to worries about constitutionality (Stone 1989). Several planned reforms of the first and second German SPD–FDP coalition governments (1969–72, 1972–6) suffered similar fates (Stone 1994a). The electoral promise to introduce compulsory profit sharing in industry, for example, was dropped, due to 'insoluble legal obstacles', the government announced.

Once a bill is submitted to parliament, open constitutional debate may begin. Special practices, more or less institutionalized, have evolved to accommodate constitutional debate (see Chapter 4). We know most about the judicialization of parliamentary governance in France and Germany. In France, many of the most tumultuous parliamentary battles of the Fifth Republic have been waged in the language of constitutional law. In the 1980s alone, dozens of bills were altered, by literally hundreds of amendments adopted in response to the threat of referral and constitutional censure. French oppositions, whether of the Right or Left, have learned to state their partisan objections to a bill in terms of constitutional law. The majority has little choice but to respond in kind.

In Germany, as Kommers (1994) puts it: 'Governments and politicians continually threaten to drag their political opponents to Karlsruhe—the location of the court. Karlsruhe's presence is deeply felt in the corridors of power, often leading politicians to negotiate their differences rather than to risk total defeat' [in the court]. Bundestag committees regularly invite leading constitutional experts, including former constitutional judges, to testify on constitutional aspects of current legislation and to predict future GFCC decisions. Committee sessions, the site of most legislative amendments, are formally closed, and thus constitutional bargaining and compromise is difficult to verify and measure. We do know, however, that three of the most controversial and important reforms ever attempted—the abortion reform (1975), the University Framework Law (1976), and the industrial codetermination bill (1976)—were subject to intense constitutional scrutiny and wholesale amendment efforts (see Landfried 1984). Fear of constitutional censure may be enhanced by a deeply embedded legalism that is said to infect German political culture. German legislators, as many students of German politics have emphasized, are 'unusually willing, even anxious, to rely on law and legal scholarship to guide their work' (literature cited in Stone 1994a). The government has even been known to repeal statutes after an abstract review referral, but before the decision of the GFCC (see Kommers 1994).

We now turn to two examples of policy-making by constitutional deliberation. Each involved extensive policy compromise, the first under conditions of high normative uncertainty, the second under an evolving tutelage of the constitutional court.

Germany: Industrial Codetermination (1972–9)

From the very first days of the Federal Republic, the strengthening of industrial codetermination, or worker's participation in corporate governance, has been a centrepiece of the Social Democratic Party's electoral programme. On winning the 1972 elections, the party sought to extend 'parity codetermination' (equal representation with management on supervisory boards), which existed in the coal and steel sectors, to the rest of industry (Katzenstein 1987: ch. 3). Debates focused principally on two conceptions of property: the constitution (article 14) guarantees the right to property, but it also states that property must serve the public good. Existing jurisprudence could not easily settle the matter, but seemed to favour the government's position. In a landmark case in 1954, the judges had declared that the Basic Law was 'neutral' with respect to the economic system, and that political authority enjoyed broad powers to shape and reshape the system (GFCC 1954). Despite reservations from its pro-business, junior coalition partner, the Free Democrats, the government, supported by unions and other labour associations, produced a bill making good the social democrats' pledge.

The debate within parliament lasted nearly two years, and was fully judicialized. A special committee heard testimony from eleven constitutional lawyers who were called in to predict the GFCC's future ruling on parity. This group split between those (five jurists) who argued that property rights were absolute and thus could not bear parity, and those (six jurists) who argued that property rights in the context of large corporations must be balanced by the interests of society and workers. In the end, the committee recommended that parliament err on the safe side, and renounce parity. The leaders of the governing majority agreed, removing parity and the bill was adopted the bill almost unanimously. According to Landfried, this autolimitation process was a disturbing case of excessive 'obedience in advance' of an GFCC ruling (Landfried, 1984: 47–63). It is also true that the pro-business Free Democrats, lobbied fiercely by business organizations, opposed parity, so much so that it is at least possible that parity would not have been supported by a majority of the Bundestag. In this case, it appears that the Social Democrats publically overestimated the constitutional constraints facing them, in order to keep peace within the coalition.

The law was later referred to the GFCC by employers and business associations who, while not expecting annulment, hoped to pre-empt future legislation. The GFCC rejected the complaints, ruling that share ownership in industry constitutes a particular form of property, one that 'requires the cooperation of employees', since their rights are also involved (GFCC 1979a). The Court refused to speculate on the constitutionality of parity; but it pointedly praised legislators for their debates on constitutionality, leaving the impression that the absence of parity may have been crucial to its approval. This at least is what business celebrated and the political left and the unions feared (Markovits 1986: 140–1).

Thus, it seems that Social Democrats used a judicialized process to renege on an important electoral promise, although they probably did not actually fear censure; yet, in the end, the renunciation of parity may have actually secured the bill's constitutionality.

France: In Search of Media Pluralism (1983–6)

During the 1983–6 period, successive governments of the Left and then Right sought to reshape regimes governing the press and audiovisual sectors. Their efforts yielded three Constitutional Council decisions, including the two longest and most complex in the Council's history. How best to secure and then guarantee 'media pluralism', defined as the possibility for French citizens to exercise meaningful choice from among a range of information sources representing diverse ideological views, proved to be one the most intractable legislative–constitutional problems encountered in the Fifth Republic (based on Stone 1992a: ch. 7).

The saga begins with the Socialist government's attempt to establish an enforceable antitrust policy to counter the rapid concentration of the French newspaper industry that began in the early 1970s. The antitrust rules then in place required a strict one person/one newspaper standard, but these rules had never been enforced. Indeed, they had been openly flouted by a Gaullist party National Assembly deputy and press baron, Robert Hersant. Hersant was able to amass—in a series of shady deals then being investigated by the courts—an empire that included 19 dailies, 7 weeklies, and 11 periodicals. After the Socialists took power in 1981, Hersant mobilized his papers, especially his flagship daily, Le Figaro, to oppose the Socialist government and to promote the emerging neo-liberal agenda of the Gaullist leader, Jacques Chirac. Thus, while the government could justly claim that its bill was designed to protect diversity in the industry and to restore respect for the rule of law, its partisan aspects were crudely evident.

The legislative battle was waged primarily in the language of constitutional law, but their subject was Hersant. Socialists argued that the collective (the State) had a responsibility to restrict the rights to property to the extent that their exercise infringes the enjoyment of non-economic rights. Freedom of the press was conceived as the right of readers to choose from among a variety of papers representing the diversity of opinion within society. This right could no longer be guaranteed, claimed one minister, because 'certain men' had engaged in 'fraud', 'cheating', and 'embezzlement'. The opposition parties on the Right argued that talk of rights only obscured the government's true motive: to take its revenge on Hersant. The Right conceived freedom of the press entirely in terms of ownership, of what Chirac called the 'inseparable principles of the freedom of expression, the right of private enterprise, and the rights to property'.

The bill submitted to parliament bore only slight resemblance to the bill adopted nearly a year later. Of the original 42 articles, 26 were substantially rewritten; most amendments were made under the explicit threat of referral to the Council. In its final rendition, the law relied on a 'fixed market ceiling' antitrust mechanism—maximum percentages of total circulation for daily newspapers that any press group could fill. The law forbade any one group from controlling more than: (1) a 15 per cent share of the national (i.e. Parisian) market or 15 per cent of the total regional circulation; or (2) 15 per cent of the national and 10 per cent of the regional markets. These rules would have forced Hersant to make a choice to keep either *Le Figaro* or his regional papers, but no mix of both. A special regulatory body, the Commission on Financial Accountability and Press Pluralism (CFAAP) was created to police the rules and to force sell-offs, if necessary. Rejected by the rightwing Senate in a motion of unconstitutionality, the Assembly overrode the Senate's veto, whereupon opposition deputies and senators referred the bill to the Council.

The Council (1984) annulled parts of ten different articles of the law. As a matter of constitutional interpretation, the Council agreed with the government that the rights of readers to choose was a constitutionally protected freedom. Relying on article 11 of the 1789 declaration (freedom of expression), the Council deduced that 'press pluralism' constituted 'an objective possessed of constitutional status'. It then went on to declare this extraordinary rule: henceforth law-makers could never weaken the protection of a constitutional right or liberty, but could only strengthen that protection—called the 'ratchet effect'. The decision none the less destroyed the bill and saved the Hersant empire. Although the Council affirmed legislative competence to set fixed ceilings, it ruled that the CFAAP could not enforce them to 'existing situations' (i.e. Hersant's) and press groups could not be forcible dismantled unless: (1) these situations had been illegally acquired; or (2) pluralism was truly threatened. The Council decided that neither condition had been met. In declaring that 'pluralism' was 'not currently weakened in a manner so serious that it would be necessary to apply [antitrust provisions] to existing situations', the Council unambiguously substituted its judgment on the state of pluralism in the press sector for that of the government and the Assembly.

What was left of the bill was promulgated. But bereft of an effective enforcement mechanism, it could not fulfil its intended purpose. Not only did the law freeze Hersant's dominance, but the press baron was emboldened to acquire more regional dailies. By March 1986, when the Right returned to power under Chirac, the Hersant press group controlled nearly 40 per cent of the national market, and 20 per cent of the regional one, including an absolute monopoly in the nation's largest multi-paper regional market, the Rhône Valley. In comparative terms, the percentage of the total French market controlled by Hersant in 1984 was greater than that controlled by any press group in any Western democracy.

Although the rightwing celebrated the Council's decision as a blow for liberty and the right to property, the decision came back to haunt it. In the 1986 electoral campaign, Gaullists promised to remove the fixed ceiling antitrust mechanism from the press regime as part of a general effort to deregulate the print and broadcast media. After decisively winning the 1986 elections, the new government introduced a law to do just that. In parliament, the Socialists attacked the absence of fixed market ceilings as unconstitutional, invoking the jurisprudence of the 'ratchet effect'. The majority reluctantly amended the bill, fixing ceilings at 30 per cent of a total unified market (Hersant's share under this formula would have fallen between 28 per cent and 29 per cent). In the end, the Council (1986*a*) annulled parts of the 1986 press law (on other grounds), but spared the antitrust mechanism, strongly implying that such a mechanism was constitutionally required.

The 1984 and 1986 press decisions judicialized the debate on the Chirac government's (1986–8) audiovisual bill, which was designed to privatize the broadcast industry and to deregulate the broadcast sector as a whole. The government argued that broadcasting was unlike the print medium in one crucial respect: since the bill would break up the State's monopoly over the radio and television industry, its effect could only be to favour pluralism. Fear of Council censure again led the government to include antitrust provisions (maximum financial interest any one person or group could acquire in privatized television channels, and fixed market ceilings for radio frequencies). The Council (1986*b*) nonetheless annulled the antitrust provisions on the grounds that they would permit unacceptably high levels of concentration, and then instructed the government on how to revise the bill. The press and audiovisual bills were 'corrected' in a new bill, adopted a few months later, enshrining the Council's preferred position.

The antitrust mechanisms now prevalent in the sector (fixed market percentages) are certainly not the only ones imaginable, nor the only means of protecting pluralism imaginable. But they have acquired a kind of indirect constitutional value of their own in France, as a result of constitutional politics. Generally, we find that multiple constitutional decisions on a cluster of related pieces of legislation result in judicialization, which is observable as ongoing restrictions of legislative discretion, and the emergence and consolidation of the authority of the constitutional court over policy.

Corrective Revision

Some constitutional decisions constitute not only the final stage of one legislative process, but the opening stage of another. This second process I call 'corrective revision': the re-elaboration of a censured text in conformity with constitutional jurisprudence in order to secure promulgation. Corrective revision processes occur after full or partial annulments. They are highly structured by case law, to the extent that the judges have already made their legislative choices explicit, and that oppositions work to monitor the majority's compliance with the ruling.

The logic of corrective revision is straightforward. Once a constitutional court has annulled a bill and then gone on to state in precise detail what a constitutional version of the bill would look like, legislators are faced with a choice. In principle, they have four options. First, they can engage in a corrective revision process, securing constitutionality by deferring to the policy preferences of the constitutional court. Corrective revision is what nearly always occurs. The governing majority knows that the surest way to secure promulgation of beleaguered legislation is to concede part of their law-making authority to constitutional judges. Second, it can forego the legislation entirely. This is rarely a viable option for important pieces of legislation, since it is usually better for the governing majority to get some part rather, than nothing, of what it wanted. Third, it could seek to circumvent the court's ruling (e.g. by creatively reformulating the legislation). In such cases, law-makers are, in effect, playing 'chicken' with the court, daring the judges to annul the bill a second time. Although they often interpret a court's ruling as narrowly as possible, to allow for maximum legislative discretion over the precise terms of the correction, I know of no important case where legislators have revised a censured bill but blatantly ignored the court's dictates.[9] A final option exists: the majority can revise the constitution in order to make constitutional those acts that had been censored, repudiating the court in the process.[10] The feasibility of this option depends on how difficult it is to revise the constitution, which is a function of two factors: the permissiveness of the rules governing constitutional revision and the relative political strength of opponents and proponents of a given revision. I know of only one important instance of overturning the court in this way (see below).

Before turning to longer case studies, two general points deserve emphasis. First, in corrective revision processes, legislators ratify constitutional rule-making. The result is court-written statutes. German legal regimes governing party finance and university education provide two good examples. Since 1958, the GFCC and German politicians have been playing an ongoing 'cat and mouse game' (Ress 1995: 213) on the financing of political parties. The Court has sought to broadly frame the reform of the party finance regime, mixing fixed rules with general principles, which the major parties have interpreted for their own purposes. In six major decisions (GFCC 1958a, 1966, 1968, 1979b, 1986a, 1992), the GFCC has elaborated technical rules governing the organization, management, and financing of political parties and electoral campaigns, including complicated formulas to determine the type, total amount, and distribution of state aid available for political parties. Several of these decisions have forced corrective revision processes (Landfried 1992), the most important of which produced the 1989 Political Parties Act, which codified most of the Court's most important holdings. In 1992, pursuant to a referral from the Green Party and the exposure of larger and larger loopholes, the Court (1992) scrapped the whole project and ordered parliament to legislate according to a new set of guiding principles (see Kommers 1997: 210–15; Ress 1995). The control

---

[9] The German government was urged to do so after the 1975 abortion ruling (Stone 1994a).

[10] The legislature would still have to readopt the law subsequent to the entry into force of the constitutional revision.

of the GFCC on outcomes in the educational sector has been so extensive that Kommers (1989: 303) has characterized the Court as 'a veritable ministry of education' (see also Weiler 1995).

Second, constitutional litigation by private individuals can also generate corrective revision and the pre-emption of legislative initiative by constitutional rule-making. The animus for many concrete review references and individual complaints is to encourage the court to invalidate undesirable laws and practices, and to establish new legal regimes by way of constitutional rule-making and corrective revision. That said, once a corrective revision process is set into motion, monitoring compliance with constitutional case law is organized by the politics of abstract review.

Although Spanish legal scholars frequently insist that *amparos* can not lead to statutes being invalidated, such is not the case (Guasch 1994). Rulings taken pursuant to an individual complaint, and to the activities of the ombudsman,[11] can lead to corrective revision. In 1982, the Constitutional Tribunal upheld the *amparo* of a man claiming a right to conscientious objection (SCT 1982*a*). Because this right was not recognized in any statute, no procedure for exempting objectors from (obligatory) military service existed. The Tribunal reacted by constructing rules on its own, and inviting parliament to legislate; in 1984, parliament adopted legislation securing the possibility of conscientious objection, and created an administrative board to screen claims. In a series of subsequent cases (SCT 1985*b*, 1987*a*, *b*), the Ombudsman attacked the work of the board for too narrowly interpreting the rules, and the SCT, agreeing with some of these arguments, mandated enhance protection of the right, forcing corrective revision efforts on the part of parliament.

We now turn to two more examples of corrective revision that began as efforts, on the part of private parties, to undermine existing legislative regimes.

---

[11] During the first Socialist Workers government, the budgets for 1983, 1984, and 1985 contained subsidies for trade unions considered to be 'the most representative', as determined by elections at the workplace level. In practice, having received more than the minimum requirement of 10% of the vote (15% in the regions), only four unions received such subsidies. Responding to complaints of unions left out of the scheme, the Ombudsman attacked these budget laws as unconstitutional, arguing that the system in place discriminated against the small unions, and thus violated equal treatment rules. The Tribunal agreed and went on to propose a proportional system (in which subsidies would roughly correspond to the percentage of the total vote obtained), a solution which was written into a new, corrected statute.

Democratizing the German University (1969–76)

In 1969, the new SPD–FDP coalition government took power promising radical reform of the education system. Although several comprehensive framework laws were ultimately adopted, they were gutted of their most controversial elements in compromises with the opposition-controlled Bundesrat, and by decisions of the Constitutional Court. The complex set of initiatives ultimately comprising the University Framework Law of 1976 is a well-documented illustration (Katzenstein 1987: ch.7). The law was promulgated after five years of tortuous debate punctuated by several crucial GFCC decisions and successive vetoes by the Bundesrat.

Perhaps the most controversial aspect of the original bill was a set of provisions to 'democratize' university governance by, among other things, diminishing the absolute authority of full professors on governing councils, and giving to untenured professors, staff, and students voting parity with professors on governing councils. The reform was designed to break up the monopoly of power possessed by full professors, a monopoly that many thought had led to inflexible university structures and the stifling of much-needed reforms (Tilford 1981). The CDU–CSU opposition laboured to defend the professors, and to retain as much *Länder* control of education as possible.

Weary with the slow pace of federal legislation, the SPD–FDP controlled *Land* of Lower Saxony adopted its own law, based on federal government drafts. Just as final touches were being made on the bill in the federal government, the GFCC ruled on the Lower Saxony statute, pursuant to individual complaints made by 398 disgruntled professors. The Court ruled (GFCC 1973a) that the law violated article 5 of the constitution, which proclaims that 'research and teaching shall be free'. Asserting that the 'special position' of professors in the administration of university education must always be maintained, the GFCC declared that professors must always enjoy a majority share of votes in decisions on teaching, 'to assert themselves against the combined opposition of other groups' in decisions pertaining to research. The dissent of two judges complained that majority had exceeded its powers, and 'placed itself in the position of the legislature'.

The ruling transformed the federal discussion in progress from a debate about the wisdom of the legislation into a debate about constitutional compliance (Stone 1994a). Under the watchful eye of the rightwing CDU–CSU opposition, which supported the full professors and threatened referral if the coalition did not fully comply with the ruling, the FCC's jurisprudence was copied into the federal law. This law not only enshrined the GFCC's preferred policy, but, as a federal law, forced the policy on those *Länder* that had delayed compliance with the GFCC's Lower Saxony decision (Blair 1978).

The case also shows how the threat of abstract review can work in tandem with an individual complaint to tighten the control of constitutional judges over policy outcomes.

Calculating Old Age Pensions in Italy (1988–93)

One of the most controversial social policy issues in Italy over the past two decades has been the calculation, on the part of government ministries, of retirement pensions (Giorgis, Grosso, and Luther 1995). In particular, the ICC has been bombarded with judicial referrals responding to claims by private individuals that differences in the formulas used for determining cost of living adjustments, both within the public sector and between the public and private sectors, violated standards of equal treatment under the law. Until 1988, the Court chose to defer to parliamentary discretion, declaring that differences in the work performed in different industries, and differences in labour–management relations, could be presumed to justify differences in treatment (e.g. ICC 1980). In 1988, the Court announced that these differences had become intolerable, and invited the legislature to enact legislation to harmonize the pensions regime across categories (ICC 1988*a*). Five years later, seemingly weary with legislative inaction, the Court ruled that the absence of such harmonization constituted a violation of the rights of employees to equal treatment. It justified its change of heart as follows

[The Court] can neither continue rendering decisions of inadmissibility [of concrete review referrals] in respect of legislative discretion, nor continue admonishing [parliament to act]. Factually irrational and discriminatory regulations, explicitly denounced in judgment 200/1988 [ICC 1988*b*] have not only persisted but have become worse. . . . To simply call again for the legislature to intervene—after having waited so long, in vain—would appear . . . as an abdication of the functions of the Constitutional Court, and a protection of legislative inertia rather than a protection of legislative discretion. (ICC 1993)

The Court then placed legislators under constitutional surveillance. It: (1) specified how harmonization must proceed to satisfy constitutional requirements; (2) ordered parliament to right the situation (in the next budget law at the latest); and (3) threatened to 'right the situation' itself if the legislature did not act, presumably by empowering the judiciary to award damages in future litigation. In the January 1994 budget law, parliament did act, explicitly acknowledging the ICC's prompting.

PRINCIPAL–AGENT ISSUES

Chapters 1 and 2 raised issues of contracting and delegation. In this chapter, I have shown that constitutional adjudication has gradually transformed the nature of parliamentary governance, by judicializing it. The contractants did not expect this transformation. Indeed, the political parties would have considered judicialization an undesirable outcome to be avoided. Further, left to their own devices (under majority rule decision-making rules), they would not have agreed to adopt most of the policy outcomes that judicialization has produced.

Although some analysts of delegation imply otherwise (e.g. Garrett 1992; Moravscik 1995; McCubbins, Noll, and Weingast 1987), there is nothing in the principal–agent (P–A) construct, *per se*, to suggest that principals are able to control their agents effectively, or that agents faithfully serve principals by pursuing the latter's revealed preferences. The interesting empirical questions concern the extent of autonomy exhibited or developed by the agent, in the course of performing its duties, and the extent to which principals are able to redirect the agent's behaviour when undesirable outcomes are produced, given the mechanisms of control available to principals (on this point, see: Moe 1987; Pierson 1998; Shapiro 1988; Stone Sweet and Caporaso 1998).

In fact, a straightforward P–A take on constitutional politics ought to lead us to expect judicialization. Consider the following three facets of constitutional politics, conceived in P–A terms. First, the nature of the delegation to constitutional courts—embedded in broad and open-ended relational contracting—constitutes an environment that is relatively permissive of agency autonomy (Chapter 2). To the extent that disputes about the constitutionality of statutes are regularly referred to constitutional courts, and to the extent that constitutional judges perform their assigned task in a minimally responsible manner, judicialization, however piecemeal and uneven across time and policy sector, is favoured.

Second, in practice, the instruments of direct control available to the political parties are difficult or impossible to wield in a consistent or sustained way. The political parties can reconstitute themselves as a constituent constitutional body, in order to revise the constitution, thus overturning or otherwise constraining the constitutional rule-making of constitutional courts. But constitutional revision requires a higher level of consensus among the parties than does legislating, and some of the most important provisions of some constitutions cannot be revised at all. Where a referendum is required to adopt proposed constitutional revisions, the electorate ultimately constitutes the principal. In short, the decision-making rules that govern the use of direct controls favour the status quo. That is, the constitutional law will likely evolve as the agent sees fit, with gradual judicialization being the result.

Third, the political parties do not constitute a unified and coherent rational actor. Indeed, they compete with one another for political power and influence in environments constituted by the constitutional law. Where abstract review exists, interparty competition to control policy outcomes generates referrals of the majority's statutes to the Court, delegating law-making authority to judges, and legitimizing constitutional rule-making in the process. The opposition, pursuing its own policy objectives, normally works: (1) to enhance judicialization; and (2) to oppose efforts on the part of the majority to reverse the effects of constitutional rule-making. Thus, some political parties always operate in complicity with constitutional judges to provoke and reinforce judicialization.

There has only been one important instance in which a constitutional court decision was overturned by constitutional amendment.[12] In 1993, the French government (rightwing), supported by large rightwing majorities in the Assembly and the Senate, revised the constitution in order to permit the promulgation of a controversial law designed to tighten immigration and asylum policy, which the Council (1993) had annulled (discussed in Stone 1996). It should not be surprising that French rules governing constitutional revision are, compared to those is place in our other three cases, by far the most permissive.

---

[12] German rules governing federalism have been revised on more than 60 occasions, sometimes to open the way for the federal government to do what the GFCC had ruled was constitutionally prohibited (Jounjan 1995). Blair (1981: 210–14) examined the first 34 amendments adopted to 1979, characterizing them as mostly 'superficial'. Few if any revisions are interpreted as reversing the court, not least since the court itself had, in many cases, pointed toward how the constitution would have to be revised in order for the desired reforms to pass muster. In Spain and Italy, some rules of jurisdiction and procedure fixed by statutes have been altered in order to reduce the constitutional court's influence. Most have been relatively minor reforms that have done little to slow judicialization. Probably the most important instance occurred in 1985, when the Spanish Socialists succeeded in abolishing the SCT's power (established in an organic law having the rank of statute) of a priori abstract review (Pérez Royo 1986). The only practical effect of the move, given that the SCT's constitutionally derived authority of a posteriori abstract review remains intact, is that oppositions can no longer use abstract review referrals to delay a law's entry into force.

Evaluating the extent to which constitutional courts constrain themselves, due to fears of being overriden constitutionally, is extremely difficult, if not impossible to do empirically. The analyst can only infer such behaviour from outcomes, and only by choosing to interpret data in one way rather than another. I have argued (Chapter 1) that all judges consider the potential impact of decisions being contemplated, because they seek compliance on the part of the parties, and because they are concerned with their own political legitimacy. In Europe, although explicit, American-style, 'political question' doctrines do not exist formally, constitutional courts have developed doctrinal formulas that amount to exactly the same thing (see Currie 1993: 170–1; Stone 1992*a*: ch. 3). These formulas allow courts to avoid those questions they would prefer not to answer, for whatever reason. It may be that when we see deference to legislative or ministerial discretion—as, for example, when the court labels an issue inherently 'political', or states that the power to act or not to act inheres in the competence to legislate—we are actually observing the judges anticipating, and then working to avoid, punishment. And it may be that they favour partial annulments, and avoid total annulments, for the same reason. In my view (see also Chapter 5), it is far more likely that constitutional courts engage in these and other practices in order to enhance their own reputations for fairness, their own flexibility in present and future cases, and the centrality of constitutional review as a mode of governance (which operates in some areas more effectively than in others). I know that constitutional judges labour continually to bolster the legitimacy of constitutional review; but I am sceptical that they do so only, or especially, because they fear being punished by elected politicians.

CONCLUSION

This chapter emphasizes the interdependence of legislating and constitutional judging, thus rejecting the view that governments and parliaments are the only 'true' law-makers, and denying claims that constitutional courts are the only 'true' judges of the constitutionality of legislation. These points, of course, challenge prevailing separation of powers notions, and implicitly raise issues of democratic theory. These latter issues are partly the subject of Chapter 5. I conclude here by briefly examining alleged distinctions between legislative and judicial rule-making in the light of this chapter's findings.

In traditional separation of powers schemes, legislatures differ from courts in that the former make law generally and prospectively. In contrast, judicial law-making, to the extent that it is acknowledged at all, is said to be particular and retrospective—a by-product of case-by-case adjudication that applies to past or existing situations. In abstract review processes, courts make law outside of litigation, employing techniques that are inherently prospective, not retrospective. In the French press pluralism case, the Council overrode parliament's judgment that press pluralism was threatened, and then went on to specify how pluralism should be protected *in the event* that a threat *might* develop. In the Spanish abortion case, the SCT's ruling looks like draft legislation with constitutional commentary attached. These are not isolated examples; constitutional courts legislate prospectively all the time.

In abstract review processes, courts behave unambiguously as legislative bodies. Yet the effects of other modes of review are not necessarily less legislative or prospective. Management's legal challenge of codetermination, for example, was motivated not by expectations of annulment, but by hopes that the GFCC would fix limits on future attempts by the German Left to extend worker's participation in corporate governance. In corrective revision processes, the distinction between parliamentary and constitutional court law-making breaks down entirely. Policies which have been laid down by constitutional courts (how pensioners must be paid, how the penal code must treat the crime of abortion) are sent to governments and parliaments for ratification. Finally, once policy space has been pre-empted by relevant case law, existing constitutional rule-making, given agency through the medium of judicialized legislative politics, broadly determines general outcomes.

4

Protecting Rights

In the previous chapter, we focused on interactions between constitutional judges and legislators within policy-making processes. In this chapter, the relative importance of constitutional politics, conceived as law-making, gives way to the relative importance of constitutional politics, conceived as the process through which the constitutional law is constructed. As will be shown, the protection of human rights is a highly structured social process, driven by ongoing interactions, or dialogues, between constitutional judges, legislators, and the judiciary.

I begin with a discussion of constitutional rights provisions, their place in the constitution, and the challenges these provisions pose for judges and legislators. I then turn to two sets of dialogues about the nature, content, and application of rights. As constitutional courts have consolidated their positions as the supreme interpreters of the constitution law, law-makers have been led to behave, in part, as constitutional decision-makers. Similarly, constitutional adjudication has breathed juridical life and agency into rights provisions, provoking ordinary judges, too, to engage in constitutional decision-making. In Europe today, the legislature and the judiciary constitute important, adjunct builders of the constitutional law.

RIGHTS, NORMATIVE HIERARCHIES, AND CONSTITUTIONAL DECISION-MAKING

The macro-setting, or 'normative structure' (see Chapter 1), of constitutional politics is, of course, the constitutional law. This law establishes—by way of language and an internal logic related to how rules are expressed in language—formal hierarchical relationships between different sets of legal norms. For our purposes, the most important of these concern the hierarchical relationship established between: (1) any given rights provision and other rights provisions; (2) rights provision and other constitutional provisions not directly associated with rights; and (3) rights provision and rules and practices embedded in other juridical orders (administrative law, the private law, the various codes, and so on). Whether any normative structure has meaningful existence apart from how specific actors use and interpret it is an enormously complex question that I will not attempt to answer here.[1] In this chapter, I proceed from the standpoint that although constitutional *meaning* is continually being (re)constituted by adjudication, constitutional *language* and constitutional *meaning* nevertheless remain analytically distinct. Constitutional provisions are sites of contestation about meaning; they organize arguments about the nature, content, and applicability of a given rule. This contestation drives constitutional development.

Placing ourselves in the position of the constitutional judge may simplify matters, if only initially. Judges are obliged to resolve legal controversies about rights which are inherently controversies about applicability in a given situation; they are also required to defend their decisions publicly, in what Europeans call a jurisprudence (what Americans call case law). Simplifying, European judges tend to present their decision-making as if it were a distinct two-stage process. First, the nature and content of the relevant constitutional provision(s) are determined. Second, a specific controversy about the meaning of the provision(s) is resolved by applying that law. The judges are telling us that, having carefully considered the language and architecture of the constitution, they are in a position to decide a particular case. In fact, the two stages are tightly interdependent, taking place more or less simultaneously within linked processes of interpretation. This simple truth turns out to be critical to our understanding of constitutional politics. In any event, because constitutional interpretation lies at the core of constitutional politics, and because constitutional language shapes constitutional interpretation, students of constitutional politics have little choice but to take normative structures and constitutional decision-making (acts of interpretation) seriously.

The Direct Effect of Constitutional Rights

When the framers of the German, Italian, and Spanish constitutions established institutions to enforce constitutional rights as higher law, they initiated a revolutionary transformation of their legal and political systems. In France, a comparable transformation was begun in the 1970s, when the French Council (1971) moved to incorporate a set of historical rights texts

---

[1] Making a single entity—the constitutional judge—the authoritative interpreter of the constitutional law does not necessarily simplify matters (see Ch. 5).

into the 1958 constitution. Prior to these revolutions, only legislative
majorities could determine if and how constitutional rights were to be
respected. Such rights had no 'direct effect', that is, they did not confer on
legal subjects judicially enforceable claims against government.[2] Litigants
could invoke 'public liberties' in court, and judges could apply them, but
only insofar as these liberties had been created by statutory law, that is, only
after legislatures had commanded judges to enforce them. Thus, in traditional parliamentary systems, rights entered into the legal order indirectly,
by virtue of a legislative act, rather than directly, by virtue of their higher
law status. Today, the positive source of individual rights is the constitution.

Chapter 2 (Table 2.1) contains a list of constitutional rights and duties in
France, Germany, Italy, and Spain. As the concept of constitutional duty
makes clear, the protection of rights is a participatory process. Not only
does the constitution provide for the protection of constitutional rights by
constitutional courts, it also commands the legislature to create the conditions necessary for the enjoyment of some rights, and to promote, encourage, and protect others. Thus, rights in Europe do not just tell state
authorities like legislators, administrators, and judges what they must not
do (negative rights), but also what they must do (positive rights). It is
partly because of the direct effect of positive rights, conceived as positive
obligations binding on the state, that we find constitutional courts commanding legislators and ordinary judges to perform certain constitutional
duties, and otherwise fixing the parameters for legislative and judicial
activity. Thus: parliaments must produce legislative regimes that guarantee
pluralism in the print and broadcasting media (Chapter 3 and this chapter); the Spanish state must protect regional languages (this chapter); and
the German penal system must operate to rehabilitate those who have committed even the most heinous crimes (this chapter).

Normative Hierarchies

The constitutional law establishes hierarchies of norms, and these hierarchies condition constitutional interpretation. The direct effect of constitutional rights, for example, establishes a simple hierarchical relationship
between constitutional text and statute: any statutory provision that
violates any rights provisions is invalid, *ab initio*. Intraconstitutional

---

[2] The 'direct effect' of a constitutional provision (see also Ch. 6) should not be confused
with the impact of constitutional courts on legislative process (which is both direct or indirect).

hierarchies are more complicated, but the law implies a privileged status for rights provisions. In Germany, Italy, and Spain, constitutional texts proclaim human rights before they establish state institutions and before they distribute governmental functions. In consequence of this fact, rights are considered by legal scholars and many judges to possess a juridical existence that is prior to and independent of the state. Doctrine has it that rights are invested with a kind 'supraconstitutional' normativity that makes (at least some of) them immune to change through constitutional revision (Table Ronde 1995). This is inherently a natural law position, although natural law is rarely explicitly invoked. The privileged status of rights is, of course, reinforced by rules governing constitutional amendment: as discussed in prior chapters, the German and Spanish constitutional law treats rights provisions as rigid and immutable, and non-rights provisions as flexible; and in Italy (discussed below), the ICC has conferred what is in effect supraconstitutional status on 'inviolable rights' mentioned—but not enumerated—in article 2 of the constitution.

By far, the most complicated hierarchical problem faced by constitutional courts appears when two of more rights provisions, which possess equivalent hierarchical status, conflict with one another in a particular case. Even a cursory glance at the list in Table 2.2 suggests the broad range of such potential problems. In a dispute about abortion law, does the right to life trump a women's right to develop freely her personality? In a libel dispute, should the press' freedom of expression or should an individual's right to personal honour be given primacy? In a dispute about expropriation, how much guidance does the constitution give judges when, on the one hand, the right to property is proclaimed whereas, on the other, property must be used for the good of the community, and can be taken by public authorities for such use? One could go on and on. What is clear is that this type of problem is both inevitable and impossible to definitively resolve. Not surprisingly, intraconstitutional tensions such as these are a great source of constitutional decision-making and development.

Constitutional Decision-making

By constitutional decision-making I mean the act of determining the meaning of a given constitutional provision (or set of provisions) in order to resolve a dispute about the constitutionality of either: (1) an infraconstitutional norm; or (2) a practice or action on the part of one or more individuals. Every act of constitutional review is an act of constitutional decision-making. In deciding, a constitutional court simultaneously makes policy *and* constructs the constitution. The policy-making function of constitutional case law is clearly revealed when we focus attention on the outcome of a given dispute in terms of the disputants involved. The resolution of the dispute establishes the law governing the interactions of the disputing parties. The constitutional development function of the case law is most evident when we attend to the court's reasoning, or justification, for why an infraconstitutional norm (or act) is, or is not, constitutional. As we saw in the previous chapter, authoritative interpretation of a constitutional text—constitutional rule-making—often produces powerful prospective effects on future policy-making and dispute resolution. It legitimates some policy routes and delegitimates others, and signals to parliament, the judiciary, and to future litigants that some lines of constitutional contestation have been closed off or narrowed, while others have been opened up.

Constitutional Rights and Decision-making

The structure of rights provisions constitute implicit delegations of enormous discretionary authority to constitutional judges. Although a few rights are declared in absolutist terms—the most important being 'equality before the law' provisions, found in all four countries, and 'human dignity' in Germany—the great majority of rights are expressly limited. To illustrate, below are a handful of expressly 'limited' rights

• In Spain, art. 20.1.a proclaims the right to free expression, which art. 20.4 then 'delimits' with reference to 'other rights, including personal honour and privacy.' Art. 33.1 declares the right to private property, while art. 33.3 provides for the restriction of property rights for 'public benefit', as determined by statute.

• In Italy, article 14.1 states that the 'personal domicile is inviolable', save for searches and seizures done 'in cases and in a manner laid down by statute in conformity with . . . personal freedom' (art. 14.2). Art. 21.1 announces that 'the press shall not be subjected to any authority of censorship', while art. 21.6 provides that 'printed publications . . . contrary to morality are forbidden', and art. 21.7 states that parliament possesses the responsibility to 'prevent and repress all [such] violations'.

• In Germany, art. 2.1 states that 'everyone shall have the right to the free development of his/her personality in so far as he/she does not violate the rights of others or offend the constitutional order or moral code'. Art. 10.1 proclaims that the 'privacy of posts and telecommunications shall be inviolable', while art. 10.2 states that 'this right may be restricted [by] statute'.

• In France, art. 11 of the 1789 Declaration of the Rights of Man declares that 'every citizen may . . . speak, write, and print freely, but is responsible for the abuse of this liberty in circumstances determined by statute'. The 1946 social and economic principles of the 1946 include the proclamation that 'the right to strike is exercised according to the laws that regulate it'.

Intraconstitutional tensions are not simply the affairs of constitutional judges. European constitutions require law-makers to engage in constitutional decision-making, that is, to ensure respect for constitutional rights *and* regulate how rights are to be enjoyed and exercised for the good of the collectivity. Although expressed in disparate provisions, this latter competence is usually conceived holistically, as a coherent set of 'constitutional interests' possessed by government: to provide for public order, to protect public morality, to secure the public weal, and so on. Although European constitutions command parliaments and judges to resolve conflicts between constitutionally protected interests of government and constitutional rights in any given case, they give little indication of how to do so. Instead, the structure of European rights provisions invites—I would say requires—what Europeans and Americans both call 'balancing': deliberation about the proper, relational limits of (1) a given constitutional right of an individual or group that has come into conflict with (2) another individual's right, or a constitutional interest of government.

Balancing

Legal scholarship, and the courts themselves, have produced an ever-growing corpus of doctrines and principles designed to explain, synthesize, and justify this kind of decision-making.[3] All elaborate on a common sequence: interpretation, balancing, proportionality (a 'rationality' or 'least means' doctrine). Constitutional judges, first, seek to interpret away intraconstitutional conflicts on the assumption that the constitution is a body of harmonious norms, and that conflicts among constitutional norms are illusory (Herzog 1992). However, when a dispute contains an inherent opposition between two rights provisions (or between a rights provision and a constitutional interest of government) that cannot be interpreted away, the judges move to balancing. In balancing, judges determine whether, and to what extent, one legal value (a right of individuals, or a constitutional interest of government) must give way to a second legal

---

[3] The published proceedings of Eighth Conference of European Constitutional Courts of 1990 (1992) were dedicated to the topic of adjudicating constitutional rights.

value. And this exercise is then governed by proportionality ('least means') tests.

Balancing is the favoured, interpretive technique used to resolve those cases in which the legal values invoked by the parties are both of equivalent status (in the hierarchy of norms), yet are opposed to one another (in the specific conflict at hand). When a court claims to be balancing two constitutional rights, or a constitutional right against a constitutionally legitimate state purpose, a proportionality test—really a 'least means' test—logically follows from the balancing exercise, and in nearly all cases actually does follow. If in balancing, the court determines that a statute which infringes the exercise of a constitutional right is nonetheless constitutional—to the extent that on balance the service of the statute to some other constitutional value outweighs the incursion—then it follows that any but the absolute minimum infringement necessary to serve the other value is unconstitutional. This is because any added curtailment of the right cannot be justified by balancing, since such curtailment adds nothing positive that can outweigh its marginal, negative effects. Put simply, it is never constitutionally sufficient, under a balancing standard, that the constitutional benefits outweigh the constitutional costs; instead, the benefit must be achieved at the least constitutional costs (least means).[4] In this kind of adjudication, constitutional judges have no choice but to answer the following question: 'Can we imagine any statutory provisions other than the ones before us that would achieve the same result, serve the same constitutional value, with lower constitutional costs?' If the answer is yes, then the imagined statute is constitutional, but the one before them is not. A jurisprudence of rights based on constitutonal balancing leads judges to put themselves in the place of the legislature, and to conduct legislative-style deliberations, which partly explains why we find constitutional courts so often commanding parliament to legislate in particular ways (see Chapter 3). A balancing jurisprudence not only gives the court great discretion, but it will inevitably caste the court into a more legislative style of deliberation and decision-making than would a jurisprudence of absolute rights.

Balancing tests and proportionality doctrines do little more than admit, albeit in a convoluted manner, the following: that protecting constitutional

---

[4] In Europe, proportionality tests are also called 'rationality' or 'reasonableness' doctrines (see Pizzorusso, Vigoriti, and Certoma 1984). Accordingly, every statutory restriction of the exercise or full enjoyment of a right is constitutional only to the extent that the limitation established is 'reasonable', or 'rational': the limitation must be derivable from an identifiable constitutional source, and must not reduce the enjoyment of the right more than is necessary to secure that interest.

rights is difficult work; that constitutional judges must possess and wield wide discretionary powers in order for them to do this job properly; and that no firm and fast rules for protecting rights can be articulated. I am not saying that courts do not seek to generate stable rules to govern this kind of constitutional decision-making (courts do), nor that decisional outcomes are random (they are not). The meaning of balancing is more profound. Constitutional courts do not protect rights without becoming deeply involved in the facts, or social context, or legislative decision-making that underlies or has given rise to the constitutional question. In this mode of decision-making, it is the policy dimension that varies, not the law *per se*, and this variance heavily conditions constitutional development by dragging constitutional judges into the lives of citizens, and the work of legislators and ordinary judges. The social logic of balancing, and some of its consequences, are further discussed in Chapter 5.

Unwritten Rights

Constitutional courts have significantly enhanced their discretionary powers by treating certain constitutional provisions as open-ended invitations to generate 'new', unenumerated rights. The Spanish Court, for example, 'insists on the necessity of a systematic and teleological constitutional interpretation, rather than strictly literal', especially with reference to what it labels the 'finality' of article 1 (Spanish Report 1992). Article 1 states that 'Spain . . . considers liberty, justice, equality and political pluralism as the foremost values of its legal order'. Thus, not only does the SCT possess jurisdiction over the most extensive enumerated list of rights in Western Europe, but all other constitutional provisions are to be interpreted in light of the objectives of liberty, justice, and equality. The German constitution opens with a relatively short series of rights provisions, but the Court compensates for this by treating article 1 ('human dignity shall be inviolable') as open-ended, and article 2.1 (the right to freely develop one's personality) as denoting 'nearly anything the individual might wish to do' (GFCC 1957). The French bill of rights, entirely the product of case law, is composed of the following: the 1789 declaration of the rights of man; the social and economic principles listed in the preamble to the 1946 constitution; and the unenumerated 'fundamental principles of the laws of the Republic' (FPRLR). The French Constitutional Council has discovered that the FPRLR contains such rights as personal liberty and inviolability, the 'independence' of university professors, the right to a legal defence, and the principle of judicial independence; it has also elevated to constitutional status certain unwritten 'general principles of law', which it borrowed from the case law of Council of State, the supreme administrative court.

Finally, the Italian Court has recently repudiated the theory (e.g. of Grossi 1972) that article 2—'the Republic guarantees the inviolable rights of man'—refers only to those rights specifically enumerated in subsequent articles. In the 1980s, supported by legal scholars (e.g. Zagrebelsky 1981), the ICC began elaborating a 'transcendental', or 'metajuridical', conception of article 2, in order to ground a 'dynamic theory of constitutional rights' (Ponthoreau 1991). By 1988, the ICC had explicitly declared that article 2 constituted an 'open norm' (ICC 1988c), through which the Court may recognize rights somehow forgotten by the framers; further, article 2 is not modifiable through constitutional revision (Pizzorusso and Rossi 1995: 140). Rights to marry, to be born, to sexual liberty, to privacy have all been generated by article 2 case law, which is now an open door to a natural law-based rights jurisprudence.

Italy: Transexualism and the Right to Sexual Identity (1979–85)

In 1979, the Italian Constitutional Court rejected a claim that article 2 included a right to determine one's own sexual identity (ICC 1979). The claimant, an individual who had undergone a male-to-female sex change operation, had sought to register as a woman with the relevant public authorities, the mayor's office, in Livorno. She did so in order to obtain certain benefits, including the capacity to marry a man and form a family under Italian law. The mayor's office rebuffed her, on the grounds that the civil code (the relevant parts of which dated from 1939) permitted changes of registration, normally made at birth, only in the event of clerical error. The woman sued the office, and the presiding judge referred the matter to the ICC.

The referral posed a delicate problem that involved multiple constitutional provisions, the civil code, and an established case law of the highest civil court, the Court of Cassation. Did article 2 cover a freedom to choose sexual identity, alone or in conjunction with the article 3.2 proclamation that Italians possess the right to 'fully develop' their 'personality'? Of what relevance was article 32, which declares a 'right to health', or article 29, which states that marriage is the 'foundation of the family' and the 'natural' basis of 'society'? In several decisions taken in the 1970s, the Supreme Court (Cassation) had consistently held that only operations performed to enhance the definition or functioning of preexisting sexual organs could be recognized by the family law provisions of the civil code. The

Constitutional Court, in its decision, implied that the Civil Code and Cassation's case law might not provide sufficient protection of individual rights; it then asked parliament to revise the law, and to 'reconcile' individual freedoms with society's interest in marriage and family.

For once, Italian law-makers acted relatively quickly and responsibly. In 1982, they legalized changes in the registration of identity pursuant to 'surgery modifying sexual characteristics'. The civil courts resisted by interpreting the new legislation as if it were in agreement with Cassation's existing policy. After a Naples woman was denied the right to alter records stating that she was male, she sued, and the case eventually reach the Supreme Court. Cassation referred the matter to the Constitutional Court, inviting it to annul the reform. According to the Supreme Court, whereas articles 2, 3.2, 29, and 32 of the constitution were designed 'to protect individuals . . . in their social life', sex change operations could only be harmful: they 'complicated' a person's already existing 'abnormality', and undermined marriage and 'normal' family development. Since, Cassation reasoned, the constitution requires the civil code to discourage such eventualities, the new law should be annulled.

The Constitutional Court disagreed, this time proclaiming that article 2 (in conjunction with article 3.2) did indeed 'guarantee the right to determine one's own sexual identity', a right that 'other members in society are obligated to respect' in the service of 'social solidarity' (ICC 1985a). Basing its decision on a much richer understanding of transexualism than Cassation's, the ICC declared that sex change operations were inherently therapeutic for those who 'feel, in a profound way', that 'they belong to the other gender', despite physical manifestations to the contrary. Far from subverting the institutions of marriage and the family, the reform would enable transexuals to remarry, and to give children from past marriages a more 'normal' family life. Given this theory of transexualism, the Court could hardly let stand the Supreme Court's solution. The ICC then ruled that the subjective, 'psycho-sexual' orientation of individuals, not the existence of unformed or non-functioning genitalia, must always be determinative. Last, the ICC praised the legislature for adopting a law that would help transexuals 'overcome the [social] isolation, hostility, and humiliation that too often accompanies their lives'. Thus, the Court reconciled a new (and radically progressive) right with traditional conceptions of relatively conservative social institutions, generating a new social duty along the way. This is constitutional rule-making of an exceptionally delicate nature.

There is no point in trying to reconcile the Italian Court's ruling of 1979 with that of 1985. Instead, the change has to be understood in the light of the participatory nature of constitutional politics. The first decision was provoked by a referral from a trial judge who apparently was seeking to undermine the Supreme Court's restrictive case law, by asking the Court to find a right to sexual identity in article 2. Declining to do so, the Italian Court none the less enlisted the legislature as an ally, in order to isolate Cassation, before proceeding to direct confrontation with the Supreme Court. By legislating as it had, parliament facilitated the Court's move to announce the new right. At the same time it provoked Cassation to request the ICC to annul the legislature's work. The ICC rejected the Supreme Court's referral in no uncertain terms—by 'constitutionalizing' the reform. In consequence, unless the Constitutional Court overrules itself or until the constitution is revised, parliament's capacity to alter this part of the civil code has been restricted.

PARLIAMENT AND CONSTITUTIONAL ADJUDICATION

Whenever legislators engage in constitutional decision-making, they behave as constitutional judges. Today, governments and parliaments do so all the time, and for three mutually reinforcing reasons. First, the constitution commands legislators to protect some rights, and to produce and maintain the conditions for the exercise of many others. This activity produces the normative context in which constitutional deliberation and decision-making takes place. Second, the adjudication of rights by parliamentarians is a facet of the struggle among political parties to control constitutional development and policy outcomes. Most of the important ideological conflicts that divide parliaments can be expressed as conflicts about the nature and application of rights, because the rights provisions generally reflect, rather than harmonize, the opposed visions of society held by the negotiating parties at the constitutional moment. In this ongoing struggle, each party seeks to implement its own version of a right, or of a proper balance between two rights. And, in much the same way, each seeks to fix relatively enduring, substantive rules of policy-making that will bind on future legislative processes.

Third, the existence of constitutional review mechanisms gives agency to constitutional commands to protect and to balance rights, and gives urgency to ideological conflicts about rights. In judicialized policy-making, each side seeks to construct constitutional law, fully aware of the prospective, symbolic effects of this construction on the legitimacy of its party programme and social vision. This behaviour is inherently 'judicial';

it constitutes a 'legal level' within a multitiered system of constitutional adjudication. Of course, such behaviour can be understood in neo-rationalist, that is, purely functional and instrumental, terms: parties anticipate the attitude of the constitutional court in order to gain reward or avoid punishment (see Chapter 3). It can also be understood as the progressive construction of a new discursive field. In this process, the behavioural norms and discursive vocabulary of constitutional law are elaborated and then absorbed into the practices and language that constitute parliamentary decision-making.

Legislating as Constitutional Decision-making

We observe parliaments behaving as constitutional judges most clearly when we pay attention to the politics of abstract review. The risk or threat of referral by the opposition triggers constitutional deliberations. These deliberations typically result in reasoned judgments about how best to protect rights, and about how best to balance rights with constitutional interests. Law-makers not only deliberate constitutional law, they defend their decisions as judges do, with reference to legal materials. This behaviour is in fact embedded in what can be conceived as an extended judicial process. When parliaments engage in constitutional decision-making, they behave as constitutional review bodies of first instance, over which constitutional courts exercise a kind of appellate control.[5]

The French case provides the ideal laboratory for research on the impact of abstract review, since abstract review is the only mode of control that exists. The Constitutional Council has been able to construct French constitutional law, now a huge and imposing edifice, only because legislators themselves have struggled to construct the constitution, through their policy-making activities. Parliamentary oppositions provide the Council with caseload, and without caseload the constitutional law would be unworthy of study. Rights provisions are the primary source of law invoked by petitioners, and are the basis for over 90 per cent of all of the Council's rulings of unconstitutionality. French rights politics are therefore a species of

---

[5] Parliamentarians recognize that their decisions at times constitute distinctly separate acts of *judicial* authority. Here is how Etienne Dailly put it during the Senate's debate on a motion of unconstitutionality against the Socialist governments 1981 nationalization bill (reported in Stone 1994a: 465–6): 'I repeat: I have never said that we would refer this bill [to the Council]. I have limited myself to arguing that it is unconstitutional . . . . Personally, I consider that we [in parliament] are judges of the first instance. But we are under the control of the Council, just as judges of first instance are under the control of the Court of Appeal'.

legislative politics, and legislative politics are part and parcel of constitutional adjudication.

That French law-makers behave as judges of the constitution can be empirically observed and evaluated. The constitution requires that every bill drafted by the government be submitted to its legal adviser, the Council of State, which reviews the legislation for 'legality'. By the mid 1980s (when referrals became more or less systematic and predictable), the Council of State had recognized the identity of legality and constitutionality; it then assumed the responsibility to evaluate inconsistencies between draft bills and the constitutional text, and to warn ministers of potential constitutional risks (Stone 1989). Once a bill has been submitted to parliament, formalized rituals organize constitutional deliberations. Any deputy or senator, for example, can raise a point of parliamentary procedure known as a motion of unconstitutionality (*motions d'irrecevabilité*). These motions, often written in the stylized form of a French judicial decision (and published in the chamber's record), interrupt legislative discussion pending a formal debate and ruling on the bill's constitutionality by the full chamber. Legislators support their respective positions by citing constitutional texts, legal scholarship, and the Council's existing case law. If the motion passes, the bill is declared unconstitutional, and it is killed. Motions of unconstitutionality are today a regular part of legislative life (Stone 1996). In the 1981–7 period, for example, the National Assembly alone voted on 94 such motions (a figure to be compared with 93 Council decisions). Subject to strict party discipline, the motions are virtually never adopted. Their importance, however, is to set the stage for the constitutional politics to come.

In Germany and Spain, the documentation distributed along with proposed legislation to parliamentarians often includes a specific chapter devoted to the relevant case law. Because this documentation is organized by the government, its position is favoured and clearly expressed. Most important, German and Spanish parliamentarians, like their French counterparts, debate and make reasoned decisions about the constitutionality of legislation, in the shadow of constitutional adjudication. If conflict has not been settled by the amendment process, majority and opposition unpack their arguments again, and send them to constitutional courts for a final hearing. The larger French, German, and Spanish political parties all employ constitutional specialists, usually university law professors, who advise them on how to attack or defend the constitutionality of a bill, and to draft abstract review petitions.

Although abstract review does not exist in Italy, procedures of the Chamber of Deputies and of the Senate also structure an ongoing dialogue between legislatures and the Italian Court. The Chamber's rules require that the ICC's decisions on the constitutionality of legislation be transmitted to the competent legislative committee,[6] as well as the Committee on Constitutional Affairs. The competent committee is then required to examine the decision, in meetings with representatives of the government and of the Committee on Constitutional Affairs, and to recommend legislative action, if necessary. Recommendations are formally communicated to the Chamber, the Senate, the Government, and the ICC.[7]

Parliamentary Law-making and Rights

It would be a mistake to dismiss parliamentary adjudication of rights as inherently less meaningful, or necessarily less 'judicial', than the deliberations of a constitutional court. The more judicialized any legislative process, the more we find parliament and the court doing the same things, using the same language, and working through the same normative materials. This should come as no surprise, since each institution makes up the targeted audience for the other; that is, each institution seeks to persuade the other institution that, by a virtuous process of principled reasoning, it has correctly interpreted the constitutional law. That parliamentary majorities and constitutional courts often disagree about how to apply the constitutional law to resolve legislative conflicts should signal to us not that parliament erred, although it may have, but that the number of potentially persuasive, reasoned positions on the constitutionality of any given bill is greater than one.

When the court annuls a bill on rights grounds, it substitutes its own reading of rights, and its own policy goals, for those of the parliamentary majority. Among dozens of examples available, the fate of gender-based electoral quotas in France suffices to illustrate the point.

France: Electoral Quotas and Affirmative Action (1982)

During the 1981 elections, the French Socialist Party promised women that it would promote gender equality by, among other things, establishing a proportional representation electoral system for local and national

---

[6] A ruling on the constitutionality of a provision of the Code of Judicial Procedure would go to the justice committee.

[7] In 1979, an *ad hoc* committee was established within the Committee on Constitutional Affairs to search for legislative gaps, brought about by the decisions of the ICC, and to be filled by parliament.

elections, and by setting aside a minimum number of slots for female can-didates on party lists. The new Socialist government's first attempt to make good on the pledge targeted local elections. A bill was produced stipulating that electoral lists for communal elections could not include 'more than 75 per cent candidates of the same sex'. The Right attacked the 1982 version as an 'unconstitutional, demagogic, and dangerous' discrimination against men, and threatened referral. Over catcalls of 'dictatorship!', and 'what about hermaphrodites?', proponents of the bill argued that constitutional-ity had been secured by the fact that the 75 per cent restriction applied to both sexes equally. With an eye to their standing among women, the op-position voted with the majority, and the bill passed with unanimous sup-port. Nevertheless, the Right referred the bill, but refrained from attacking the quota.

The Council annulled the provision anyway, relying on article 6 (1789), which guarantees equality under the law (Council 1982b). What was not said was deafening. The Council ignored altogether the constitutional command, contained in the 1946 social principles and cited constantly by the Left during the legislative debates, that equal rights between women and men shall be guaranteed by statute. As an act of policy-making, the Council had vetoed an important provision of the 1982 electoral law. But it had also constructed the constitution: the ruling is today read as pro-hibiting affirmative action, not just in electoral matters, but in all matters of public policy.

In this kind of case, it would be nonsense to suppose that the constitu-tional court has functioned as some kind of bulwark against the tyranny of majority rule. In fact, the Socialists sought to promote the rights of an under-represented category of citizens, by activating a constitutional pro-vision that had been all but ignored up to that point in time. The Council blocked this effort, on the basis of the parliamentary opposition's reading of the constitution. This part of the outcome raises another general point. In reviewing prior, parliamentary acts of constitutional decision-making, the constitutional court rarely if ever protects rights that would otherwise be ignored by parliament. Instead, the court makes a choice about how best to protect rights from the 'menu' of policy options that has already been elaborated in parliamentary debates about the constitutionality of the bill in question. Constitutional judges, more often than not, choose from this menu, precisely because parliamentarians, more often than not, target in on the salient constitutional issues and debate them intensely.

Balancing (again)

When governments and parliaments engage in balancing, 'judicial' and 'legislative' behaviours blend: each constitutes the primary activity of the other; they cannot be dissociated. Just as legislators often consciously work to protect and to strengthen the exercise of rights, they also engage in balancing, on their own, without prior prompting from constitutional judges. The evidence of such behaviour is published, in parliamentary debates and in the internal structure of the statute itself. In referring the statute, oppositions are, in effect, requesting a ruling on a point of constitutional law *and* a final legislative 'reading' of the bill. The court can not do one without doing the other—any more than parliaments can. In approving of how legislators have balanced contending claims, as in the case of a Spanish region's efforts to promote its native language (below), or in disapproving, as in the German saga to liberalize abortion (below), new rules governing policy-making are produced by courts, and these will impact on future legislative processes.

Spain: Language Rights in Catalan (1994)

Resolving disputes concerning the proper division of competences between the national government and the governments of the autonomous regions is one of the Spanish Constitutional Tribunal's most difficult and important tasks. The 1978 constitution, the product of a complicated web of delicate political compromises among many parties, established an ill-defined, quasi-federal system. Generally, the governments of the autonomous regions have sought to exercise, defend, and extend their competences (Clark 1989). Regions have attacked national legislation as unconstitutional before the Tribunal, and have adopted legislation that pushes their own authority to, and often beyond, constitutional limits. For its part, the national government has produced 'framework' laws to shape or restrict how regional autonomy would be used. In part due to the insufficient clarity of the constitutional rules governing Spanish federalism (Arce Janariz 1989; García de Enterría 1989, 1993), in part due to these politics, the Tribunal has become a kind of permanently constituted forum for the clarification and revision of the constitutional rules governing Spanish federalism (Velàzquez Vidal 1994).

Some rights issues overlap issues of regional autonomy, none more so than the relationship between linguistic and educational rights, and the regions' competence to promote regional languages and to regulate education. To the extent that rights are implicated, concrete review and individual complaints may enter into play, as in the following case.

In 1983, the Catalan legislature, taking advantage of opportunities afforded by the Constitution, adopted a law making the Catalan language one of two co-official languages of the region (see Kasha 1996). The second co-official language is Castilian Spanish. Since the 16th century, the central authorities have sought to suppress Catalan, in favour of Castilian, with no success. The regional government now sought to promote the spread of Catalan to users of Castilian by exploiting the competences of regions in the education realm. The 1983 law mandated: that all students attending Catalan schools achieve fluency in both official languages by the time they end their studies; that after primary school, all subjects would be taught in Catalan, and not Castilian; that diplomas would not be issued to those who did not achieve minimal proficiency levels in both languages; and that Catalan would be the 'medium of normal expression' in the schools, and in communications between the schools and the community. Anxious to secure constitutionality, the government included provisions: giving all children a right to be educated in their mother tongue, but only in the primary schools; exempting students who had been educated outside of the region from the obligation to learn Catalan; and requiring every student to take at least one non-language course taught in Castilian, each term.[8]

Within months after the new school year began, a father of a Castilian-speaking student sued in court. After more than ten years of legal manoeuvring and appeals, the Supreme Court asked the Constitutional Tribunal to review the law, making it clear that it considered it to be unconstitutional. There were good reasons to suppose that it was. In prior decisions, the SCT had ruled that, although public authorities had an obligation to promote regional languages, individuals did not have a duty to know them (e.g. SCT 1983). Further, article 3 places every Spaniard under a positive obligation to know Castilian; article 27 of the constitution proclaims the right to a free education, and a state duty to provide it; and article 149.1.30 confers on the national government the 'exclusive authority' to issue diplomas. The Supreme Court therefore argued that the region, in requiring students to know Catalan in order in order to obtain an education, and to receive a diploma, had violated the rights of those whose first language was Castilian, and had exceeded its competence in the education field. On the

---

[8] For the purpose of simplicity, I discuss the law and the implementing decrees as if they were one and the same. The suit alleged that the decrees violated the constitutional rights of Castilian speakers, and the concrete review petition was made because the legality of the decrees depended upon the constitutionality of the law.

other hand, article 148.1.18 grants to regions the power to 'promote . . . instruction in the language of the autonomous community'.

The Tribunal ruled for Catalan, approving how the government had balanced the rights and duties of citizens and government (SCT 1994). The right to an education, the judges declared, requires that the education provided can not be 'appreciably inferior to that which they would have received had they received education in their mother tongue'. The SCT looked favourably on Castilian-speaking students being able to begin instruction in their first language. To the extent that 'the Catalan language will be used progressively until all students develop a command of it', it stated, the law 'protects' the students' 'basic right to be educated in a language that they know'. The Tribunal, somewhat disingenuously, declared, without real discussion, that the region had taken steps to promote Catalan (which is a constitutional duty of government) but not to require students to know Catalan (which is prohibited). Similarly, the Tribunal tersely ruled that the government's authority to withhold diplomas derived from its authority to manage the school system generally, since only by completing requirements could students earn diplomas. Finally, the SCT noted that the law required the use of Catalan in official communications only by school officials (constitutional), not by private parties in their dealings with the schools (unconstitutional).

Germany: Liberalizing Abortion (1975–92)

The subject of intense political controversy since the late 1960s, German abortion policy is now, as in the United States (Craig and O'Brien 1993) fully judicialized (Neuman 1995; Prützel-Thomas 1993).

Sections 218–220 of the German penal code, the core of which dates from 1871, makes abortion one of several 'crime against life'. A century later, these provisions remained virtually intact, prescribing one- to five-year prison sentences, excepting operations performed to preserve the mother's health. Given the stranglehold of the Catholic Church on the social policies of the Christian Social Union (CSU)—the rightwing political party that has always governed the post 1949 state, Bavaria, and the coalition partner of the Christian Democrats at the federal level—liberalization became politically feasible only after the CDU–CSU went into opposition for the first time, in 1969.

The rank and file of the two new coalition parties, the Social Democrats and the Free Democrats, supported the legalization of abortion in the first trimester of pregnancy, and afterwards on other grounds. At the November

1971 conference of the Social Democrats, delegates supported such a solution by a vote of 638–59, and polls showed public support hovering at about 75 per cent (Braunthal 1983: 250–2). After intense two-year negotiations with critics (especially the Catholic Church), the government produced a timid bill, relaxing penalties only for cases of medical necessity, rape, and social emergencies. In the Bundestag, however, the SPD and FDP deputies rewrote the bill in conformity with party resolutions.

The parliamentary majority sought to achieve a harmonious balance of two rights found in article 2 of the constitution: the protection of the constitutional 'right to life' of the foetus, a right whose existence no political party denied; and the right of women to control their reproductive lives, which the majority derived from 'the right to freely develop one's personality'. The law finally adopted enshrined a 'stage of pregnancy' solution: in the first twelve weeks, after mandatory counselling, abortions would be legal; in the first twenty-two weeks, abortions would be allowed only in cases where the woman's health was endangered or where the baby would likely be born with serious birth defects; after twenty-two weeks, abortions would be permitted only when the woman's life would be endangered by carrying the foetus to term.

The GFCC, which received the law on reference from 193 deputies and five states controlled by the opposition, annulled the law on 'right to life' grounds (GFCC 1975). The Court ruled that, because post-Nazi Germany had a special obligation to protect human life, including the embryonic, abortion could never be formally decriminalized. It then went on to propose draft legislation containing a 'reasons' formula to replace a 'stage of pregnancy' one. Although abortion could not be legalized, *per se*, the procedure could nonetheless go unpunished: (1) after mandatory counselling; and (2) when justified by eugenic (birth defects probable), medical (heath risk for the mother), criminal (pregnancy the result of rape), or social hardship reasons. Despite protests from SPD–FDP deputies, the government decided, 'regretfully', to respect the Court's ruling. It drafted a new law, grafting, virtually word-for-word, the salient parts of the Court's ruling onto what was left of the bill's architecture. Thus, during the first twelve weeks of pregnancy, abortions could go unpunished, when criminal or social reasons had been properly certified, or up to twenty-two weeks when birth defects were likely, or when the mother's health was seriously jeopardized. In 1976, the law was promulgated.

The reform did not calm controversy. Proponents of legal abortions complained that the 'reasons' test was being applied more strictly in some federal states than in others, as evidenced by the abortion-tourism industry. In the 1980s, some 40,000 abortions annually were being performed on German women in the Netherlands alone. Opponents of abortion protested that the procedure was far too easy to obtain, as evidenced by the fact that the percentage of 'social hardship' cases had risen steadily, from 60 per cent in 1977 to 89 per cent in 1990 (Prützel-Thomas 1993: 472).

Both sides sought to undermine the law through the courts. German women appealed, unsuccessfully, to the European Court on Human Rights (Kommers 1989: 360). The GFCC invoked procedural grounds to avoid ruling on the constitutionality of public funding of abortions (GFCC 1984). And in Bavaria, prosecutors charged doctors and nurses with too liberally interpreting the 'social reasons' and counselling requirements, sentencing some to imprisonment, and levying fines of up to DM3,200 on hundreds of women (Prützel-Thomas 1993: 473). By 1990, the GFCC had a stack of abortion cases pending, including a reference by the Bavarian government to the effect that the law was being too liberally administered in various other *Länder*.

Both the fall of the Berlin Wall and the reunification of Germany required law-makers to deal with the problem. In East Germany, the right to choose to terminate pregnancy in the first trimester had acquired the status of an entitlement—'one of the few areas where the omnipresent . . . State had not intefered' (Prützel-Thomas 1993: 468). After delicate negotiations, the Unification Treaty of August 1990 sidestepped settling the issue, but obligated the German parliament to adopt a new abortion law, by 31 December 1992.

In June 1992, after nearly two years of debate, a revision of articles 218 and 219 of the criminal code was adopted by the Bundestag.[9] The CDU–CSU group, the largest party delegation in the Bundestag, had drafted a bill to make it even more difficult to obtain abortions, but the Social Democrats, the Free Democrats, the Greens, and smaller parties from the former East Germany negotiated their own bill which carried by a vote of 355–283. The bill is an elaborate product of constitutional decision-making and balancing. To protect the woman's right to choice and 'free development', the bill legalized abortion in the first twelve weeks, after counselling. But the Bundestag sought to protect the foetus in two ways. First, legislators maintained criminal penalties for terminating pregnancies beyond the twelve-week limit, subject to certain (mostly medical) exceptions. Second, the bill including comprehensive, wide-ranging provisions designed to address many of the social hardships many poorer women

---

[9] The CDU replaced the SPD as the coalition partner of the Free Democratic Party.

would face if they carried to term. Thus, the bill, entitled 'Law to Assist Pregnant Women and Families', provided for heavily subsidized child care for preschool children, the construction of low income family housing, free contraception for individuals 21 years old and under, and the establishment of a widely available network of counselling offices. *Der Spiegel* reported that although the estimated annual cost of the bill would top DM10 billion, after startup costs of over DM40 billion, polls showed that more than 75 per cent of Germans favoured the bill, including 69 per cent of CDU voters. On promulgation, the law was referred to the GFCC by Bavaria and 248 Christian Democrats of the Bundestag.

The Court, by a 6–3 vote, annulled the revision of article 218, holding essentially to its 1975 ruling: the State's obligation to protect embryonic life meant that abortion could not be legalized, even in the first trimester, but that abortions performed for medical, eugenic, and criminal reasons could still go unpunished (GFCC 1993*a*). The social hardship standard, however, was tightened and recast in terms of 'unreasonable burden': abortions would be tolerated by the criminal law if carrying a foetus to term would impose 'heavy and unusual burdens' going well beyond 'reasonable sacrifice'. The Court made it clear that such tolerance could only be sustained to the extent that the State actively sought to discourage women from choosing to terminate. By a 5–3 vote, the GFCC laid down detailed instructions for redrafting the counselling requirement of article 219, among these, that: the sole purpose of counselling is to make women aware of the unborn's own right to life' and to 'encourage' them to 'accept their tasks as mothers'; counsellors must employ 'scientifically developed "conflict counselling" that require a woman to reveal her motives', because 'an uninvolved "it is up to you" demeanour is unacceptable'; and counselling facilities must be separated from facilities providing abortions. Although the Court praised the legislature for working to enhance housing and child care for low income families, it ruled that neither public nor private health insurance could be used to pay for abortions.

A corrective revision process enshrined the Court's referred policy. But future controversies—concerning what constitutes a 'heavy and unusual burden', and the constitutionality of creative, alternative funding schemes—are assured.

Corrective Revision

We cannot begin to understand European systems of rights protection if we do not pay attention to parliamentary decision-making, both before and after the constitutional court decides. The German abortion cases—but no more than many other examples—show just how seriously parliament can take its responsibility to protect rights and to engage in constitutional decision-making prior to the intervention of constitutional judges. After the rulings, legislators acted as agents of the GFCC, implementing the Court's preferred policy in corrective revision processes.

Concrete review referrals and individual complaints organize the protection of rights outside of parliamentary space. While designed to restore or protect individual rights that have already been violated, such procedures none the less have the capacity to generate or restructure ongoing and future legislative processes.[10] The most obvious examples occur when the constitutional court commands parliament to legislate or to revise legislation, or suffer future censure. The wide-ranging public discussion of the constitutionality of life imprisonment triggered by decisions of the German Court taken in the 1970s, provides an example (but there are literally hundreds of similar instances). In 1977, partly in response to the ban on capital punishment imposed by the European Convention on Human Rights, the German parliament sought to require mandatory life sentences for those convicted of murder in 'wanton cruelty'. A judge attacked the reform in a concrete review petition, laying out a complex brief to the effect that the bill was unconstitutional, including an argument to the effect that the legislator, being motivated out of the desire for 'revenge', had violated what was in effect a prisoner's right to be 'resocialized' by the state (technically, the state's duty to use imprisonment to resocialize). The GFCC, relying on the constitutional right (article 1) to 'human dignity', declared that because the state has a constitutional responsibility to rehabilitate criminals, mandatory life sentences could only be imposed under certain, strict conditions (GFCC 1977). The ruling suspended the reform's application until these conditions were incorporated into the code by the legislature (Kommers 1997: 306–12; van Zyl Smit 1992).

One of the most important Italian examples concerns the dismantling of the state's broadcast monopoly, and the emergence of a mixed public–private system (the most comprehensive treatment is Volcansek in press: ch.7). In 1974, the ICC declared elements of the state monopoly on radio and television broadcasting to be in violation of the constitutional principle of pluralism (the right to be exposed to a wide range of 'political, social, and cultural tendencies and currents of thought'), a corollary of freedom of expression and opinion (ICC 1974*a*; *b*). In subsequent decisions

---

[10] See Ch. 3.

(including ICC 1976, 1981, 1985*b*, 1986, 1988*d*), the Court all but begged parliament to regulate a transition to a mixed public-private broadcasting regime by, among other things, creating specific kinds of antitrust rules, and establishing an independent regulatory agency to oversee the allocation of broadcast frequencies and to supervise compliance with competition rules (Pace 1990). The usual partisan bickering and parliamentary paralysis (several governments have fallen over the issue since 1986) were not overcome until 1990, when a framework law was finally passed. The law conformed to the main lines of the ICC jurisprudence (Barendt 1991). The reform did not still constitutional controversy. Indeed, private actors have since generated a long series of cases challenging the law's antitrust provisions, and other aspects of how the law has been applied (Volcansek in press: ch. 7). Nevertheless, it bears emphasis that, before 1990, government ministers regulated the sector, without any meaningful, external controls over their decision-making. Today, the domain is governed by rules generated by a fluid and complex set of interactions between: private actors (who challenge the legality of public acts); judicial officials (who certify concrete review referrals and resolve disputes); constitutional judges (who elaborate supralegislative rules binding on law-makers); and legislators (who write and revise the relevant statutes).

THE JUDICIARY AND CONSTITUTIONAL ADJUDICATION

The development of constitutional review has transformed the role and function of the law courts, a development that some European legal scholars refer to as 'the constitutionalization of the law', or the 'constitutionalization of the legal order' (Bon 1991; Favoreu 1990; Pizzorusso 1985; Quint 1989). By constitutionalization, I mean the process through which (1) constitutional norms come to constitute a source of law, capable of being invoked by litigators and applied by ordinary judges to resolve legal disputes, and (2) the techniques of constitutional decision-making become an important mode of argumentation and decision-making in the judicial system. Constitutionalization is partly the logical, normative consequence of the direct effect of rights provisions, and in part the product of complex dialogues between constitutional judges and the judiciary.

Constitutionalization has subverted three very powerful, deeply entrenched dogmas about the character and functioning of Continental legal systems. First, the traditional notion that the various legal codes in each country constituted more or less autonomous realms, governed by different sources of law and different principles of adjudication, is gradually being replaced by a new view, Kelsenian in inspiration, that the constitutional law unifies these domains into a more or less coherent legal order. Second, the quasi-official myth of judges as slaves of the codes, prohibited from creatively interpreting and rewriting the laws, has been shattered, in a very public manner. The very existence of constitutional review subverted the 'sacred' nature of statute within the legal order; and the practice of doing constitutional review, by processing concrete review referrals, for example, socialized judges into a new role—that of protecting the legal order from any legal acts contaminated by unconstitutionality. Third, orthodox accounts of the division of powers between: (1) constitutional judges, who do not involve themselves in the facts or in how judicial conflicts are actually resolved, but simply answer constitutional questions posed to them; and (2) all other judges, who do not make reasoned judgments about constitutionality, but instead refer constitutional questions to constitutional courts, are unhelpful. Indeed, they are totally outmoded. The fact that these dogmas persist has much to do with the inability of judges and legal scholars, faced with constitutionalization, to reconstitute the legitimacy of the juridical order differently than they have in the past. New paradigms have been offered, but they have also met with resistance (Chapter 5).

The discussion below seeks to account for these outcomes, commonalities among our four cases, while explaining important differences. It bears emphasis in advance that major comparative research on the impact of constitutional review on the judiciary does not exist. There is also a startling scarcity of empirical work documenting relationships between national judiciaries with their own constitutional judges. What follows is therefore necessarily schematic, a first thrust at comparative analysis. Generalizing across cases, the greater the level of interaction between the constitutional court and any given court system, the more the distinction between constitutional jurisdiction and ordinary jurisdiction collapses. That is, as constitutionalization deepens, ordinary judges necessarily behave as constitutional judges—they engaged in principled constitutional reasoning and resolve disputes by applying constitutional norms. And, as constitutionalization deepens, constitutional judges become more deeply involved in what is, theoretically, in the purview of the judiciary: they interpret the facts in a given dispute, and they review the relationship between these facts and the legality of infraconstitutional norms. As constitutional judges increasingly do so, the codes gradually loosen their grip on ordinary judges. Ordinary judges begin to treat the codes, more overtly and explicitly than they had previously, less as a set of sacred commands issuing from the sovereign, and more as a system of rules that must be co-ordinated with other systems of rules in light of changing conditions.

Cross-national differences in the scope, pace, and intensity of constitutionalization appear to be closely tied to the existence, or non-existence, of particular modes of review. In Germany and Spain, where abstract review, concrete review, and individual complaint procedures coexist, extensive constitutionalization has proceeded rapidly. In Italy, the absence of an individual complaint mechanism has reduced the capacity of the constitutional court to control judicial outcomes, much as the absence of abstract review mechanisms has reduced its capacity to control legislative outcomes. In consequence, constitutionalization has been more gradual and piecemeal. In France, where promulgated statute retain their formal, sovereign character, and no formal links between ordinary and constitutional jurisdictions exist, a primitive form of constitutionalization can nevertheless be observed.

The Constitutionalization of Law in Germany, Italy, Spain

In orthodox Continental legal theory, rights do not possess direct effect. Instead, rights provisions that did exist were viewed as programmatic statements, at most expressing a set of guidelines for legislative protection, but not judicial enforcement, of rights. In proclaiming rights and providing for a means of protecting them, new constitutions posed the knotty problem of direct effect, and its scope. Few denied the juridical status of rights within the public law. By definition, rights are restrictions on the power of the state, designed to protect individuals in their relations with public authority. In Germany, Italy, and Spain, the impact of constitutional rights on judicial outcomes became visible almost immediately in the domains of tax and social security law, and other forms of administrative law.

But the juridical status of constitutional rights outside of the public law provided a tougher test for constitutionalization. Two questions were raised. In relationships between private persons (e.g. employers with employees, associations with individuals, individuals with other individuals), did a violation of constitutional rights provide a basis for legal actions and remedies in the courts? If so, would not ordinary judges be required to enforce, and perhaps even interpret, the constitution? Traditionalists answered 'No' to both questions, since: (1) the private law (family law, labour law contracts, torts, etc.) constituted a sphere outside of the reach of the constitutional law; and (2) only the constitutional court possessed the power to interpret and enforce constitutional rights. Others disagreed, arguing that: (1) the constitution—of which rights are an integral part—comprised the source of all legality and justice, including the legality of private relationships; and (2) that since all judges are bound to uphold legality and promote justice, all judges automatically assume the responsibility of defending rights.

Although the outcome was by no means programmed in advanced, in Germany, Italy, and Spain, both questions have been definitively answered in the affirmative. The German experience represents the paradigmatic case of constitutionalization, an experience largely reproduced in Spain. It can be summarized by the following sequence. Immediately following the founding of the Federal Republic, ordinary judges began to behave as constitutional judges, on their own, without prompting from the constitutional court (Quint 1989: 254–9). The constitutional court legitimized this behaviour, in its review of the constitutionality of judicial decisions. The GFCC then went further, in effect ordering all judges to work to balance constitutional rights and interests in light of sweeping proportionality tests, and announcing that it would use its individual complaint jurisdiction to review this balancing behaviour on a case-by-case basis. Thus, the GFCC required all judges to engage in exactly the same kind of constitutional decision-making in which it engages. Such a requirement necessarily led the constitutional court to become deeply involved in the work of the ordinary judges (fact finding, choice of law, etc.), and led the latter to behave much like the former.

Germany: Freedom of Expression and the Private Law

The resolution of conflicts between traditional 'public liberties' enshrined in the Civil Code and the constitutional right to free speech served to formally constitutionalize German private law. The landmark constitutional decision involved a suit brought by the producer and distributor of the 1950 film, *Immortal Beloved*, against a minor bureaucrat in the Hamburg state government, Erich Lüth (GFCC 1958b). Lüth had called on Germans to boycott the film, as a protest against the rehabilitation of its director, Veit Harlan, an anti-Semitic film-maker whose work for the Nazis had led a court to convict him for crimes against humanity. The producers based their action on section 826 of the Civil Code, which prohibits 'intentional injury against another person in a manner contrary to good morals'. The lower court found that Lüth's activism had indeed caused injury, and ordered him to desist. Lüth appealed directly to the Constitutional Court, which (extraordinarily) waived the usual requirement that remedies be exhausted. The GFCC found for Lüth, using its decision to clarify the relationship between constitutional and private law. Most important, the Court proclaimed that the 'value system' expressed by the constitution 'affects all spheres of law', and that therefore 'every provision of the private law must be compatible with this system of values, and every such provision must be interpreted in its spirit'. The Court then declared that 'the constitution requires the [ordinary] judge' to verify the conformity of the private law with basic rights, and at all times to interpret the former as if it were in harmony with the latter. In the private law, constitutional rights thus possess what in continental legal parlance is called *indirect effect*, since the judge is obliged to (re)construct code law in light of rights provisions. 'If he . . . ignores the influence of constitutional law', the Court ruled, 'he violates objective constitutional law'.

The GFCC also made it clear that no simple formula for accommodating the private law to constitutional rights exists, that indeed accommodation could only be made in case-by-case acts of constitutional decision-making, itself structured by the requirements of balancing and proportionality (Thwaite and Brehm 1994). Because, in the Court's words, the Constitution 'desires' the establishment of 'an equilibrium . . . between the mutually contradictory and restrictive tendencies of the constitutional rights and the general laws [e.g. the Civil Code]', judges must 'weigh the values to be protected against each other', and give precedence to the most important of the interests at stake in any given case while maintaining maximum integrity for the interest to be subordinated. Thus, according to the GFCC, the constitution obliges the civil law judge to engage in balancing, as conditioned by proportionality, and these obligations are reinforced by the threat of review, via appeals and the individual complaint procedure.

In *Lüth*, the GFCC examined the facts and then determined that Lüth's right to free speech outweighed damages suffered by the film-makers. In subsequent cases in which plaintiffs sought damages caused by defendant's speech acts, the Court went on to develop multiple lines of jurisprudence, some favouring free speech, others favouring interests inherent in the Civil Code (Quint 1989). Thus, in *Blinkfeuer* (GFCC 1969), the Court quashed a Federal Supreme Court ruling to the effect that a call for a news vendor boycott of a pro-Communist weekly constituted protected speech. The Supreme Court had relied on *Lüth*. Before finding for the leftist weekly, the constitutional court walked through the case step-by-step, sifting through the facts and reconstituting its context. It concluded that: 'an assessment of the conduct of the defendant . . . shows that the Federal Supreme Court went too far in its interpretation of the protective scope of the constitutional right to free expression of opinion'. In such instances, alleged distinctions between the work of ordinary and constitutional judges are obliterated.

In Germany, and I would argue as a general rule, the constitutional court's capacity to provoke constitutionalization and control judicial outcomes depends significantly on the existence of the individual complaint procedure. Virtually all such complaints attack the constitutionality of judicial decisions, effectively positioning the constitutional court as a super-appellate body (see Youngs 1996: 228–31). This is the German situation, post-*Lüth*. The story of the gradual constitutionalization of the Spanish civil code parallels the German, in that the *amparo* mechanism provoked and then sustained the Spanish Tribunal's efforts to consolidate constitutionalization (see Díez Picazo 1994*a*).

Spain: Freedom of Expression and Rights to Privacy versus Personal Honour

In 1982, the Spanish Supreme Court[11] declared that the rights enumerated in the new constitution possessed programmatic force, encouraging the legislator to ensure their respect in legislation, but did not express a set of juridical commands capable of being enforced by the courts. The Supreme Court's ruling reflected a view that had reigned in Spanish civil law circles since the late 1930s (Bon 1991: 39). The constitutional court annulled the decision on *amparo*, asserting the constitution's binding normative status, a ruling subsequently accepted by the Supreme Court (SCT 1982*b*). Absent the *amparo* mechanism, the pace of constitutionalization in Spain would have depended entirely on intrajudicial comity and cooperation. The *amparo* enabled the constitutional court to impose its preferred solution, a wide-ranging set of doctrines that established the direct and indirect effect of rights.

As in Germany, the protection of fundamental rights in a case-by-case approach, governed by balancing and proportionality tests, has led the SCT to intervene, more or less systematically, in what was thought to be the exclusive domain of the judiciary. To take a very clear example, in 1987 a journalist working in the province of Soria published a satirical piece spoofing the foibles of a local mayor. Offended, the mayor sued, claiming a violation of his personal honour. The judge of second instance agreed with

---

[11] The highest appellate court for the entire judiciary.

the mayor and ordered the journalist to pay a small fine. The journalist referred the matter directly to the constitutional court, which annulled the judge's decision on the grounds that the judge had not given enough weight to the journalist's right to free expression (SCT 1986). Indeed, the SCT held not only that the judge must balance the conflicting rights of the two parties in this case, but also must always give special consideration to the right of free expression in all such cases. The Tribunal referenced a prior decision (SCT 1982c) to the effect that article 20 possessed special status given to its role in 'guaranteeing' other rights, and democracy itself.

The judge of second instance deliberated again, but again found for the mayor, although he carefully cited the SCT's case law on free expression. A second *amparo* ensued, and the SCC again quashed the decision, this time doing the balancing job for the civil judge and, accordingly, insisting that the journalist must win the case (SCT 1987c). In a long series of subsequent cases, the SCT has demonstrated its enormous capacity to reach deeply into the private law and to reshape it. The Tribunal, in effect, 'teaches' ordinary judges how to behave as constitutional judges, including intervening when necessary in their, normally 'autonomous', fact finding and dispute resolving activities. The ever-present threat of an individual complaint reinforces the authority of this pedagogy.

I do not mean to imply that the SCT and GFCC always seek to determine specific judicial outcomes. Rather, these courts, in reviewing the constitutional decision-making of judicial officials, do—often enough to matter a great deal—settle litigation. Both courts normally answer questions asked in concrete review referrals in such a way as to guide but maintain the discretion of the presiding judge, although the exercise of this discretion is always reviewable.[12]

That said, in Spain conflicts between the Supreme Court and the Constitution Tribunal have flared in recent years. In 1994, the President of the Supreme Court gave a speech in which he argued that the SCT has increasingly behaved as a 'supercassation court', a kind of appellate instance for judicial decisions, and that only one solution to this problem was possible:[13] the ordinary courts should be given the authority to protect fundamental rights on their own, without having to refer questions to the SCT first (Sala Sanchez 1994). A small group of law professors have even begun pressing for a move to an American-style, 'diffuse' rather than 'con-

---

[12] 'The death of a bullfighter' story told by Arechederra (1991) is a good example.

[13] In 1994, after having been overruled on substantive grounds by the SCT, members of the Supreme Court formally appealed to the King, who refused to become involved (Tomás y Valiente 1994).

centrated', system of review, in which all judges are empowered to adjudicate rights claims (Aragón Reyes 1987; Díez Picazo 1994a; Renoux 1994).

Italy: the 'War of Judges' and the Peace

The Italian situation contrasts sharply with the German and Spanish cases. Constitutionalization has proceeded, but only through a drawn out 'war of judges' (D'Amico 1991; Merryman and Vigoriti 1967) that has finally ended in a relatively stable stalemate. The crucial issue to be resolved was the extent to which interpretations of the constitutional court were binding on the civil courts. When the ICC was created, it was assumed—as in Germany and Spain—that ordinary judges retained substantial autonomy over dispute resolution—fact finding and applying the law—whereas constitutional judges answered questions about constitutional interpretation. As should by now be clear, constitutional judges do not do their jobs without invading the domain of the legislator and of the ordinary judge. In Germany and Spain, the authority of the constitutional court's interpretations is ultimately secured by the individual complaint. In Italy, the constitutional court's position can be strengthened, but not guaranteed, only by annulling legislation (thus provoking a confrontation with the legislature).

The fate of article 392 of the Code of Judicial Procedure provides a classic example. In 1955, the Code was comprehensively revised in order to remove some of its worst, fascist elements and to harmonize it with constitutional rights. The new article 304 established the right to counsel at various stages of judicial investigation and during trial hearings, in line with article 24.1 of the new constitution ('A legal defence is an inalienable right at every stage of legal proceedings'). Article 392, however, denied the right to counsel in proceedings wherein no investigation or evidence gathering was necessary (e.g. when the proof of the crime was not in question). In 1965, after a lower court judge referred a challenge to article 392 to the ICC, the constitutional court declared that article 304 must govern at all stages of the proceedings, including those covered by article 392 (ICC 1965a). Thus, the ICC chose not to annul article 392, presumably out of deference to the legislature, and instead ordered the ordinary courts to simply pretend that it did not exist. Two months later, the Supreme Court (Cassation), citing legislative debates, declared that it was not bound by the ICC's ruling, but only legislative intent. Given no choice, the ICC then annulled the offending provision, erasing it from the code; it blamed refusal of Cassation to accept its interpretive authority (ICC 1965b). The constitutional court's position had been won, but at the price of bringing the legislature into the equation. Further, in a series of subsequent skirmishes on the effect of the annulment, the Supreme Court rejected the ICC's position that the annulment of article 392 had retroactive effect (to the date of promulgation), ruling instead that the provision was void only from the date of the ICC's decision. Absent jurisdiction over individual complaints, and given Cassation's refusal to refer the question of retroactivity to the ICC, the constitutional court possessed no means to control the outcome, and article 392 was declared operative.

Eventually, the ICC and the Supreme Court have been able to forge a kind of truce, in the form of two related rules, both of which had fully emerged by the early 1980s. The ICC articulated and has since reaffirmed many times, what scholars call the 'doctrine of the living law' (Pizzorusso 1989; Zagebelsky 1988). According to this notion, the power to interpret authoritatively statutes is the power to make rules that are binding on the judiciary (ICC 1984). Although the ICC reserves the power to review this judicial law-making, it nonetheless recognizes, and has in effect constitutionalized, the Supreme Court's interpretive autonomy. The Supreme Court, for its part, has agreed in principle to accept the ICC's reasoning, and not just the formal effects of its rulings, as binding. The practical result of the doctrine of the living law is to require each court, within concrete review processes, to engage the work of the other. Ordinary judges behave as constitutional judges when they decide how to frame and then ask questions in their concrete review referrals. Constitutional judges take into account how the living law accommodates the constitutional law, in their reception of these questions, and in the answers given. At times, the legislature may brought into this game in order to tilt the balance one way or the other (e.g. the controversy surrounding transexualism and the right to sexual identity, discussed above).

France: Constitutionalization without Appellate Review?

The Constitutional Council's case law has given the 1958 constitution a judicial agency that French constitutions have never before possessed. Most important, the Council's incorporation of a bill of rights has gradually made it possible for the ordinary courts to apply the constitution to resolve litigation before them. In so doing, ordinary judges necessarily behave as constitutional judges. Further, the Council has issued what in Chapter 3 were called 'binding interpretations'—decisions declaring that certain statutory provisions are only constitutional under one specific interpretation—pronouncements that all public authorities, including judges, are expected to respect.

The Council's rights jurisprudence has gradually led the civil courts to openly, if somewhat tentatively, engage in activities long considered to be prohibited by separation of powers principles and certain statutes. The Supreme Court (Cassation), for example, now routinely engages in principled construction of statutes, what that Cassation calls the 'constitutional correction of legal norms'. (The practice has been accelerated and reinforced by the growing influence of the European Convention on Human Rights, which is now recognized, in all four of our cases, as possessed of direct effect.[14]) According to the tenets of this doctrine, civil judges are obliged to interpret all legal norms, including code law, as if they were in harmony with constitutional rights. When legislation and the constitution conflict, judges in effect rewrite the former so as to conform to the latter. After all, in the presence of a law deemed unconstitutional, all French judges can do is correct the law by rewriting it, since a law once promulgated is immune to review by the Constitutional Council.

Not surprisingly, litigants have begun to invoke constitutional rights in their arguments before the civil courts, a practice that the Advocate General has supported.[15] In 1988, the Supreme Court heard a suit brought against a tyre manufacturer by an employee who had been fired for having talked to a journalist about the poor working conditions at his company. The Court found for the plaintiff, in effect, incorporating the right to free expression into the Labour Code (see Cartier 1995). During his summation, the Advocate General had passionately argued that fundamental rights were both prior and superior to the codes, and therefore must prevail in any conflict with any other norm, including legislative ones.

The task of the high administrative court, the Council of State has been somewhat more incremental, although no less revolutionary. During the Fourth Republic, the Council of State had succeeded in cataloguing in its case law, under the banner of 'general principles of law', a long list of restrictions on administrative action. Most of these principles, like 'individual liberty', 'equality before the law', 'freedom of conscience', and 'nonretroactivity', function, in fact, as rights. In the 1980s, the Council of State

---

[14] Although the outcome may appear paradoxical, the provisions of the European Convention on Human Rights are more directly applicable in the French legal order than are constitutional provisions, not least because litigants can appeal the decisions of ordinary judges to the Commission and Court of Human Rights.

[15] The advocate general presents the case to the Supreme Court and suggests how it ought to be resolved. The Court is not bound by the Advocate General's opinion.

simply began to convert the general principles into constitutional rights that it enforces, a move that secures the permanence and higher law status of their prior case law. It appears that the Council of State took pains to follow the Constitutional Council's lead, only converting into rights those principles that the constitutional judges had promoted to a constitutional rung.

The legal status of the binding interpretations announced by the Constitutional Council is much more contested. In the 1980s, following the example of the Italian and German courts, the Council began rendering these interpretations as a means of softening the impact of review on the work of parliament. The percentage of decisions containing these pronouncements has increased over time, in some years to as high as 60 per cent. The Council has further declared, following jurisprudence dating from 1962 (Council 1962), that its reasoning is binding on all public authorities. Binding interpretations raise the problem of judicial compliance with the Council's reasoning, and therefore of co-ordination among judges. Recall that such interpretations declare that a given statutory provision can only have one precise meaning if it is to pass constitutional muster. In the absence of either a concrete review or an individual complaint mechanism, the institutional position of the Council in any struggle to control outcomes, is far worse than even that of the Italian Court. To simplify a complicated politics, the position of the Supreme Court is that 'there is no legal obligation to follow binding interpretations' (Table Ronde 1995: 279–80). Some judges are openly hostile to being placed under the tutelage of the Council.[16] The Council of State likewise insists that it is not legally bound by the Council's reasoning; it has nevertheless incorporated binding interpretations in several of its decisions since 1988, and has, at times, even employed the exact language of the Council's case law. Absent expansion of the Council's review jurisdiction, it is unlikely that this problem will be resolved in any definitive manner. More important, the Constitutional Council, the Council of State, and the Supreme Court are today consciously working to harmonize a coherent jurisprudence of rights, in the interest of coherence and judicial security (predictability).

---

[16] In August 1993, for example, the Professional Association of Judges issued a communiqué calling on judges and prosecutors to ignore binding interpretations, which they characterized as nothing but 'trivial gloss' (*Le Monde*, 9 August 1993).

Prospects for Reform

In 1990, the Rocard government, with the full support of President Mitterrand and the President of the Council, formally proposed a constitutional amendment to establish limited concrete review. The change would have permitted litigants to challenge the constitutionality of legislation on the grounds that the legislation had violated their constitutional rights. Once requested, a joint delegation from the two high appellate courts—the Council of State and the Court of Cassation—would decide if the challenge was serious and, if so, would refer the matter to the Council. The revision would have placed the Council in contact with litigation and the judiciary, and allowed it to consolidate both its 'judicial' status and its position as the defender of constitutional rights in France.[17] The amendment was rejected by the rightwing Senate,[18] and opposed by the leading constitutional scholar in France (Favoreu 1994). A similar proposal was debated again in 1993, with the same result. The Right opposes the revision on the grounds that the Council already possesses too much power; it argues further that an expansion of the Council's right jurisdiction would only be acceptable once a 'real' bill of rights has been written and adopted by the representatives of the people. Neither the revision nor a new charter of rights has any chance of being adopted in the near future.

CONCLUSION

The structure of European rights provisions, as developed by constitutional courts, has recast the work of parliament and the judiciary, reinforcing the centrality of constitutional decision-making as a general mode of governance. Law-makers and judicial officials regularly behave as constitutional judges, and constitutional courts recognize, welcome, and even insist on this behaviour. In consequence, a huge range of outcomes—registered in parliaments and courts of law, on the lives of private persons, and on the content of the constitutional law and the various codes—can only be understood by taking into account the constitutional decision-making of those who do not sit on constitutional courts.

When we conceptualize protecting rights as an extended social process, involving multiple state actors and private litigants, we notice that

[17] A similar set of arguments was made in Italy to support a 1989 proposal to introduce an individual complaint procedure (D'Amico 1991: 95).

[18] The Senate possesses an absolute veto only with respect to constitutional changes.

orthodox models of legislative and judicial authority, and between constitutional law and other legal orders, fail to tells us much of value about how
judges and legislators actually behave and interact with each other. On the
one hand, recent history reveals an increasing judicial capacity to construct
and reconstruct the very meaning of legislative authority, and to impinge
directly on how that law-making authority will be exercised. On the other
hand, traditional models of legitimation—separation of powers doctrines,
juridical theories of the state, and so on—appear increasingly insufficient,
if not irrelevant. Efforts to construct a new logic of legitimacy, rooted in
ideologies associated with the new constitutionalism, are taken up in the
next chapter.

5

The Politics of Judging

Previous chapters have demonstrated the great extent to which constitutional politics have undermined orthodox understandings of how legislative and judicial powers are exercised in Western Europe. Traditional separation of powers notions were employed as benchmarks for evaluating subsequent developments, and certain logics of delegation were used to help explain the move to constitutional review. But I did not explicitly deal with what Cappelletti (1989) has rightly called the 'mighty problem' posed by review: the question of its democratic legitimacy. In this chapter, I examine how this question is most commonly addressed in Europe, by grafting Kelsenian constitutional theory on to the classical (but not therefore Kelsenian) distinctions between 'law' (the judicial function) and 'politics' (the legislative function). I then offer a very different perspective on the question, arguing that the legitimacy of constitutional review is a product of the participatory nature of constitutional adjudication.

JUDGING, LAW-MAKING, AND SEPARATION OF POWERS DOCTRINES

In 1973, the German Federal Constitutional Court ruled on an individual complaint, brought by the newspaper, *Die Welt*, attacking a decision of the Federal Supreme Court. The Supreme Court, the nation's highest civil law jurisdiction, had upheld an award for damages in favour of Madame Soraya, the wife of the former Shah of Iran. *Die Welt* had published what turned out to be a completely fabricated interview with Soraya, in which it revealed embarrassing, intimate details of her personal life, leading her to sue. The Supreme Court, proceeding forward from a line of case law dating from the 1950s, found that articles 1 and 2 of the German constitution created a damage remedy, within the framework of the Civil Code, in situations wherein one individual has violated another individual's 'general right of personality' (the functional equivalent of 'privacy' in US law). The

Civil Code, however, explicitly prohibited damage awards in such instances, and the Bundestag had twice rejected (1959, 1967) proposals to grant such a remedy. The newspaper argued that judicial authorities had violated constitutional separation of powers doctrines: the courts had not only ignored clear statutory commands, but had amended the Civil Code on their own.

In its decision (GFCC 1973*b*), the Court ruled that ordinary judges have a duty to ignore relevant statutory provisions that would lead, if applied, to fundamentally unjust results. Instead, when necessary to achieve justice, judges are to reconstruct and even add provisions to the codes, in light of the structure of constitutional rights. The decision not only comforted the position of the Supreme Court. It effectively 'constitutionalize[d] natural law by requiring the [ordinary] judge to reject fundamentally unjust laws' (Currie 1993: 212), to reconstruct creatively, outmoded ones, and to fill gaps caused by legislative inaction. When 'legislation has not kept up with the rapid pace of social development . . . and a changed society's substantive notions of justice', the Court declared: 'One cannot blame the judge, if compelled to decide every case submitted to him and convinced that he cannot rely upon [the] future intervention of the legislature, he does not adhere to the literal meaning of the existing written law in a case where adherence would largely sacrifice justice'.

As Quint (1989: 281) has it, the *Soraya* decision embodies 'the natural implication of the influence of constitutional rights on private law in German constitutional doctrine', post-*Lüth* (see Chapter 4). But it is also symptomatic of a more general phenomenon: European judges are breaking free of the traditional boundaries that have long circumscribed their work. I have largely focused on the activities of constitutional judges, but consider the following examples drawn from the world of the ordinary courts

• In Italy, beginning in the 1970s, 'progressive judges' began to mould, by creatively interpreting, the various codes, in order to 'adapt' them to constitutional principles and values (documented by Bognetti 1982). Judges, and especially those sitting on lower courts, now typically develop rights provisions, including: equality before the law; rights to work, free expression, and health; due process standards; and the open-ended norm of 'personal freedom'. They do so for their own purposes, without first referring questions to the constitutional court. As important, their reading of these rights are now often in advance of the ICC's case law. Italian statutes 'have undergone . . . a process of internal transformation' (Bognetti 1982: 440), subverting legislative intent, but also the monopoly of the constitutional court on constitutional interpretation.

• In Spain, general labour contract law, ostensibly governed by statute, is also being transformed, as judges on the labour courts gradually incorporate constitutional principles, such as freedom of expression and privacy rights, into their understanding of the labour code. As in Italy, ordinary judges have gone beyond, and at times have even contradicted, more restrictive interpretations of rights issued by the Spanish Constitutional Tribunal (del Rey Guanter 1995). Labour judges often prefer to reconstruct statutory provisions in the light of their own versions of constitutional rights, rather than attack statutes before the SCT as unconstitutional. In bypassing the Tribunal, they enhance their own autonomy, and avoid potentially undesirable decisions (which, once pronounced, could be enforced against them by the *amparo* mechanism).

• In France, the Council of State (France's highest administrative jurisdiction), once hostile to the notion that the Constitutional Council's case law could constitute a source of law binding upon it, today actively engages in creative constitutional decision-making of its own. In a recent case involving the right to property (Errera 1998), an apparent conflict between the constitutional court's jurisprudence and the Council of State's own doctrines provoked the administrative judges to find creative ways of blending their own case law with the Constitutional Council's, thus reconfiguring rules—now part (judge-made) administrative law, part statute, and part (judge-made) constitutional law—governing the taking of property by local authorities.

Ordinary judges today regularly use the techniques of constitutional law adjudication to manage the problems that confront them in their workplace. Judges may even be using such techniques to enhance their own policy-making authority, *vis-á-vis* legislatures and constitutional courts. The brute empirical reality is that parliaments have lost their implied monopoly on law-making, constitutional courts today share their authority to interpret the constitution, and ordinary judges—certainly not *slaves to the codes*[1]—participate in constitutional politics. Stated differently, it has become increasingly obvious that traditional separation of powers doctrines, however deeply embedded in consciousness we might suppose them to be, are increasingly less relevant to the realities of European governance.

[1] I do not mean to imply that parliaments really did exercise continuous control (parliaments did not), or that ordinary judges did not make the codes their own (judges did). But, today, judges do so overtly.

The Challenge of the New Constitutionalism

Separation of powers doctrines underpin theories of the state, reflecting, but also conditioning, how political legitimacy is to be understood and assessed. Such doctrines are deeply normative constructs. Read descriptively, as rule systems, they purport to model the relationship between structures and functions in any complex system of governance. Read prescriptively, as sets of idealized expectations how about structure and function ought to be related, they provide standards for evaluating the appropriateness of official conduct.

Traditional, Continental separation of powers doctrines are in deep crisis. Conceived as a set of prescriptions, they appear increasingly obsolete and incoherent. Conceived as descriptions, they obscure more than they clarify what is actually going on in the world. Although other very important factors are at work,[2] systems of constitutional justice have operated— inherently, in my view—to undermine the utility and relevance of the classic doctrines. Structural differentiation, but overlap in functions, are the norms. We can easily list the institutional characteristics that distinguish a European legislature from a European court; but today judges legislate, parliaments adjudicate, and the boundaries separating law and politics—the legislative and judicial functions—are little more than academic constructions.

If all this is so, some readers may be asking if and why they should bother with such formalities. This is a serious question, to which I have two quite different responses. First, many social scientists probably do not have any immediate reason to concern themselves with the fact that constitutional politics have undermined separation of powers doctrines, or the question of what, if anything, ought to be done about it. After all, such doctrines, excessively formal simplifications of how political systems are organized, operate at levels of abstraction that are often too high to be of practical use in research. For most purposes, it is probably enough to take seriously the fact that judges (constitutional and ordinary) play an increasingly active, sometimes crucial, role in a wide range of policy domains.

My second response takes the form of an alert. How such controversies are deliberated and settled will likely shape the deep changes in European law and politics already underway. Separation of powers doctrines help those who govern (e.g. government ministers, members of parliament, judges, and administrators) make sense of their own role in the political

---

[2] The growth in the state, social welfare, the complexity of government given modern communications, etc.

system, and of how they are expected to interact with other actors. They thus constitute not only models of the polity, but models of action. To the extent that these models actually condition how governmental actors take decisions, they deserve our attention. Today, judges and legislators not only participate in constitutional politics, but their work is deeply impacted by the evolution of constitutional rules, and these behaviours are not modelled well by traditional separation of powers doctrines. Consider the following description of the judicial function in Europe:

the focus of all law-making authority within the state is the sovereign legislature; law is a closed system of logically arranged and internally coherent rules; all legal disputes must be resolved by reference to such rules; courts of law, independent of the legislature, are the proper agencies for interpreting law; courts should interpret law literally and in strict accordance with the legislator's will; their function, therefore, is to administer the law as written. (Kommers 1997: 124; see also Merryman 1985)

We know that constitutional courts often dictate statutory provisions that legislators ratify; that constitutional politics create gaping holes in the legislature's law, once presumed to be closed; and that ordinary judges increasingly behave as if they recognized a higher duty to interpret statute as if it were in conformity with the constitution, thus participating directly in the legislative function. Nevertheless, how the relationship between law and politics is most commonly conceptualized has lagged far behind what is actually happening.

The emergence and consolidation of a new model of the relationship between legislative and judicial power, one that incorporates the normative logic of the new constitutionalism in Europe, would effectively complete the transformation of European governance that I have been describing. Not only would such a model gradually replace the existing one by, among other things, serving to discredit the traditional dogmas as outdated, and those who espouse them as not sufficiently versed in the niceties of constitutional law. A new model would accelerate and reinforce the movement already taking place, operating to legitimize it. At stake, then, is how the nature of European democracy is to be redefined, albeit in the form of a quasi-official state ideology, given that existing separation of powers doctrines are no longer tenable.

The process of developing this new model has already begun. It is most visible in the work of legal scholars, especially in the activity of constitutional lawyers, but judges are also intimately involved. It bears mention in advance that although aspects of these debates echo those found elsewhere, they remain distinctly European. The institutional logic of parliamentary democracy, the historically rooted suspicion of judicial power, and a tradition of highly formalist legal scholarship give them a specific character. Contemporary North American ideas about judicial review and its legitimacy are available, but American and Canadian debates have had no sustained or serious influence on how Continental legal scholars understand the work of their own constitutional courts.[3]

Three general approaches or orientations to the question of the legitimacy of constitutional review are current. The dominant approach (e.g. Brewer-Carias 1989; Favoreu 1988, 1990, 1994; Von Brünneck 1990, 1992; García de Enterría 1991) is explicitly Kelsenian, in that its proponents invoke his constitutional theory (see Chapter 2). It entails reconceptualizing traditional separation of powers principles in light of Kelsen's ideas about constitutional legality, taking into account the formal requirements of contemporary systems of constitutional justice. The constitution, which expressly provides for the exercise of review, is the ultimate source of legitimacy. Although tinkering with the classic doctrines has been unavoidable, scholars have also tried to show that they have retained as much of the traditional separation of powers edifice as possible.

The second approach (e.g. Ponthoreau 1991; Troper 1995; Gascón Abellan 1994; Guastini 1991), a distinctly minority one, is commonly labelled 'realist'. For realists, the constitutional law, and therefore the polity, is constructed through processes of interpretation, which breathes life and agency into the law, expanding its domain and import. Realists argue that the constitutional law is developed within interpretative communities, comprised not only of constitutional judges, but also of legislators, administrators, ordinary judges, scholars, and the interested public. The monopoly of the constitutional judge, presumed by the Kelsenians, is therefore rejected. The perspective is broadly congruent with my own, to the extent that realists see the building of the constitutional law as a participatory process, involving a wide range of actors, public and private.

The third approach is critical, but even less representative of typical academic discourse. The expansion of judicial authority and the attendant 'juridification' of political life are viewed as inherently oppressive phenomenon (e.g. Habermas 1986, 1992; Teubner 1987), and stifling of what is needed—a liberating, 'deliberative' democracy. In this view, the law—and particularly academic discourse about the law—tends to construct the out-

---

[3] The extent of transatlantic cross-fertilization is insignificant. American constitutional law scholars are especially insular in their approach to judicial review, know little or nothing about constitutional review elsewhere, and therefore rarely address European concerns.

side environment in a particular way, by favouring the reproduction of the law's own internal logic, insulating the law from the world 'external' to it, and by recasting social problems as legal ones (see King 1993; Beck 1994). Of course, the more any project to legitimize constitutional review succeeds, the worse off we are. Although there are connections between this approach and my own,[4] I will not deal with it further except insofar as I treat the work of legal scholars, which I do find insular and expansionist, as an important stage in the construction of the law.

We now turn to the Kelsenian orthodoxy. I focus only on those elements that are related to conceptualizing sources of legitimacy; I simplify (or ignore altogether) many otherwise important arguments.

THE KELSENIAN MODEL

Kelsen and his latter-day followers have been concerned, above all else, with the problem of legal validity, in particular, how public acts come to be invested with normativity, that is, with their formal authority as binding law. Put as a question: how do we determine which public acts constitute authoritative rules, binding on their subjects, backed up by the enforcement capacities of the state? Simplifying, Kelsenians argue that any given act is only valid, or normative, if it is enabled by, and does not conflict with, a specific—and formally superior—legal rule. Furthermore, all legal rules, in order to confer validity to lower order rules, must be enforced by some authority (a judge or 'jurisdiction'). A closed, self-referential, hierarchically ordered, system of norms is thereby established: every legal rule is lawful by virtue of another, higher order, legal rule. Thus, a ministerial decree or a police action taken in pursuance of a statute must respect the terms of that statute or be invalid, as controlled by judicial authorities; and the statute itself must conform to constitutional dictates or be invalid, as controlled by constitutional judges. The legality of the norm, which reduces ultimately to constitutional legality, and the legitimacy of the legal system, are virtually one and the same thing.

In today's Europe, the common source of all legality, and therefore of political legitimacy, is the constitution—the summit of the hierarchy. Modern European constitutions:

---

[4] I have tried to show that constitutional review has generated an expansive (rather than simply narrow) and relatively participatory (rather than exclusively elite-dominated) deliberative mode of governance, a mode of governance that would not have emerged in the absence of constitutional review.

(1) establish state institutions and confer on them the power to make and enforce other legal rules;
(2) lay down procedural rules that govern the production of other legal norms, like statutes, and the constraints (like rights) on legislating that must be respected;
(3) fix the rules through which constitutional revision can take place, firmly distinguishing these rules from those governing the production of infraconstitutional law, like statutes;
(4) authorize constitutional courts to defend the normative superiority of constitutional law *vis-à-vis* all other legal rules.

To this point, Kelsen's modelling of the constitution as a system of higher order—but, nevertheless, a *positive* body of—norms adequately describes how Continental legal systems are, in fact, organized. The constitutional law, as adopted by the sovereign people, comprises both a positive source of law, and the common source of legitimacy for all other legal norms. Further, Kelsenian constitutional theory and principal–agent (P–A) models of delegation are broadly congruent with one another.[5] A simple P–A model of constitutional politics links, as in a chain, authoritative acts of delegation from one set of official actors to another (see Chapters 1–3). The sovereign people (first order principals) decide—albeit through their representatives—to be governed by a constitution. The constitution is the normative instrument through which the people have delegated power to governmental bodies, like legislatures. And the statute is the normative instrument through which governments and legislatures (agents of the electorate, but second order principals *vis-à-vis* ordinary judges and administrators) delegate certain specific responsibilities and powers to the courts and the administration. Different sets of principals exercise different types of controls depending on the normative act at hand and the precise terms of the delegation. But the ultimate source of authority, and legitimacy, is the constitution, which is assumed to express the will of the sovereign people.

As a formal construction, the legitimacy of European constitutional review can hardly be questioned, flowing as it does from specific, authoritative acts of delegation from one ultimate source of legitimacy: the sovereign people. However, when we look in detail at how constitutional politics actually operate, other aspects of the model quickly run into difficulty. At its core are two views of the world that are increasingly at odds with reality. First, although the point does not follow from Hans Kelsen's

---

[5] This connection is never made.

own writings,[6] Kelsenians today reproduce the separation of law and politics that is basic to the state theory that reigned prior to the advent of the new constitutionalism. The boundaries separating law-making from judicial functions, although breached by the introduction of constitutional review, are otherwise supposed to have retained their integrity. Second, Kelsenians insist that the erosion of legislative sovereignty has been no more than necessary to guarantee the normative superiority of the constitution through constitutional review.

An attempt to show that the European state, and especially the juridical order, can accommodate constitutional review with minimal subversion of legislative supremacy animates the argument. Kelsenians argue that the constitutional court is the sole judge of the constitutionality of statute, whereas the ordinary courts are judges of how statutes are to be applied (Renoux 1994). Further, although the constitutional court necessarily possesses the power to invalidate unconstitutional legislation, its law-making function is purely 'negative', while the government and parliament act as 'positive' legislators (see Chapter 2). Undeniably, the monopoly of the constitutional court on constitutional interpretation of statutes has broken down, and in some places—like Germany—was never established (see Quint 1989). Just as clearly, constitutional courts act as positive legislators: not only do they regularly say no to legislators, they also draft and amend legislation, commanding legislators to behave in certain ways, and not in others.

We know why this modern-day Kelsenian model, as a description of what is going on, is in trouble. Theoretically, the project is incoherent, for reasons that Kelsen himself would be quick to identify. Kelsen knew that establishing review would fatally subvert the separation of political and judicial functions (see note 6), by politicizing the judge. He warned against codifying rights in the constitution precisely because he knew that codification would politicize constitutional judges even further, making of them not only legislators, but supreme legislators. Although legal scholars today appear to be parroting Kelsen's constitutional theory, they also claim that constitutional courts inherently function to protect constitutional rights, and that this function is basic to the legitimacy of review. Further (see Chapter 4), the orthodox position of modern Kelsenians, and many judges,

---

[6] For Kelsen, law-making is political in that law constitutes the formalization of politics, or the will of those authorized to make the law. Constitutional courts, because they have been delegated the authority to interpret and therefore to make the constitutional law, are recognized by Kelsen to perform a political function. I thank Michel Troper for reminding me of this point. For further discussion, see Ch. 2.

is that rights possess 'supraconstitutional' status (their contents can not be altered by constitutional revision), which is akin to a natural law, not a positivist, position. In a sentence, orthodox constitutional scholarship in Europe only selectively embraces elements of Kelsen's constitutional theory, while implicitly rejecting the fundamental positivism of the rest of his thinking. In consequence, Kelsenians are led to defend what cannot be defended, namely, that constitutional judges are only negative legislators.

Empirically, the move to a judicially enforceable constitutional law, replete with human rights (and positive rights) possessed of direct effect, did more than just undermine legislative sovereignty in a formal sense. The new constitutionalism created opportunities for a range of non-judicial actors to pursue their interests through the constitutional law, and made judges responsible for developing and exercising new powers of decision-making. The more judges have effectively resolved the constitutional disputes referred to them, the more opportunities for more litigation, and more constitutional rule-making, expand. Although those who negotiated the constitution (the leaders of political parties) did not intend as much, the construction of a self-sustaining, expansive constitutional politics—which gradually but inevitably weakens the hold of statute on judging, and gradually but inevitably diffuses the techniques of constitutional adjudication, as a general mode of governance, to judicial and legislative actors—has been the general outcome. In P–A terms, because constitutional and ordinary judges operate in relatively permissive environments, guided by rules that they themselves curate, it is no surprise that their activities routinely escape mechanisms of control available to their principals. The hierarchy of rules and controls assumed by the hybrid-Kelsenian—and the P–A—model is in fact little more than an assumption.

Although this model remains dominant, and in France reigns as quasi-official dogma, some legal scholars, and even a few judges, have begun to raise questions. There is growing awareness, for example, that the distinction between the positive and the negative legislator can not be sustained; at the same time, it is constantly asserted that this distinction remains basic to how the legitimacy of constitutional review is normally conceived (e.g., Auguiar de Luque 1987; Díez Moreno 1986; Pizzorusso 1990; Rubio Llorente 1988*a*, 1991). Thus, Gascón Abellan (1994: 75) complains that 'the distance that separates the constitutional court [of today] from the Kelsenian court is abysmal'. And Rubio Llorente (1988*b*: 170–85), a law professor and former vice-president of the Spanish Constitutional Tribunal, has noted the 'awkwardness' and the 'insufficiency of the theoretical model inherited from Kelsen', and has called attention to the fact that the so-called 'negative legislator' too often 'assume[s] the role of legislator *in toto*'.

Why not simply acknowledge that constitutional courts sometimes act as positive legislators, and that ordinary judges sometimes act as constitutional judges? To do so, Kelsenians fear, would effectively destroy classical separation of powers schemes—'the very foundation of all constitutional architecture' (Rubio Llorente 1988*b*: 174–5); judges would then be left exposed to charges of usurpation of the political function. In my own view, the fact that European constitutions explicitly establish their own normative superiority[7] provides all of the formal legitimacy needed (although formal legitimacy is only part of the equation). Further, in practice if not always in scholarship, the dictates of the new constitutional law tend to overwhelm rules derived from traditional Continental separation of powers schemes, rather than vice versa.

Four 'Functions' of Constitutional Review

In Europe, doctrinal commentaries on the constitution and on case law comprise the vast bulk of research in public law; surprisingly little is written on constitutional courts and their relationships with other actors, such as parliament and ordinary judges. Nevertheless, there exists an important strain of scholarship, again Kelsenian in inspiration, that seeks to legitimize constitutional review with reference to the (always virtuous) impact of review on parliamentary systems of governance (e.g. Brünneck 1990, 1992; Favoreu 1986,1988, 1990, 1994). It is claimed that constitutional courts perform four basic 'functions': (1) they operate as a 'counterweight' to majority rule; (2) they 'pacify' politics; (3) they legitimize public policy; and (4) they protect human rights.

These functions are essentially regulatory. First, as Favoreu puts it (1994: 560; see also Brünneck 1990: 40) constitutional courts act as 'either a counterweight' against a parliamentary majority that is 'too powerful' [e.g. in France and Spain], or as a 'substitute' legislator where a parliamentary majority 'does not exist' (e.g. Italy). Second, constitutional review tends to 'pacify' politics: 'quarrels' that before would have been fought out in partisan terms, unrelentingly, are 'appeased', and settled more reasonably—with reference to the constitutional law (Favoreu 1986: 62; 1988: 19, 39). As Brünneck (1990: 41–2) writes, 'in society, characterized by extreme politicization and by the total supremacy of majority principles', constitutional

---

[7] That is, by (1) distinguishing between legislative procedures and procedures for revising the constitution, and (2) conferring review powers on a constitutional court.

review not only settles conflict about the legality of any parliamentary act, more or less permanently, it also facilitates the building of a consensus in favour of other democratic principles, including 'the safeguarding of rights' and the 'principle of legality'. Third, although they deny that constitutional courts ever 'block', 'veto', 'censor', or 'prevent' decisions taken by parliament, judges act to 'guide', 'direct', 'authenticate', and 'correct' decisions (Favoreu 1988; Brünneck 1990; Vedel 1988), 'putting reforms on the right normative track . . . the constitutional one' (Favoreu 1994: 578). Thus, far from obstructing the will of the majority, constitutional judges legitimize it. Last, in the absence of constitutional review, the argument goes, human rights would enjoy no protection.

I have evaluated these formulations elsewhere (Stone 1992*a*: chs. 4, 6, 7; Stone 1994*a*), and will not repeat these criticisms here. It is enough to note (as Kelsen himself would have) that constitutional judges can fulfil these functions effectively only to the extent that they in fact behave as (very powerful) 'positive' legislators. If, for example, constitutional judges did not annul legislation as unconstitutional and, at the same time, tell (or at least signal to) legislators how they should go about their legislative business, then constitutional review could function neither to 'correct' statutes nor to put law-makers 'on the right track'. To take another example, the safeguarding of rights may very well provoke, rather than appease, partisan controversies; clearly this occurred in the German abortion cases (Chapter 4), and in the French media pluralism decisions (Chapter 3). Modern-day Kelsenians seemingly do not notice, let alone explore, these points. Instead, Brünneck (1990: 46–7), after elaborating on these functions, simply reasserts the distinction between the negative and positive legislator, and declares that 'nearly everyone' insists that the distinction remains robust. For Favoreu (1994: 578; see also Vedel 1992), even if it is admitted that the constitutional court may at times appear to block the majority's will, or to usurp the legislator's discretionary prerogatives, constitutional rule-making can always be voided by constitutional revision

What grounds the legitimacy of the constitutional judge is that [an annulment] is to be analysed not as barring but as redirecting the legislative act: further, whatever obstacle has been erected by the constitutional judge is not definitive and can be removed by the adoption of a constitutional revision.[8]

---

[8] The argument recalls one made by Kelsen (1942: 187): the ultimate source of unconstitutionality is that the majority decided to adopt the desired reform as a statute, rather than as a constitutional revision.

We are thus thrown back into the world of principals, agents, and direct mechanisms of control (see Chapter 3) which, we know, are far less effective than Kelsenians suppose.

CONSTITUTIONAL POLITICS AND LEGITIMACY

Given that constitutional review subverts the schema that has traditionally served to legitimize judicial power on the Continent, how do we account for the fact that European constitutional courts have succeeded not only in enhancing their capacity to shape legislative and judicial processes, but have at the same time seen their own institutional legitimacy, *vis-à-vis* other governmental institutions,[9] increase? I approach this question not as a legal theorist or political philosopher might, but as a social scientist.[10] I wish to explain, as simply and clearly as possible, why specific actors behave as they do, and how these behaviours produce specific, relatively predictable, outcomes.

I argue that the political legitimacy of constitutional review has been constructed over time, in interactions among three sets of actors: (1) litigants, those who activate constitutional review processes; (2) judges, those who adjudicate constitutional disputes; and (3) academic lawyers, those who work to build the constitutional law through their scholarly activity. I reject the law/politics distinction on empirical grounds. The decision-making behaviours that constitutional review engenders are always both 'judicial' and 'political'; and institutions that participate in constitutional review processes necessarily engage in each other's activities. Equally important, as a matter of causality, the politicization of constitutional review processes, by litigants, comprises the essential first step, the trigger mechanism, that enables judicialization; and judicialization processes serve to legitimize constitutional review, by establishing and continuously reinforcing the centrality of constitutional case law within legislative and judicial processes. Underlying this argument, indeed underlying the account of constitutional politics in this book, is a theory of action. This theory of action integrates strategic behaviour and normative reasoning.

In Chapter 1, we examined the relationship between rule structures and self-interest. I argued that, in any complex set of social behaviours, norms,

---

[9] Opinion polls regularly show higher public support from citizens than do other governmental institutions.

[10] I do not deny the contribution legal theory or political philosophy can make, and indeed make use of it.

and interests are likely to become intertwined in ways that are often difficult or impossible to unravel. We know that people often obey rules routinely, without giving much thought to them; but we also know that people
also weigh the potential consequences of choosing behaviour that does not
conform to normative expectations. More complicated yet, sometimes
what we observe as the enactment of rules may actually be the surface man-
ifestation of the desire, on the part of individuals, to avoid punishment or
to access desired benefits.

In the discussion that follows, I assume that all three sets of actors behave
strategically all of the time: they seek to maximize their well-being given the
constraints they face. In constitutional politics, however, actors can pursue
their interests only through normative argument, and effective normative
arguments can only be fashioned by reasoning through rule structures. In
such a social system, interests are constantly reconstituted as legal discourse,
a fact which has heavy consequences for how the system develops. At any
given point in time, perfect information about the precise nature of the most
important set of constraints, the constitutional law, rarely if ever exists;
rather constitutional adjudication and its associated practices lead to the
clarification of these constraints. As we will see, each of the three sets of
actors use normative discourse for their own purposes; but each does so with
different priorities in mind, and seeks different kinds of outcomes.

Litigating

Individuals activate constitutional review processes—they *politicize* constitutional justice—in order to alter policy outcomes in their favour. They
know that the constitutional court can overrule parliaments and courts,
and that the court can also control legislative and judicial behaviour in
other ways. Individuals litigate if the potential benefits of obtaining an
annulment or revision of a law (or public policy, or private practice) outweigh the costs of the legal challenge. Litigants will make the best possible
legal arguments on their own behalf, but such arguments will express,
rather than disguise, motivations. Constitutional challenges constitute an
instrumental, relatively porous form of normative discourse, one provoked
by, and open to, social facts (e.g. the details of a particular dispute, the relative power of disputants, the distribution of resources in society, and so
on). It is through litigation that the constitutional law secures and maintains its political relevance and vitality.

Constitutional litigation helps to legitimize constitutional review in at
least two ways. First, in activating constitutional review litigants delegate,

to constitutional judges, policy issues that could have been dealt with in other, non-constitutional, forums. Acts of delegation are (at least implicit) acts of legitimation. Consider the politics of abstract review. Governing majorities often complain, after an annulment, that constitutional judges have thwarted democratic principles and subverted legislative sovereignty. Yet, when these same parties are in opposition they do not hesitate to make use of abstract review, and they characterize their victories as strengthening democratic principles embodied in the constitution. Parliamentary oppositions could choose to defer to the wishes of the majority, after losing parliamentary votes, as the price to be paid for losing elections; instead, seeing the opportunity to alter the majority's legislative programme, they initiate abstract review.[11] In this way, legislators—across the political spectrum—have participated, willingly and continuously, in processes that reduce the scope of their own authority and discretion, and to enhance that of the constitutional court. More generally, we find more, not less, constitutional litigation over time, across Europe, for the simple reason that individuals find it useful to pursue their interests through constitutional review. That legislative and judicial processes are increasingly conducted in the shadow of the constitutional court is important empirical evidence of the enhanced social legitimacy of review itself.

Second, in activating constitutional review, litigants help to build the constitutional law. Litigation not only transfers questions of social, economic, and political import to judges; it provokes constitutional rule-making.

Judging

In resolving disputes, constitutional judges seek both to preserve the normative superiority of the constitutional law and to ensure that the constitution becomes, or continues to be, the essential reference point for the settlement of like cases that may arise in the future. Judges know that their activities will be evaluated by two groups: (1) present and future litigants, and (2) doctrinal authorities. The judges are cross-pressured. Litigants hope to win the case and to see their own political values enshrined as authoritative constitutional law. Failing that, they hope not to lose too much, or see values that they oppose enshrined as case law. Legal scholars expect constitutional courts to exercise their rule-making powers in ways that enhance the overall coherence of the constitutional architecture,

[11] There are no systematic differences, across countries or among political parties within countries, in how or why political elites make use of abstract review.

which they have helped to build. At a minimum, this means producing decisions that can be read as being consistent with antecedent case law and established doctrinal understandings.

To succeed at their task, the judges deploy several techniques. First, they avoid declaring either side a clear loser, preferring, wherever possible, to issue partial victories, splitting the difference between the disputants. Of course, for those who challenge a statute's constitutionality, even a partial victory equates as a loss for those who supported the law (since, in the absence of constitutional challenge, the law could not be challenged). None the less, in abstract review processes, for example, it is striking how few total annulments have been issued by constitutional courts. Instead, the judges remove those provisions considered to be contaminated by unconstitutionality, allowing the rest of the law to be applied; or they tell the legislature how it must correct the law if it wishes to pursue a given legislative reform. This point is seemingly never noticed, and certainly not commented upon publicly, probably because it would focus attention on non-normative, extraconstitutional elements of constitutional adjudication.

Other, explicitly legalistic, aspects of constitutional decision-making help judges counter suspicion that constitutional review produces clear winners and losers, over time. In developing balancing and proportionality tests (Chapter 4), for example, judges exploit the social logic of long-term reciprocity among potential litigants (society), and construct the law as a flexible instrument of dispute resolution. These tests make it clear: that each litigant's legal interest is a legitimate one; that the court none the less must take a decision, by weighing each side's interest against the other; and that future cases pitting the same two legal interests against one another may well be decided differently, depending on the facts. Balancing and proportionality tests hold sway precisely where: (1) the law is most indeterminate; and (2) most in danger of being constructed in a partisan way.[12] Balancing tests constitute normative tools for managing this indeterminacy over time; they also enable the judges to maintain their own room to manoeuvre in cases likely to come before them in the future.

Second, constitutional judges labour to portray their decision-making process as inherently 'judicial', and therefore meaningfully distinct from 'political' (i.e. legislative) processes. They have borrowed procedures from ordinary courts for example, in order to make more 'concrete' what would otherwise be essentially abstract processes of decision-making. Thus,

[12] For example, when two rights claim conflict, or when a right conflicts with a constitutionally derived public interest being pursued by government

although no written rules require such practices, the French Constitutional Council solicits from the government and parliamentary majority briefs that respond, point-by-point, to legal arguments contained in referrals from the parliamentary opposition (see Stone 1992*a*: ch. 5). The other courts, too, have actively sought to enhance the adversarial quality of constitutional review procedures, to increase the perception of fairness, to enhance the 'judicial' qualities of the proceedings, but also to encourage those actors being controlled to engage in the kind of rule-governed reasoning that the court does.

In any event, the judges are cognizant of what litigants wants, and what doctrinal authorities expect. The administrative staffs of the courts under consideration compile dossiers that contain, in addition to litigants' briefs, discussions of the pertinent case law and relevant scholarly commentaries. In abstract review cases, all of the parliamentary debates, committee reports, and other documents that issue from the legislative process are included. In concrete review cases, the court receives the essential documents related to the litigation that generated the referral.[13]

Although the socio-political stakes of constitutional litigation are always apparent, the judges will nevertheless push private interests and social facts further into the background, repackaging them as inherently normative arguments. Thus, the French government had a long list of reasons why every important French bank needed to be nationalized in 1981–2, and these reasons were iterated and reiterated for months leading up to the constitutional adjudication stage of the legislative process. The French Council recognized these arguments, which had nothing to do with the constitution, only in so far as they could be said to constitute a 'public interest', which the constitution had authorized the French government and parliament to pursue. But because the 1789 declaration of the rights of man contains a provision guaranteeing citizens the right to property and fair compensation in the event of expropriation, the Council proceeded to what were, in effect, balancing and proportionality tests, and then found the Socialist's bill lacking (Council 1982*a*). My point is not only that constitutional judges are fully aware of the partisan, or instrumental, nature of the litigation that comes before them, but that they also react by requiring such interests to be expressed in the rule-governed discourse that constitutional decision-making generates.

Finally, and most obviously, constitutional courts portray their decision-making as if it were a pure exercise in logic. The logic is ultimately

---

[13] For reports on the internal procedures, staffing, budgets, and so on, of European constitutional courts, see Table Ronde (1990, 1994).

expressed as a syllogism: the constitution, as higher law, requires x; the act which has been attacked as unconstitutional falls either within or outside category x; to the extent that said act falls outside of category x, it is void as unconstitutional. Of course, in order to arrive at this point, judges have reasoned through the case and through the pertinent rule structures. Often this reasoning is complex, sometimes tortuous. Nevertheless, in that final, crucial instance in which the law is determined, the decision perfects its own internal normativity. And it is this normativity that gets passed on to doctrinal authorities and future litigants, as part of the law.

The Decision

Constitutional courts are, by law, required to justify their decisions in written form. Yet how they do so has more to do with their own quest for legitimacy, given the environment in which they find themselves. Judges seek to create the conditions under which constitutional review will not only survive, but thrive; that is, they seek to reconstruct their environment in ways that are conducive to the continuing vitality of constitutional review. To thrive, constitutional review must draw other actors into the rule-governed discourse of adjudication; and the court must also convince its audiences that how it exercises its powers is meaningfully constrained by rules internal to normative reasoning (and therefore are not arbitrary powers). Michel Troper (1995: 294–5), a French legal theorist, has put these points together elegantly

The internal constraints on the constitutional judge's power are essentially those linked . . . to the need to justify the judge's decisions. This need does not relate exclusively, or even principally, to the requirement to provide justification . . . The judge in fact intends to give his decisions the [highest] level of effectiveness possible. In other words, he wants to hand down a decision that will produce effects, not just *in concreto*, thanks to the annulment of the law, but also *in abstracto*. . . . The norm which will have thus been established can then be imposed on other constitutional authorities, such as parliament, because it is obvious that any future law which contradicts this decision will in turned be deemed constitutional, as well as other courts, because they likewise could not, without difficulty, avoid basing their own decisions on this same norm, except by establishing the objective existence of another more general principle which would justify the exception. The justification is thus an attempt to enclose the other bodies within a logical conclusion from which they cannot escape. However, this logical conclusion also constrains the constitutional judge himself, because once he has confirmed the objective existence of a norm, he cannot therefore ignore it.

What is peculiar to the political power exercised by constitutional judges is that, in deciding, they not only constrain the activities of governments, parliaments, administrators, ordinary judges, and the citizenry. They constrain themselves.

Opinion Styles and Dissents

Two models of opinion-writing styles coexist in Europe. The first, represented by France and Italy, is the more traditional. The French and Italian constitutional courts follow conventions established by the high administrative and civil courts. Decisions are relative short and declaratory of the law; they invoke the precedential authority of prior case law through the use of linguistic formulas that are pointedly repeated. The second model, developed first in Germany but quickly adopted in Spain, more resembles American practice. Constitutional decisions are longer, more wide-ranging, even literary. Each important point of law raised by each litigant may be argued through to its conclusion, in the light of existing case law and alternative (but ultimately rejected) lines of argument. The German and Spanish courts commonly cite the work of legal scholars and even other courts, like the US Supreme Court. Although a decision written in the style given by the first model could never be confused for one written in the style of the second, French and Italian constitutional rulings have, over time, become much longer, more openly argumentative, and less terse and syllogistic. I interpret this change as a predictable response to the increased politicization of constitutional justice. As constitutional judges know, the politicization of their offices by litigants can only be effectively countered with more and better normative arguments.

In Germany and Spain, votes are published and dissenting opinions allowed; in France and Italy, dissents are prohibited. Those who favour the practice argue that dissents enhance the court's legitimacy by showing 'that the arguments of the losing side were taken seriously by the court' (Landfried *ed.* 1989: 231). Opponents invoke the legitimizing power of public unanimity. A small handful of studies on voting patterns in the German and Spanish courts exists, which show that groups of judges do tend to vote together, and that judges appointed by the same parties tend to belong to the same groups (e.g. del Castillo Vera 1987). These tendencies, which are quite weak, are often overwhelmed by disagreements about the law and constitutional doctrine (Lamprecht 1992).

In Italy, but not France, there exists a vigorous debate over whether to allow dissenting opinions (e.g. Panza and Reposo 1981; Roselli 1994). In any case, the style of opinion-writing in Germany and Spain more easily accommodates dissents. If France or Italy did move to permit the publication of minority opinions, it is likely that a more literary, discursive model of opinion-writing (such as that found in the US, Germany, and Spain) would gradually emerge.

The Precedential Authority of Case Law

It is commonplace in comparative law to note, first, the formal absence of the doctrine of *stare decisis* in Continental legal systems and then to assert that this absence constitutes a crucial difference between legal systems. However, the best systematic research has shown, in Summers and Taruffo's summation (1991: 487), 'that there are no great differences in the use [of precedent] between the so-called common law and civil law systems'. Courts, and especially higher courts, constantly invoke the authority of prior decisions. In Spain, scholars now openly debate whether or not the principle of *stare decisis* has in fact already emerged (Díez Picazo 1994b). In Germany, lawyers can be fined for failing to invoke relevant precedents in their pleadings. The notion that judicial decisions could not create binding precedent inhered in traditional separation of powers doctrines, since to admit otherwise would have required recognizing that judges participated in the legislative function. Today, with legislative sovereignty in full retreat, judges more openly exploit the legitimizing resources that asserting precedent provides. In contemporary Europe, virtually all of the constitutional law that matters is case law.

Decisions rendered by constitutional courts are recognized as formal sources of binding law in all four countries. In France, Germany, and Spain, how courts arrive at their decisions—the judges' reasoning—is also binding; in Italy, the doctrine of the 'living law' gives the Supreme Court (*Cassazione*) some latitude to interpret constitutional case law in light of its own, judicially constructed, doctrine and cannons of statutory interpretation (Chapter 4). Finally, in Germany and Spain, failure on the part of any public official to abide by the terms of constitutional case law constitutes grounds for individual complaints. In France, some judicial authorities continue to resist the authority of the Council's reasoning (Chapter 4).

Doctrinal Activity

Legal scholars work to construct the law as a coherent body of rules, by elucidating the content and meaning of specific norms, and by defining the relationship of any given norm to the greater normative system. Constitutional case law grounds the scholar's work, conditioning while not entirely determining it. One function performed by the legal scholar is to explain the constitutional court's jurisprudence, and to integrate the court's rule-making into the law; still the constitutional law, as curated by the legal scholar, remains analytically distinct from case law. As a form of normative discourse, doctrinal activity is—relative to litigating—maximally opaque: it self-consciously ignores the world external to the law itself. Put differently, doctrinal activity reconstructs the law as a radically autonomous discursive structure, cut off from the greater socio-political environment to which the law, and the judges of the law, would otherwise belong.

In Europe, the social power of public law scholars has depended critically on their capacity to insulate the law from the social world, and especially from 'politics': the world of political parties, ideologies, interests, and 'non-legal' values.[14] This way of doing things—the maintenance of the law/politics distinction as an article of disciplinary faith—has reproduced itself over many generations. That Continental legal scholarship is highly formalist, relatively immune to critical perspectives on the law, largely disinterested in questions of legal interpretation, but none the less committed to enhancing the prestige and legitimacy of doctrinal and judicial power are tendencies that have been widely commented upon (e.g. Merryman 1985; Stone 1992*a*: chs. 1, 4). For our purposes, what is important to emphasize is that legal scholars, in pursuing their own corporate interests, operate to legitimize the court and its case law.

They do so in several ways. Constitutional scholarship, first, refrains from being too critical of any decision. Confronted with an aspect of a decision that appears inconsistent with prior case law, or with established understandings of the constitution, for example, doctrinal authorities will typically downplay the 'mistake', narrowing its relevance to the specific case at hand, and reasserting the full scope of the prior version of the law in all other relevant cases. Scholars have thus invited the constitutional court to correct itself in the future, and shown the court how to do so without having to admit that an 'error' had ever been made.

Second, scholars extract from the case law those purely normative elements that can be incorporated into the rule system they are building, all but ignoring other elements. They do so almost instinctively, so normal has the reflex become. Thus, most standard texts on constitutional law in

[14] In the public law, relative to the private law, this task has proved to be especially difficult (see Stone 1992*a*: chs. 2, 4).

Germany, Italy, and Spain, make little or no mention of who litigates and why, what kinds of legal arguments were made and rejected, or even how the constitutional court reasoned through rules. (In fact, most students of constitutional law in German, Italian, or Spanish universities do not read any case law for their courses, but rather a treatise—a 'synthesis' of the law written by a constitutional scholar.) In France, scholars have even produced a *Code Constitutionnel* (Renoux and de Villiers 1994), that combines exegesis of the constitution, provision by provision, with discussion of how relevant decisions have clarified the meaning of the constitutional text. In constructing a 'pure' system of constitutional law, scholars enhance the court's authority, to the extent that constitutional rule-making is portrayed as the by-product of purely normative reasoning.

Bernard Schlink, one of a very small number of constitutionalists who have written reflectively on their discipline, is quite critical of this result, which he characterizes as a kind of 'constitutional court positivism', wherein constitutional scholars seek to 'canonize the constitutional court's case law', by 'harmoniz[ing] these decisions into a coherent doctrinal corpus' (1993: 730–1). If the legal scholar appears to treat the constitutional court as if it were 'the mouth' of the constitution, the scholar appears to be 'the mouth' of the constitutional court. What is clear is that the relationship between constitutional adjudication and doctrinal activity is pervasively symbiotic. Scholars need an authoritative, 'judicial' interpreter of the constitutional law, to structure, but also to give salience and urgency, to their own activities; and constitutional courts rely heavily on legal scholars to disseminate and explain their decisions to politicians, judges, the interested public, and, often enough, even to the constitutional judges themselves.[15]

Although my argument is that the scholarly impulse towards systematizing the constitutional law helps to legitimize that law, I do not mean to imply that scholars are blind to the politics of constitutional review. On the contrary, legal scholars actively participate in these politics other than through their doctrinal production. For obvious reasons, the more authoritative a legal scholar is within the academy, the more likely that scholar will be solicited by potential litigants, such as governments and political parties, for advice and for drafting referrals. Further, in all four of the countries under consideration here, eminent public law scholars have not only been named to, but have dominated, constitutional courts. I argue, instead, that the drive towards systematizing the law constitutes a deeply ingrained

[15] Judges rely on and use doctrinal materials; they also consult, and have even been known to discuss important decisions with doctrinal authorities.

response to the fact that constitutional law only develops in reaction to politicization. The constitutional law is, inherently and by definition, political law, but legal scholars rightly insist on that law's normative qualities. In doing so, they help to constitute and perpetuate their own authority.

Summary: Constructing the Constitutional Law

One important measure of the social legitimacy of constitutional review is the extent to which review has provoked normative discourse. In Europe, constitutional courts have drawn an ever-widening range of actors, public and private, into participating in, and perpetuating, that discourse. Although I have argued that each set of actors participates in constitutional politics with different purposes in mind, the core activities of each tends to push for more, not less, constitutional review, and for more, not less, rule-governed discourse. The result is that constitutional review process function as permanently constituted forums for the construction of the constitutional law.

Figure 5.1 summarizes and depicts the argument. This process of constructing the law, represented as the line moving from left to right, involves three sets of actors: litigants, judges, and legal scholars. As we move from left to right, the nature of the normative discourse changes. Litigation activity, the far left-hand pole, requires that self-interests—private or partisan—be expressed as legal interests; the discourse is overtly instrumental. Doctrinal activity, the far right-hand pole, produces a relatively 'pure'

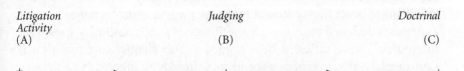

Litigation   Judging   Doctrinal
Activity
(A)   (B)   (C)

FIG. 5.1. *Constructing the constitutional law.*
Note. The figure depicts three stages of the process through which the constitutional law is constructed. The line, a continuum, is constituted by the relative presence of policy considerations within three kinds of normative discourses. At point A, litigants express (in the form of normative arguments) specific, identifiable socio-political interests, which they hope will be furthered by subsequent constitutional decision-making. At point B, judges co-ordinate socio-political interests and normative structures, by taking policy decisions, but also engaging in constitutional rule-making. At point C, legal scholars represent the law as an autonomous, apolitical, rule system, eliminating as far as possible the policy-relevance of constitutional innovation.

normative discourse, as divorced as possible from socio-political interests. Judges co-ordinate abstract rule structures and concrete disputes and, in doing so, build the constitutional law. Litigants keep the law open, and legal scholars work to close it. The court is advantaged by both activities. To use an analogy, litigation pours in, turning the mill; constitutional judges operate the mill, separating the wheat from the chaff; and legal scholars produce neat loaves that are easily stacked.

Last, it bears emphasis that I consider each of these stages to be equally, and profoundly, political processes. Governance is, in my view, how rules are adapted to the experiences and exigencies of those who live under them. If political scientists have reason to care about how rules are produced and stabilized within social systems like political systems, than they have reason to take seriously the sources and consequences of normative deliberations.

CONCLUSION

Chapters 2–5 show that legislating, litigating, and constitutional adjudication are—increasingly—mutually constitutive processes. Under certain conditions, each establishes the context for the others. The empirical findings lead us to deny the utility of traditional separation of powers schemes. Such schemes do more to obscure than to illuminate how laws are made, how judges take decisions, and how the constitution evolves.

Separation of powers ideologies, of course, are less suited to the accurate description of how the world of government actually works than they are to putting in order that (potentially chaotic) world. Moreover, they ground arguments designed to secure the legitimacy of public authority, including the judicial. Nevertheless, I have argued in this chapter that traditional, Continental separation of powers notions provide an inherently weak basis for discussions about the political legitimacy of constitutional review. I conclude by sketching three different ways to conceptualize the legitimacy of the constitutional judge, each of which admits (at least partly) the policy-making consequences of constitutional review.

The first is drawn from the logic of delegation and hierarchy of laws notions. Kelsen argued that the exercise of constitutional review could effectively operate not to obstruct but to legitimize the work of the legislature, but only if constitutional judges were not given jurisdiction over rights provisions. There existed no logical means, he demonstrated, for judges to defend rights without at the same time supplanting the legislator.

Kelsen's prognosis was correct: if Europeans wish to have judicially enforceable rights then they must accept that constitutional judges will fully participate in the legislative function. It follows that the legitimacy of constitutional rule-making is ultimately tied to the legitimacy of rights provisions. The calculus: is the polity better off without constitutional rights?; and should legislators alone decide how constitutional rights are to be enjoyed and protected in law? The answer to both questions, in most of Europe today, is a clear and resolute *No*.[16]

Second, if we accept that constitutional judges behave as adjunct legislators, that this is a core component of their job description, provided for by the constitution, then legitimacy issues are recast in important ways. Most debates about the legitimacy of constitutional review are debates about whether or not constitutional courts behave as 'judicial bodies' are expected to behave, that is, as adjudicators (applying pre-existing law to resolve disputes) not law-makers; and these expectations are derived from outmoded separation of powers schemes. But constitutional courts were neither meant, nor originally intended, to be 'judicial bodies' traditionally conceived (which is not to say that the ordinary courts make less law than do constitutional courts).[17] The founders recognized the mixed politico-legal nature of these new jurisdictions, just as they recognized the mixed nature of constitutional law. Constitutional courts were instead expected to participate in the legislative function. We get closer to reality if we go beyond the question of whether constitutional judges legislate when they protect rights, and ask instead: do constitutional judges, in fact, protect rights better than governments and parliaments do, or would do in the absence of constitutional review? To the extent that we can answer this question in the affirmative, the legitimacy of constitutional review is that much more secure.

This book, and the latter part of this chapter suggests a third argument, one that will be revisited in the concluding chapter. The legitimacy of constitutional review, like the development of the constitution, is constructed,

[16] Recall that everywhere but France, the constitution explicitly delegates the responsibility and the powers to constitutional judges to protect rights.

[17] According to Golay (1958: 183; see also Kommers 1994: 12), the founders of the German Basic Law 'recognized . . . that in many issues on which it is called to adjudicate, [the GFCC] acts as a kind of third legislative chamber, whose decisions have the same effects as legislation . . .'. In France, neither legal scholars nor politicians understood the Constitutional Council to be a 'judicial' body until the late 1970s (Stone 1992*a*: ch. 4). And in Italy, opponents of constitutional review regularly characterized the proposed ICC as a 'superparliament' or 'third parliamentary chamber' (Pizzorusso, Vigoriti, and Certoma 1984: 334).

over time, by practice, by constitutional politics. The development of the constitution, as organized by constitutional rule-making, tends to draw other actors into specific kinds of legal discourses, thus reinforcing the centrality—and legitimacy—of constitutional justice within the polity.

6

Constructing a Supranational Constitution

The European Court of Justice (ECJ), the judicial organ of the European Community (EC),[1] is the most powerful and influential supranational court in world history. Its unique achievement is to have fashioned a judicially enforceable constitution out of international treaty law, transforming the European polity in the process. In a series of innovative decisions initiated in the 1960s, the ECJ effectively 'constitutionalized' the European treaty system, thereby constructing the conditions that enable and sustain judicialization.[2] As judicialization has proceeded in the EC, a quasi-federal, rule-of-law polity has emerged in Europe.

This chapter examines the sources and consequences of this evolution. After a brief introduction to the European political system, we turn to the ECJ and its moves to constitutionalize the legal order. The impact of constitutionalization is then examined in terms of two linked dialogues: (1) between the ECJ and the national courts, on how to accommodate the supremacy of Community law within national legal orders; and (2) between judges and legislators in the making of public policy.

EUROPEAN INTEGRATION AND
SUPRANATIONAL GOVERNANCE

In the aftermath of World War II, Belgium, France, Germany, Italy, Luxembourg, and the Netherlands established a treaty-based, supranational

---

[1] Although the 'European Union' is now commonly used to denote the European polity, I use European Community most of the time in this chapter. Formally (in the structure of European treaty law), the EC remains distinct from the Union, and the EC is the most inclusive term for how the legal system functions most of the time. In any case, at this point, the normative logic of 'constitutionalization', and its attendant political consequences, applies almost exclusively to the system constituted by the 1958 Treaty of Rome and subsequent amendments to that Treaty.

[2] Constitutionalization made possible the forging of powerful causal linkages between social exchange and third party dispute resolution. Judicialization can occur in purely interstate regimes (see Stone Sweet 1997, 1999 on the GATT–WTO), but opening up litigation processes to individuals all but guarantees it.

political system that was firmly in place by 1958. They sought a long-term solution[3] to a pressing problem: how to channel political and economic reconstruction, and particularly that of Germany, to common and peaceful ends. European integration provided that solution. The EC has survived and prospered, helping to make war unthinkable within Western Europe, and powerfully stimulating economic growth among its members. Anxious to share in the benefits of integration, the original six member states were joined by Denmark, Britain, and Ireland in 1973; by Greece in 1981; by Spain and Portugal in 1986; and Austria, Sweden, and Finland in 1995. Thus, today there are fifteen member states in the EC.

The classic core of the Community project is economic integration, the process through which the economic and regulatory functions of the nation state are replaced by a common market: those supranational rules that govern the production and provision of goods and services within the territory comprised by the member states. The European common market includes: (1) a zone of free movement, wherein restrictions on the movement of labour, goods, services, and capital within the area have been abolished; (2) a collective external customs policy, whereby goods imported from outside the area are subject to uniform treatment; and (3) an EC-wide regulatory system, whereby common legislation and other public policies are made by the EC's governing bodies.

Economic integration, and the emergence of supranational governance, has taken place within an institutional framework laid down by the treaties, especially the Treaty of Rome establishing the European Economic Community (1958). As integration has proceeded, the priorities of supranational governance have expanded. Establishing and maintaining the zone of free movement animated the Community's governing bodies in the 1960s and 1970s. Yet as this project moved forward, new issues—of fiscal and monetary policy, gender equality, social policy and healthcare, consumer and environmental protection, and human rights—steadily moved onto the agenda. In the Single European Act (1986), the Treaty of European Union (1993), and the Treaty of Amsterdam (signed in 1997, now in the process of being ratified), the member states formally incorporated some of these and other policy domains into the Rome Treaty, and expanded supranational competences to govern to domains outside of the EC framework.

---

[3] The 1958 EEC treaty was adopted for an 'unlimited period' (art. 240).

Governing Institutions

The treaties comprise the EC's constitution. Like all constitutions, they distribute governing authority among functionally differentiated institutions and establish procedures to produce legislation. The EC, however, does not fit easily into traditional typologies of political systems. This is because it blends in complex, often fluid, ways, elements of governance found in international law and organization, with elements akin to national constitutional law and federalism. Simplifying, institutionalized forms of interstate cooperation, or 'regimes' (Krasner *ed.* 1983), are commonly understood in *intergovernmental* terms. Representing sovereign states, national governments establish and maintain these regimes as a means of achieving better results more cheaply or easily than they could acting alone (Keohane 1984). Intergovernmental analyses of these regimes focus on the crucial position of the member state, a position bolstered by the presumption in international law that a state cannot be bound without its consent. The intergovernmental mode of governance is therefore one of negotiation among member states in search of unanimity. International regimes can also be understood in *supranational* terms. Such analyses commonly focus on the interplay between the regime's own institutions and the member states. In the supranational mode of governance, intergovernmental bargaining is present and at times crucial to political outcomes. The regime's institutions, however, may also possess an independent capacity to structure this bargaining or to generate political outcomes, alone or in conjunction with transnational (private) actors.

The EC is principally governed by four institutions:

1. The Commission, which combines legislative and executive powers, and is the supranational nerve centre of the Community system. The Commission possesses the exclusive authority to draft and propose legislation. It also monitors member state compliance with EC law, and has the power to initiate enforcement actions against member state governments, including before the ECJ. There are currently 20 commissioners, named by member state governments and responsible to the European Parliament, who collectively manage a large bureaucracy based in Brussels, Belgium.

2. The Council of Ministers (Council), composed of sitting ministers of member state governments,[4] is the intergovernmental centre of gravity in

---

[4] The Council's actual composition is determined by the legislative subject matter being discussed. When the subject matter is agriculture, the agricultural ministers of the member states constitute the Council; when the subject matter is the environment, the environmental ministers meet, etc.

the EC. The Council is often characterized as the Community's legislature, since it usually takes the final decision on important EC legislation, and can block unwanted legislative proposals. Each member of the Council possesses a weighted vote, roughly determined by size.[5] The Council has developed its own Brussels-based bureaucracy, organized along national lines, to monitor the Commission's activities and to help the ministers defend their government's interests.

3. The European Parliament (EP) is the only Community institution whose members are directly elected (since 1979). The EP's powers are generally reactive, as befits a weak, 'arena' legislature in the terms of Chapter 2. It possesses the right to be consulted on legislation; it sometimes has the power to make amendments, which normally can be overridden by the Council; and, in rarer circumstances, it possesses a veto. The Parliament, now composed of 626 members (after the 1997 elections) meets both in Strasbourg, France, and Brussels. Members serve five-year terms.

4. The ECJ is a constitutional court roughly based on the European model. The Court resolves legal disputes that arise between the various EC organs, between EC institutions and the member states, and between the member states themselves. It also provides authoritative interpretations of European law to national judges, by way of a preliminary reference procedure that closely resembles German, Italian, and Spanish concrete review. The ECJ's fifteen members (appointed by, and drawn from each of, the member states) serve six-year, renewable terms.[6] The Court sits in Luxembourg.

The evolution of supranational governance must be understood in the light of permutations in the Community's decision-making processes. Simplifying, the original understanding of these processes distinguished between: (1) treaty amendments (e.g. the accession to the Treaties of new member states, an alteration in the weighted votes of Council members or in legislative procedures, the transfer of new powers from the member state to the Community); and (2) legislation—called secondary legislation—made pursuant to the treaties. Treaty amendments would be governed, as in traditional international law, by the rule of unanimity (i.e. every member state

---

[5] After the 1995 accession, the weighting of Council votes was as follows: France, Germany, Italy, and Britain, 10 votes each; Spain, 8 votes; Belgium, Greece, the Netherlands, and Portugal, 5 votes; Austria and Sweden, 4 votes; Denmark, Finland, and Ireland, 3 votes; Luxembourg, 2 votes.

[6] According to art. 167, judges must be 'chosen from persons whose independence is beyond doubt and who possess the qualifications required for appointments to the highest judicial offices in their respective countries' or who are law professors.

would possess a veto). Secondary legislation, including most legislation concerned with the construction of the common market, would be proposed by the Commission, and then amended and adopted by a supermajority (about two-thirds) of the weighted votes of the Council (what is called 'qualified majority voting'). Unanimity is an intergovernmental mode of governance, whereas qualified majority voting tends toward supranationality, since a member state can be bound by a policy it has not voted for.

The Treaty of Rome fixed a timetable for the completion of the common market, through two types of integration processes. The first constitutes negative integration: the obligation of all member states to remove barriers to free movement within EC territory. It is negative because governments renounce their authority to regulate a range of economic transactions within their borders. States were obliged by the Treaty to reduce progressively and ultimately eliminate (by 1969) all import tariffs and quotas, for example. The second type is positive integration: the creation of new rules to regulate problems common to all member states. The two processes were meant to go hand-in-hand. Successful negative integration would erase whole classes of national laws and regulations, leaving important 'holes', which positive integration would then fill with EC laws. The kaleidoscope of disparate national laws that functioned to hinder trade in 1958—such as taxes, duties, and rules governing health, licensing, and environmental protection standards—would be replaced by uniform, or 'harmonized', Euro-rules by the end of the 1960s. Most harmonization, according to the Treaty, would proceed, beginning in 1966, by qualified majority voting.

This is not what occurred. Just as the deadline approached, France's President, Charles de Gaulle, provoked a constitutional crisis. He distrusted the supranational elements of the Community, including the Commission and qualified majority voting. The crisis was resolved by the 'Luxembourg Compromise' of January 1966, an intergovernmental understanding among the member states. The compromise permits a member state, after asserting that 'very important interests are at stake', to demand that legislation be approved by unanimity rather than by qualified majority voting. In other words, each member state, on the grounds of the national interest, could veto Community legislation. The veto radically strengthened the intergovernmental element of the Community—the Council and the member states—and positive integration appeared to stall.

Qualified majority voting was only reinstated as the dominant legislative process for achieving the common market by the Single Act in 1986 (extended to other areas by the 1993 Treaty on European Union). Since the mid 1980s, the EC has developed a powerful momentum of its own evidenced by, among other things, institutional reform bolstering the position of the Parliament, the development of juridical notions of European citizenship and rights, the emergence of a formal treaty basis for foreign policies and new modes of political cooperation in policing and border control (under the guise of the 'European Union'), and the move to a European central bank and a common currency.

Theoretical Issues

This is not the place to survey the complex scholarly debates concerning how best to understand the integration process and the expansion of supranational capacities to govern. Instead, I will simply make the following three sets of points.

First, these debates have been dominated by two groups: those who employ 'intergovernmental' theories and perspectives (e.g. Garrett 1992; Moravscik 1991, 1993, 1995); and those who, following the development of integration theory by Ernst Haas (1958, 1961), employ more 'supranational', or 'neo-functional', perspectives (e.g. Burley and Mattli 1993; Sandholtz 1993, 1996; Sandholtz and Zysman 1989; Sandholtz and Stone Sweet *eds.* 1998). Intergovernmentalists argue that member state governments, operating in the Council of Ministers and in regular summit meetings, are the 'gatekeepers' of integration, controlling its scope and pace. Governments, responding to specific domestic interests, acting in order to enhance their own autonomy *vis-à-vis* domestic actors, or seeking means to resolve problems that are inherent transnational in nature, bargain out the details of transfers of authority to supranational institutions. The Commission and the Court then pursue the purposes of these intergovernmental bargains, as part of their own organization agendas. The heirs of Haas' neo-functionalism (see, e.g. Stone Sweet and Sandholtz 1997) argue that supranational governance tends to follow from increasing levels of transnational activity—exchange and cooperation across borders—as shaped by the work of the EC's supranational institutions. Transnational activity tends to provide opportunities for EC's institutions to push their own agendas, namely, the deepening of integration and the expansion of supranational governance. To the extent that EC institutions succeed, they expand the opportunities for the further development of transnational society. Although governments occupy a crucial position in the treaty-making and legislative processes, neo-functionalists argue that the context for intergovernmental bargaining is generated by larger integrative dynamics that governments do not fully control.

Second, intergovernmentalist theory has failed to explain European legal integration, the construction of a constitutional legal order for the EC. Intergovernmentalists (e.g. Garrett 1992; Kilroy 1996; Moravscik 1995) commonly adopt principal–agent (P–A) imagery as the preferred mode of analysing the Court's role and impact; and they argue that the Court, on balance, faithfully serves the interests of its principals, the member states. Indeed, Garrett argues (1992: 556–9), ECJ case law will tend to codify the policy preferences of the dominant states. Recent, more systematic research on legal integration has shown that the legal system operates not to comfort the legal positions of the member states, but to facilitate the expansion of transnational society and supranational authority to govern (Stone Sweet and Brunell 1998*a*; Stone Sweet and Caporaso 1998). As discussed in the next section, this result depended heavily on the prior development of a system through which individual litigants could pursue their private interests, in their own national courts, through law and procedures provided by European law.

Third, the rules governing the relationship between principals and agents—between the member states on one hand, and the European Court on the other—are permissive (see Chapter 3). Member state governments can overturn an ECJ decision interpreting a treaty provision, but only by revising the treaty, and that procedure requires unanimity among the member states followed by ratification of the revision (governed by national constitutional law).[7] Court decisions interpreting the Treaty constitutionalized the EC legal order. Although powerful governments have opposed these and most other important decisions taken by the Court, governments have not been successful at blocking constitutionalization, or at limiting the judicialization that has ensued. It bears emphasis that the EC principal is not a unified actor, but an aggregate composite of fifteen sets of national representatives of the member states. Because member state governments are usually scattered across different points along any relevant politico-ideological spectrum, one or more states will welcome the policy changes produced by innovative case law—and it only takes one state to block revision of the European constitution. Under most circumstances, the EC's constitutional law develops as the Court-as-agent, not member state governments-as-principals, see fit. Judicialization—the adaptation on the part of the EC's law-makers to the evolution of constitutional rules—follows.

---

[7] Reversing interpretations of secondary legislation is normally easier, requiring a second legislative process.

We now turn to the construction of the EC's legal order, focusing on litigation and adjudication within the context provided by the Treaty of Rome.

THE CONSTITUTIONALIZATION OF THE EUROPEAN COMMUNITY

The phrase, 'the constitutionalization of the treaty system', is used to capture the transformation of the EC from an international regime, founded on the precepts of international law, into a multi-tiered, quasi-federal polity, founded on higher law constitutionalism (see: Burley and Mattli 1993; Lenaerts 1990; Mancini 1991; Shapiro 1992; Stein 1981; Stone Sweet and Brunell 1998*a*; Stone Sweet and Caporaso 1998; Weiler 1991, 1994). Under classical conceptions of international law, only sovereign states possess 'legal personality' (i.e. only states enjoy rights and bear obligations). In the higher law constitutional polity described in Chapter 1, legal personality is diffused, and judges have the power to control all uses of public authority, including the activities of sovereign states (governments). To define our terms more precisely, constitutionalization refers to the process by which the EC treaties evolved from a set of legal arrangements binding upon sovereign states, into a vertically integrated legal order that confers judicially enforceable rights and obligations on all legal persons and entities, public and private, within EC territory.

The ECJ is the supreme interpreter of the EC's constitution. Its functions are to enforce compliance with the treaty, and to ensure that EC law is applied in a uniform manner across the Community. With constitutionalization, these two functions have become one and the same. Although the outcome was not intended, the vast bulk of the Court's caseload is generated by preliminary references sent by national judges responding to claims made by litigants before them. This procedure is governed by article 177 of the Treaty of Rome. According to article 177, whenever an EC legal norm is material to the settlement of a dispute being heard in a national court, the presiding judge may—and final courts of appeal must—ask the ECJ for a correct interpretation of that law. This interpretation, called a preliminary ruling, is then applied by the national judge to settle the case. The procedure is designed to enable national courts to understand the nature and content of EC law, and to apply it correctly and uniformly throughout EC territory. As a mode of constitutional adjudication, the preliminary reference procedure functions much like the concrete review found in national constitutional systems (see Chapter 2).

Constitutionalizing the Treaties

The relationship between international law and national law is normally governed by national constitutional rules, rules usually classified as either more or less *monist,* or more or less *dualist.* Simplifying, in monist systems, the international and national legal orders are considered to comprise a single legal order, wherein international law takes juridical precedence in any conflict of norms. Although there are exceptions (e.g. the Netherlands), European legal systems have traditionally tended toward dualism: treaty law enters into the national legal order after having been *transposed*— or ratified—by parliament. Once transposition has been achieved, statute and treaty law, having been produced by equivalent acts of the legislature, occupy the same rung on the hierarchy of norms (both are binding, as parliamentary acts, on ordinary judges, and both are inferior to constitutional norms). In most dualist systems, the juridical relationship between statute and treaty law is governed by the doctrine of *lex posteriori*: when an irresoluble conflict between the two arises during the course of litigation, the judge must apply the most recently produced legal norm. Thus, when international rules conflict with a subsequent legislative act, the latter prevails in court, on the theory that parliament's last word on the matter controls.

What is innovative—what appears constitutional—about the ECJ's jurisprudence is that it requires national judges to treat EC law as if it were a source of law that is superior to, and autonomous from, national statutes, and capable of being applied, directly, within the national legal order, by national judges. Through this case law, the European Court has firmly sought to constitute the Community legal order on the basis of a sophisticated monism, demanding, among other things, that the orthodoxies of constitutional dualism, like *lex posteriori,* be abandoned.

The constitutionalization process has been driven—almost entirely—by the relationship between private litigants, national judges, and the European Court, interacting within the framework provided by article 177. Simplifying, there have been two waves of constitutionalization. In the 1962–79 period, the Court secured the core, constitutional principles of supremacy and direct effect. The Court made these moves despite the declared opposition of some member states, formally expressed in briefs to the Court.[8] The *doctrine of supremacy,* announced in *Costa* (ECJ 1964), lays

---

[8] Belgium, Germany, Luxembourg, and the Netherlands submitted briefs opposing the direct effect of treaty provisions ultimately declared by the ECJ in *Van Gend en Loos,* and Britain opposed the extension of direct effect to directives in *Van Duyn.* Italy opposed supremacy in *Costa* and *Simmenthal.*

down the rule that in any conflict between an EC legal norm and national rule or practice, the EC norm must always be given primacy (discussed further below). Indeed, according to the Court in *Simmenthal II*, every EC rule, from the moment of its entry into force, 'renders automatically inapplicable any conflicting provision of . . . national law' (ECJ 1978). The *doctrine of direct effect* holds that, under certain conditions, EC rules confer on individuals rights that public authorities must respect, and which must be protected by national courts. During this period, the ECJ found that certain treaty provisions (*Van Gend en Loos*, ECJ 1962) and a class of secondary legislation called directives (*Van Duyn*, ECJ 1974a), were directly effective, and the Court strengthened the direct applicability of another class of secondary legislation, called regulations.[9]

The Treaty of Rome makes regulations directly applicable in national legal orders, but does not do the same for Treaty provisions or directives. The ECJ's pronouncement that directives could be directly effective has been controversial. The Treaty, after all, explicitly leaves it up to national authorities to determine how to implement directives into the national order once adopted by the EC legislator (they are obliged to do so, by enacting, in the form of a national statute, the logic and social purposes that underly directives). In the leading case (ECJ 1974a), the Court was faced with a clear conflict between an EC directive and a national rule. In 1973, Yvonne Van Duyn, a Dutch national, sued the British government in an English court after having been denied entry into the country due to her religious beliefs. She had been offered a job as a secretary of an English branch of the American Church of Scientology. The government, having declared that the Church was a 'socially harmful' institution that bred 'authoritarian' tendencies in its members, had ordered immigration officials to refuse work permits to Church members beginning in 1968. Ms Van Duyn claimed that this order violated a 1964 directive prohibiting restrictions on free movement of persons excepting those 'based exclusively on the personal conduct of the individual concerned'. Britain had not transposed this directive into national law. The Court sided with Van Duyn, declaring that the directive established, in a sufficiently clear and precise manner, rights 'enforceable . . . by the courts of the member states'. The ECJ thus served notice, reinforced in a long line of subsequent cases,

[9] As noted above, regulations are the only class of EC legislation recognized by the EEC Treaty to be 'directly applicable'. The ECJ has strengthened this applicability by, among other things, declaring that national implementing measures are 'contrary to the Treaty' if they 'have the result of creating an obstacle to the direct effect of Community Regulations' (ECJ 1973).

that it would scrutinize whether and how the member states transposed directives into national law, and that it would censor national measures functioning to deprive individuals of rights conferred on them by EC law.

In the second wave of constitutionalization, the Court supplied national courts with enhanced means of guaranteeing the effectiveness of EC law. In the 1980s, the *doctrine of indirect effect* was established, according to which national judges must always interpret national rules as if they were in conformity with EC law (*Von Colson*, ECJ 1984). In *Marleasing* (ECJ 1990*a*), the Court announced that when a directive has either not been transposed or has been transposed incorrectly into national law, national judges are obliged to interpret this law in conformity with that directive. The doctrine empowers national judges to rewrite national legislation—an exercise called 'principled construction'—in order to render EC law applicable, in the absence of implementing measures. Once national law has been so (re)constructed, the EC law (in the guise of the national rule) can be applied in legal disputes between private legal persons (i.e. non-governmental entities). Thus, indirect effect substantially reduces the problem that the Court's doctrine of direct effect only covers disputes between a private person and a governmental entity. Finally, beginning with *Francovich* (ECJ 1991*a*), the Court has developed the *doctrine of governmental liability*. According to this doctrine, a national court can hold a member state liable for damages incurred by individuals due to a member state's failure to transpose properly a directive. The national court may then require member states to compensate such individuals for their losses.

The European Court and the National Courts

Constitutionalization constituted a bid, on the part of the European Court, to integrate national and supranational legal systems, and to establish a decentralized enforcement mechanism for EC law. Direct effect enables individuals and companies to sue member state governments or other public authorities for either not conforming to obligations contained in the treaties or regulations, or for not properly transposing provisions of directives into national law. Supremacy prohibits public authorities from relying on national law to justify their failure to comply with EC law, and requires national judges to resolve conflicts between national and EC law in favour of the latter.

In this jurisprudence, the Court has sought to enlist national judges in a working partnership to construct a constitutional, rule of law Community. As the ECJ has imagined this partnership, national judges become agents of the Community order—they become Community judges—whenever they resolve disputes governed by EC law. The Court obliges the national judge to uphold the supremacy of EC law, even against conflicting subsequent national law; encourages her to make references concerning the proper interpretation of EC law to the Court; and empowers her (even without a referral) to interpret national rules so that these rules will conform to EC law, and to refuse to apply national rules when they do not. The ECJ has derived as much from the doctrine of supremacy.

The success of the ECJ's gambit depended heavily on the willingness of national judges to use the article 177 procedure, and to faithfully implement the ECJ's interpretations of EC law. In general, national judges have heard the Court's message and responded, with some reservations discussed below, positively. The first article 177 reference was sent to the ECJ in 1961; references climbed to over 100 per year during the 1970s, and over 175 in the 1980s. Today, the Court regularly receives about 200 references annually. The scope of litigation of EC law in the national courts has also steadily expanded. In the 1971–5 period, more than half of all references concerned just two sectors: the free movement of goods, and agriculture. In the 1991–5 period, these two domains accounted for only 27 per cent of total references, while new areas, such as environmental protection, commercial policy, and competition, are becoming increasingly important (data in Stone Sweet and Brunell 1998*b*).

There is a vigorous debate about why national judges have been so willing to play the 'Euro-law game' (for overviews, see: Slaughter, Stone Sweet, and Weiler *eds.* 1998; Stone Sweet and Brunell 1998*b*). The question is an important one, given that in some national jurisdictions supremacy required judges to abandon certain deeply entrenched, constitutive principles, such as the prohibition against judicial review of legislation; and direct effect required some judges to set aside whole classes of traditional rules governing their jurisdiction and procedures (such as standing and recognition), and to evolve new ones. I will focus on only two approaches to the question of why judges have been willing to participate in article 177 processes, since the evidence gives broad support for both.[10]

The first, the 'judicial empowerment thesis', assumes that judges work to enhance their own authority to control legal (and, therefore, policy) outcomes, and to reduce the control of other institutional actors, such as national executives, parliament, and other judges, on those same outcomes. Two academic lawyers, Eric Stein (1981) and Joseph Weiler (e.g.

---

[10] Comprehensive data on art. 177 has recently been collected and analysed, allowing some testing of extant explanations (Stone Sweet and Brunell 1998*b*).

1981, 1991, 1994) pioneered studies of the strategic choice-contexts facing European judges, in the context of emerging constitutionalization. Weiler argued that the evolution of EC law and of the incentive structure facing both ECJ and national judges all pushed in the same direction—in favour of integration. The ECJ needed national judges to provide it with caseload and, therefore opportunities for building EC law; and, in doing so, national judges could acquire (many for the first time) the power to control state acts previously beyond their reach, such as statutes. Although exploiting supremacy is potentially risky, article 177 affords both judicial levels a good deal of protection from political fallout. The European Court responds to preliminary questions, as the Treaty requires, but the ECJ does not apply EC law within the national legal order; the national court sends the ECJ questions, but only 'implements' the Court's preliminary rulings, as the Treaty requires. Thus, at critical moments, each court can claim to be responding to the requirements of the law, and the demands of the other court. Once national judges understood that they were advantaged by participating in the construction of EC law, a delicate mixture of the active and the passive (and of normative requirements and self-interest) flowed naturally, gluing the two levels together.

The second approach builds on the first, but focuses intensively on the role of private actors in activating and sustaining European legal integration. Litigants and their interests are understood to be fuelling the machine (Burley and Mattli 1993; Stone Sweet and Brunell 1998*a*; Stone Sweet and Caporaso 1998). In this view, European legal integration has proceeded according to a self-sustaining logic: in announcing the doctrines of supremacy and direct effect, the ECJ opened up the European legal system to private litigants, undermined certain constitutional orthodoxies in place in Continental legal systems, and radically enhanced the potential effectiveness of EC law within the member states; private actors, motivated by their own interests, provided a steady supply of litigation capable of provoking article 177 activity; preliminary references generated the context for judicial empowerment, which proceeded in the form of a nuanced, intrajudicial dialogue between the ECJ and national judges on how best to accommodate one another; and, as the domain of EC law expanded, this dialogue intensified, socializing more and more actors— private litigants, judges, and politicians—into the system, encouraging more use. The approach is broadly consistent with contemporary versions of neo-functionalist integration theory (see Sandholtz and Stone Sweet *eds.* 1998), and with the theory of judicialization underlying this book (Stone Sweet 1999).

THE CONSTITUTIONAL POLITICS OF SUPREMACY

Although legal integration has proceeded steadily, and the most important structural hindrances to constitutionalization have been gradually overcome, national courts have not been passive actors in the process (Slaughter, Stone Sweet, and Weiler *eds*. 1998). Clearly, the logic of judicial empowerment and dynamics associated with transnational litigation do not apply equally across national jurisdictions. Those courts that regularly process litigation involving EC law are the most active suppliers of preliminary references, and the most active consumers of ECJ case law. But some judges have resisted participating in the construction of EC law, believing that the ECJ's case law could undermine their own carefully crafted jurisprudence in certain sectors. Further, and most important for our purposes, national constitutional courts have been the least willing to accept constitutionalization without reservation. Not only do constitutional courts not adjudicate conflicts about EC law (except insofar as questions referred to them raise issues of the compatibility of EC law with national constitutional law), they could hardly welcome the development of a 'constitutional' EC legal order that would subsume the national constitutional order.

In this section, I focus on the role of national constitutional courts and other high courts in sustaining a set of dialogues with the ECJ on the relationship of EC to national constitutional law (based partly on Stone Sweet 1998*b*). As we will see, these dialogues have: (1) produced a wide reaching supremacy doctrine; (2) induced the construction of an enforceable charter of rights for the Community; and (3) provoked a still unsettled controversy about the underlying democratic legitimacy of the EC polity.

Supremacy and the Problem of Constitutional Review

The ECJ's supremacy doctrine developed out of a delicate, often conflictual, dialogue between it and the Italian Constitutional Court. Indeed, the evolution of the Italian constitutional law of treaties and the doctrine of supremacy have gone hand-in-hand. The story begins in 1962, when Mr Costa went on trial for refusing to pay a three dollar electrical bill in protest of the nationalization of electrical companies in Italy. Costa, a shareholder in one of the companies expropriated, defended himself on the grounds that the nationalization violated article 37 of the EEC Treaty ('national monopolies' are not to be managed in a discriminatory manner). The trial judge referred the matter both to the ECJ and the ICC.

The Italian Court, which disposed of the case first, was faced with determining the relative primacy of two sets of constitutional provisions. The first governs the relationship between international and national law: article 10 provides that 'the Italian legal order conforms to the general principle of international law', and article 11 authorizes the state to 'limit' its sovereignty in order to 'promote and encourage international organizations' like the EC. The second, article 80, states that treaty law enters into force upon an act of parliament. In its decision (ICC 1964), the ICC declared that because treaty law occupies the same rung on the hierarchy of norms as legislation, the *lex posteriori* rule controls, and Costa lost his case.

Five months later, the ECJ rejected Costa's claim as unfounded, while announcing the doctrine of supremacy (ECJ 1964). The Court emphasized that the Treaty of Rome had 'created its own legal system which, on the entry into force of the Treaty, became an integral part of the legal systems of the Member-States and which their courts are bound to apply'. The Court continued

[T]he law stemming from the Treaty, an independent source of law, [can]not, because of its special and original nature, be overridden by domestic legal provisions, however framed, without being deprived of its character as Community law and with the legal basis of the Community itself being called into question.

The decision thus repudiated all national *lex posteriori* doctrines to the extent that they would inhibit the effective application of EC law in national legal orders.

Ignoring the ECJ's jurisprudence, the ICC let stand its position on *lex posteriori* until 1997 (ICC 1977). Simplifying, whereas in *Costa* the ICC had allowed article 80 to govern the case, it now shifted control to articles 10 and 11. At this point, however, the ICC's conception of constitutional review got in the way. Arguing that the prohibition of judicial review (because it forbids the review of the legality of a parliamentary act) denies ordinary judges the authority to enforce EC law against subsequent, conflicting legislation, the Court declared that Italian courts would only be permitted to abandon the *lex posteriori* rule, on a case-by-case basis, on authorization by the ICC pursuant to a concrete review referral. Thus, in cases where the supremacy doctrine comes into play, the applicability of EC law would be subject to the enormous delays attending Italian constitutional review processes. From the perspective of EC law, directly applicable, legal rights would be held hostage to an idiosyncratic, national procedure.

Some Italian judges, apparently hoping to gain a measure of autonomy from the Italian Constitutional Court, worked to undermine the ICC's case law. The crucial case involved the importation of French beef into Italy by the Simmenthal company. In 1973, Italian customs authorities billed Simmenthal nearly 600,000 lire to pay for mandatory health inspections of its meat as it crossed the border. The border inspections, required by Italian legislation passed in 1970, conflicted with the EEC Treaty, and with two EC regulations adopted in the 1960s. Simmenthal challenged the border inspections before an Italian judge, who referred the matter to the ECJ. The European Court (ECJ 1976*a*) ruled that the border inspections violated principles of free movement and EC regulations, and authorized the Italian judge to order the Italian government to return Simmenthal's payment. The Italian government appealed the judge's order, partly on the grounds that, in the Italian constitutional systems, only the ICC could authorize an Italian judge to set aside national legislation. At that point, the trial judge requested the ECJ to declare the ICC's jurisprudence incompatible with the ECJ's supremacy doctrine!

The European Court (ECJ 1978) agreed, declaring that EC norms, from their entry into force, become immediately enforceable in every courtroom throughout the Community. Consequently, 'any provision of a national legal system and any legislative, administrative, or judicial practice which might impair the effectiveness of Community law'—such as a mandatory concrete review process—'are incompatible with . . . *the very essence* of Community law'. Despite the clarity of the European Court's statement, the ICC waited more than fifteen years to decide that EC law could be directly applicable by ordinary judges, without a preliminary reference to the ICC.[11] In its decision, the ICC (1984) was careful to stress that the Italian constitution, not the ECJ, governed the relationship between Community law and national legislation, and that, contrary to the European Court's vision of the world, the European and national legal orders are 'independent and separate' of one other.

In this saga, both the ECJ and the ICC have remained stubbornly attached to their own 'inalienable conceptual orders' (Barav 1985: 314). Nevertheless, the ICC has been forced to adapt to the case law of the European Court, rather than the other way around. The ECJ, for its part, has refused to back down, using its interactions with the Italian Court to clarify and extend its message. In comparing the reception of this message cross-nationally, we notice that it was in those states where constitutional

---

[11] The ICC finessed the constitutional review issue, ordering judges simply to ignore national law conflicting with antecedent EC law. On discovering a conflict between national and EC norms, the ordinary judge must choose not to recognize the existence of the former, although this is not considered to be judicial review of legislation.

review by constitutional courts exist—France, Germany, and Italy—that supremacy proved to be the most problematic.

In France, despite what looks on the surface to be friendly terrain, the story was, until recently, one of confusion and fragmentation. The constitution of 1958 is strongly monist, article 55 states that treaty law is both part of French law and superior to statute. Each of France's three high courts, however, had to determine whether and how EC law was to be enforceable within the scope of its jurisdiction. In 1975, in a decision having no relationship to EC law, the Constitutional Council (1975) ruled (contrary to the ICC's position) that constitutional review of statute and the review of the conformity of national legislation with treaty law were inherently different juridical exercises, and that its powers were limited exclusively to the former. Although this decision is now commonly read as a kind of constitutional authorization to the judiciary to accept supremacy (Favoreu and Philip 1997: 305–29), the fact is that the civil courts needed no such authorization.

In 1971, four years before the Council's ruling, a Paris trial court had set aside certain customs rules, adopted in a law of 1966, taxing imports from other EC countries more than the same products produced in France. The French administration had argued that the civil courts could not ignore the *lex posteriori* doctrine without 'making themselves judges of the constitutionality of laws'. The trial court disagreed, basing its decision on article 55 and on the autonomous nature of EC law. The ruling was subsequently upheld by the Paris court of appeal and by the high civil court, the *Cour de Cassation*, which ruled that the supremacy of Community law over conflicting, subsequent national law inhered in both the nature of EC law and in article 55 (reported in Stone Sweet 1998*b*).

France's administrative courts, however, refused to accept supremacy until a decision of 1989. Before 1989, the Council of State's position was that while article 55 provided for the supremacy of treaty law over statute, the administrative courts could not enforce this supremacy, because: (1) judicial review was prohibited; and (2) the authority to set aside legislation conflicting with a constitutional provision rested exclusively with the Constitutional Council. In 1989, the Council of State simply empowered itself and the administrative courts to enforce article 55, at the same time avoiding mention of the ECJ, the status of Community law, *Cassation*'s case law, or the Constitutional Council's jurisprudence on article 55 (reported in Plötner 1998).

The sometimes tortuous accommodation of supremacy by the French, Italian, and—as we will shall soon see—the German legal systems contrast sharply with how smoothly supremacy was received by judiciaries of the other three original members of the EC. In the Netherlands, the constitutional prohibition against judicial review was simply overridden by a strongly expressed monism. Articles 93 and 94, which date from the 1950s, provide both for the direct applicability of international law and their primacy in any conflict with national legal norms. Even more extraordinary, the consensus of legal scholars is that this supremacy clause bestows on international agreements supremacy even over the constitution itself (see Claes and deWitte 1998). In Belgium and Luxembourg, dualist constitutional orders, provided tougher tests. Nevertheless, the high courts in both countries quickly and easily swept aside entrenched *lex posteriori* doctrines, without formal constitutional or political authorization.

One would expect supremacy and direct effect to have met their chilliest reception in the courts of Britain, a relative latecomer to the EC (joining in 1973). In Britain, the organizing precept of constitutional law is the doctrine of parliamentary sovereignty: the only legal limitation to legislative power is that a parliament of today cannot, with legislation, bind a parliament of tomorrow. The doctrine prohibits judicial review of legislation, and implies a rigid *lex posteriori* solution. Further, Britain constitutes the archetype of a dualist regime.[12] Nevertheless, Britain's high court, the House of Lords, formally accepted supremacy of EC law (but not the supremacy of any other species of international law) in 1991. Prior to 1991, British judges either: (1) applied the British norm, under the guise of an 'implied repeal' of the antecedent EU norm, a solution in open conflict with the ECJ's supremacy doctrine; or (2) engaged in 'principled construction of the UK statute', reading it—as far as possible—as if it were adopted in the light of requirements of EC law (see Craig 1998). The change caps a long process through which British judging has been 'Europeanized' (Levitsky 1994), to the detriment of traditional conceptions of parliamentary sovereignty (Craig 1991).

Supremacy and the Problem of Fundamental Rights

One enormously important, but wholly unintended, consequence of the ECJ's elaboration of the supremacy doctrine has been the progressive construction of a charter of rights for the Community. The EEC treaty originally contained no such charter, although several of its provisions—

---

[12] That is, any international legal norm that modifies the legal rights and obligations of British citizens must be transposed to have effect within Britain. This law is then subject to implied repeal (*lex posteriori*).

including the principles of non-discrimination based on nationality (article 7), and equal pay for equal work among men and women (article 119)—can be read as rights provisions. Their purpose was not so much to create rights claims for individuals, as to remove potential sources of distortion within an emerging common market. In 1959, the ECJ declared itself to be without power to review Community acts with reference to fundamental rights (ECJ 1958); in 1969 the Court ruled that it had a positive duty to ensure that Community acts conform to fundamental rights (ECJ 1969); and, in 1989, the Court secured the power to review the acts of the member states for rights violations (ECJ 1989). The Court has thus radically revised the treaties, 'wisely and courageously' in Weiler's terms (1986: 1105–6).

The move, however, was not voluntary.[13] An incipient rebellion against supremacy, led by national courts, drove the process. Just after the doctrine of supremacy was announced, Italian and German judges noticed that supremacy could work to insulate EC law from national rights protection. They began challenging—in references to the ECJ and to their own constitutional courts—the legality of a range of EC legislative acts, on the theory that these acts violated national constitutional rights. The *International Handelsgesellschaft* case provides an important example. The case involved a financial penalty (the forfeiture of an export deposit) permitted by EC regulations adopted in 1967, and administered against a German exporter by the German government. In its referral to the ECJ, the administrative court of Frankfurt complained that the regulations appeared to violate German constitutional rights. In its response, the ECJ declared that EC law could not be overridden by national rights provisions 'without the legal basis of the Community itself' (i.e. supremacy), 'being called into question'. But recognizing the seriousness of the challenge, the Court declared that 'respect for fundamental rights'—'inspired by the constitutional traditions of the member states'—'forms an integral part of the general principles of law protected by the Court of Justice'. Although the German government argued that the Court had no power to do so, the ECJ then reviewed the regulations for their conformity with these fundamental rights, but found no violation (ECJ 1970).

The case did not end there. Disappointed with the ECJ's ruling, the Frankfurt court asked the German constitutional court to declare the EC rules unconstitutional. Although the GFCC (1973*c*) refused to do so, it declared (by a 5–3 vote) that '*as long as* the integration process has not

---

[13] Mancini and Keeling (1994) argue that the ECJ was not 'bulldozed' but only 'forced' by national courts into recognizing fundamental rights.

progressed so far that Community law also possesses a catalogue of rights
... of settled validity, which is adequate in comparison with a catalogue of
fundamental rights contained in the [German] constitution', the GFCC
would permit German constitutional review of EC acts. The decision is
today known as the *Solange I* (the first 'as long as') decision.

In response to cases like these, the ECJ became increasingly explicit
about the fundamental rights it had promised to protect. Thus, in *Nold*
(ECJ 1974*b*), the Court declared that it would annul '[Community] measures which are incompatible with fundamental rights recognized and protected by the constitutions of the member states'. In the same case, the
Court also announced that international human rights treaties signed by
the member states, including the European Convention on Human Rights,
would 'supply guidelines' to the Court. The Court has thereafter referred
to the Convention as if it were a basic source of Community rights, and has
invoked it in review of member state acts (e.g. *Rutili*, ECJ 1975; *Commission
v. Germany*, ECJ 1986*a*). Although some uncertainty remains, national
courts have generally been persuaded by these moves. In 1986, the GFCC
set aside *Solange I*. In *Solange II*, it declared that 'a measure of protection of
fundamental rights has been established ... which, in its conception, substance and manner of implementation, is essentially compatible with the
standards established by the German constitution'. The GFCC then prohibited concrete review references '*as long as* the EC, and in particular the
ECJ, generally ensures an effective protection of fundamental rights'
(GFCC 1986*b*).

The European Court's jurisprudence of supremacy and fundamental
rights are tightly linked, to each other, and to a particular vision of the
Community. Without supremacy, the ECJ had decided, the common market was doomed. And without a judicially enforceable charter of rights,
national courts had decided, the supremacy doctrine was doomed. The
ECJ could have maintained its original position which, in effect, held that
fundamental rights were part of national—but not Community—law; the
courts of the member states could have begun to annul EC acts judged to
be unconstitutional. Legal integration might have been fatally undermined. Despite the potential threat, no EC act has ever been censored, by
the ECJ or a national court, for violating Community or national rights
provisions, although the ECJ, in cooperation with national courts, have
begun to review member state acts for their conformity with Community
rights provisions.

In consequence, an expansive constitutional politics of rights, closely
resembling the politics examined in Chapter 4, is emerging at the

Community level. A 1989 decision, *Wachauf* (ECJ 1989), illustrates the main features of these new politics. The case involved Hubert Wachauf, a German farmer who, along with his parents before him, had built a thriving dairy business on leased land over a period of twenty-five years. After having been denied a renewal of his lease by the landowner, Wachauf decided to take advantage of a 1984 EC regulation providing for monetary compensation to dairy farmers who agreed to downsize or abandon their milk production.[14] The federal government, charged with implementing the regulation, refused to grant this compensation (about DM150,000) on the grounds that the EC rule required, in cases where land leases were involved, the consent of the landowner. The landowner, in an attempt to profit from Wachauf's labours, had denied his consent. The case was brought before the Frankfurt administrative court which, in its reference to the ECJ, offered 'a suggested interpretation' to the effect that the implementation of the EC rule had 'deprived [Wachauf] of the fruits of his labour', and 'amounted to an unconstitutional expropriation without compensation'. The ECJ agreed with this interpretation but declined to annul the regulation. It instead declared that the EC act could be construed to include compensation in cases like Wachauf's, despite the language of the regulation to the contrary, in order to render the act compatible with 'fundamental rights in the Community legal order'. The ECJ left it to the national court to determine if Wachauf's rights had indeed been violated, and the Frankfurt court subsequently awarded the farmer compensation and trial costs.

The decision has far-reaching implications, three of which deserve emphasis. First, the ECJ announced that it was now in the business of balancing rights claims against the interests of government (using proportionality tests, see Chapter 4). The Court stated

The fundamental rights recognized by the Court are not absolute . . . but must be considered in relation to their social function. Consequently, restrictions may be imposed on the exercise of these rights . . .. provided that these restrictions in fact correspond to objectives of general interest pursued by the Community and do not constitute, with regard to the aim pursued, a disproportionate and intolerable interference, impairing the very substance of those rights.

Second, member state governments, when they administer EC law within their territory, are considered by the Court to be *agents of the Community*, and thereby bound by Community rights provisions. Third, national

---

[14] The regulation was adopted as part of a general scheme to reduce chronic surpluses in the EC agricultural sector.

courts are enlisted to monitor respect for Community rights, and the ECJ is present to authorize national judges to annul member state acts that violate these rights. Taken together, *Wachauf* has strengthened the capacity of the ECJ, in partnership with the national courts, to control policy outcomes.

Coppell and O'Neill (1992) have argued that the Court's jurisprudence on rights can be divided into two stages, corresponding to two different judicial strategies. In the first period, the authors argue, the Court adopted a 'defensive' posture, engaging in a rights discourse to preserve what was far more essential—supremacy. In the present period, inaugurated by the *Wachauf* decision, the Court deploys a rights discourse 'offensively'—to 'extend its jurisdiction' and 'to expand the influence of the Community over the activities of the member-states'. Highlighting these strategic (empowering) aspects of the Court's moves, the authors criticize the ECJ for not 'taking rights seriously', and for promoting a double standard in which national acts are controlled more strictly than are EC acts.[15] There is no reason, however, to suppose that a posture of 'taking rights seriously' is incompatible with strategic judicial behaviour. Indeed, as I have argued in Chapters 4 and 5, the more a court relies on rights discourse to pursue its own institutional interests, the more a court seeks to construct a compelling jurisprudential foundation for that discourse. Further, the elaboration of a new line case law should not only be interpreted as a record of empowerment, which it partly is, but also a record of how the Court has also constrained itself in future cases.

In summary, although conflictual in origin, the dialogue on fundamental rights has served to deepen legal integration, to widen the scope of EC constitutional politics, and to strengthen the supranational aspects of the Community.

Supremacy and the Constitutional Limits to Integration

Interactions between the European and national constitutional courts have led to stable accommodations on rights and the obligation of ordinary courts to enforce EC law. But they have not resolved another fundamental problem posed by supremacy: who has the *ultimate* authority to determine the constitutionality of EC acts? The problem is in fact irresoluble. On the one hand, the logic of supremacy suggests that the ECJ alone should have such authority, as guardian of the constitutional order of the EC, and the

[15] In an exhaustive analysis of the Court's rights jurisprudence, Weiler and Lockhart (1995*a*, *b*) have sought to refute Coppell and O'Neill's double standard thesis.

Court has declared as much in *Foto Frost* (ECJ 1987). On the other hand, national constitutional courts, guardians of their own constitutional orders, stubbornly view Community law as a species of international law which must either conform to national constitutional rules or be invalid as law. These courts, even at their most integration-friendly moments, have always been careful to reserve for themselves the final authority to determine the legality of EC acts.

The most far-reaching ruling in this regard is the German constitutional court's decision on the Treaty on European Union, signed at Maastricht in January 1992. The ruling sent shock waves through the Community that are still being felt. Because of its far-reaching scope, the Maastricht Treaty required an accommodation between the European and national constitutions. The Treaty of European Union (which also commits EC member states to enhanced cooperation in foreign policy, security, and social policy) established European citizenship for all EC nationals and a step-by-step process to European Monetary Union (EMU). These provisions forced most member states to amend their constitutions: the granting of a right to vote in local elections to all EC citizens, wherever they lived within the Community, conflicted with those constitutional provisions restricting voting rights to nationals; and the transfers of sovereignty involved in the EMU, the core of which is a single European currency managed by an independent European Central Bank, also required constitutional authorization. In December 1992, four articles of the German constitution were amended to enable ratification, and the German Bundestag (by a 543–25 vote) and the Bundesrat (unanimously) then ratified the Treaty. In amending the constitution, the government and the legislature were careful to pay tribute to the GFCC's jurisprudence on legal integration. Article 23, for example, now states that Germany

shall cooperate in the development of the European Union in order to realize a united Europe which is bound to observe democratic . . . principles . . . and which guarantees the protection of basic rights in a way which is substantially comparable to that provided by this constitution.

Further, rules (article 23) governing transfers of governmental authority from Germany to the EC were tightened: such transfers, which previously could be effected by a simple majority, now must be approved by two-thirds of the Bundestag and the Bundesrat.

The law ratifying the Treaty was suspended[16] after four members of the German Green Party, joined by a former German EC Commissioner,

---

[16] The German President refused to sign the bill pending the GFCC's decision.

attacked its constitutionality in separate constitutional complaints. Although a dozen often contradictory arguments were invoked, complainants focused on the alleged 'democratic deficit' afflicting the EC: that the expansion in the Community's policy-making powers had so far outpaced democratization in the Community that in many areas Germans do not effectively participate in their own governance.

In a long and complex ruling rendered in October 1993 (GFCC 1993*b*), the German Court dismissed the complaint as unfounded, thus clearing the way for German ratification of the Treaty. Given the care in which article 24 and other constitutional provisions had been revised, this aspect of the decision was hardly surprising. Nonetheless, the Court used the opportunity to introduce a new basis in which to challenge EC norms: the *ultra vires* nature of EC acts. (*Ultra vires* acts are governmental acts that are not legally valid to the extent that the governmental entity taking them has exceeding its legally prescribed authority.) The ruling thus conflicts with the ECJ's doctrine in *Foto Frost*.

The decision rests on two interpretive pillars, both revelatory of how the Court understands the nature of the EC polity and Germany's place within it. First, the Court subjugated article 23 to article 38, which establishes that the Bundestag is to be elected by 'general, direct, free, equal, and secret' elections. The GFCC read article 38 to mean not only that Germans possessed a right to participate in such elections, but that 'the weakening, within the scope of article 23, of the legitimation of state power gained through an election' was prohibited. Thus, a vote of the Bundestag, issuing from legislative elections, constitutes the sole means of conferring legitimacy to acts of public authority within Germany, *including acts of the EC*. Second, the GFCC announced that it would view the expansion of supranational governance as compatible with the German constitution to the extent that member state governments 'retain their sovereignty', and 'thereby control integration'. Wilfully ignoring reality, the GFCC declared the EC to be a strictly 'intergovernmental Community', in which the government of each member state is a 'master' of the treaties, possessing the power to veto Community acts and the right to withdraw from the EC.

The operative part of its ruling is derived from these two interpretive moves. Most important, the Court declared that integration must, in order to conform to constitutional dictates, proceed 'predictably', that is, intergovernmentally. At the Community level, the German government negotiates and authorizes, by treaty law, whatever there is of EC governance; at the national level, the Bundestag legitimizes and transposes these authorizations in national law. The Court then asserted its jurisdiction over EC acts:

If . . . European institutions or governmental entities were to implement or develop the Maastricht Treaty in a manner no longer covered by the Treaty in the form of it upon which the German [ratification act] is based, any legal instrument arising from such activity would not be binding within German territory. German state institutions would be prevented, by reasons of constitutional law, from applying such legal instruments in Germany. Accordingly, the GFCC must examine the question of whether or not [these] legal instruments . . . may be considered to remain within the bounds . . . accorded to them, or whether they may be considered to exceed these bounds.

Thus, the GFCC possesses the authority to void any EC act having the effect of depriving German legislative organs of their substantive control over integration. In terms of constitutional review processes, litigants now possess the right to plead the *ultra vires* nature of Community acts before all German judges, who would then be obliged to initiate concrete review processes before the GFCC.

Not surprisingly, the GFCC's decision has been the target of sharp criticism, particularly by Community lawyers who see a repudiation of the underlying bases of European legal order. Weiler (1995), for example, sees a 'sad and pathetic decision' that employs 'a surface language of democracy', but ultimately rests on a 'deep structure' of ethno-centric nationalism. A glaring irony runs through the decision. Supranational aspects of the Treaty of European Union, such as the enhancement of certain powers of the European Parliament and the establishment of a general right to vote in local elections, sought to close, however slightly, the Community's democratic deficit. The revision of the German constitution, necessary for ratification of the Treaty, also strengthened democratic controls over integration.[17] Nevertheless, in privileging a traditional international law and organization approach to the EC, the Court legitimizes the very source of the alleged deficit: the Community's intergovernmental elements. The irony can be drawn out further. The process by which the treaties were constitutionalized, widely viewed as both strengthening the supranational and the democratic character of the Community/Union, escaped the control of national governments. Had the rules the GFCC laid down there been in place two decades earlier, the construction of an EC charter of rights, which the GFCC itself required in the name of democracy, would presumably have been unconstitutional.

---

[17] In addition to the revisions of art. 23 discussed above, the powers of Bundestag and Bundesrat committees to be informed of and to scrutinize the government's activities at the EC level were enhanced.

Summary

The constitutionalization of the treaty system generated a dynamic and inherently expansive set of dialogues between the ECJ and national judges on the nature of the relationship between the national and the Community legal orders. I have focused on the relatively formal attributes of these dialogues in this section. It is crucial to stress, however, that the evolution of the supremacy doctrine has steadily upgraded the capacity of both the ECJ and the national courts to intervene in policy processes, to shape political outcomes, and thus to provoke judicialization. In Chapters 4 and 5, I discussed the steady erosion of the principle according to which ordinary judges are prohibited from reviewing the legality of national statutes or refusing to apply them in conflicts that come before them. The elaboration of supremacy has worked in the same direction, further freeing ordinary judges from the dictatorship of statute (and legislative intent), while enhancing the ECJ's position as the locus point for the elaboration of EC constitutionalism. Supremacy, when coupled with the doctrine of direct effect, opens up the EC legal system to individual litigants, and thus potentially to the kinds of constitutional politics examined in Chapters 3–5.

CONSTITUTIONAL POLITICS AS LEGISLATIVE POLITICS

We now turn to constitutional politics in the European Community, focusing on the European Court's impact on policy processes and outcomes, and adapting the approach developed in previous chapters of the book to the study of integration.

The ECJ and Negative Integration

Negative integration (discussed above) is the process through which national barriers to intra-Community economic activity are removed. The European Court, activated by article 177 references, sustained this project during the post-Luxembourg Compromise period of intergovernmental stalemate, systematically removing national rules and administrative practices that hindered labour mobility and trade beginning in the 1970s. One such line of decisions, on the free movement of goods, turned out to be crucial to the politics that culminated in the Single European Act (SEA) of 1986. The SEA repudiated the Luxembourg Compromise, and reinstated qualified majority voting as the dominant legislative process for regulating the common market.

Free Movement of Goods and the Single Act 1969–86[18]

Articles 30–36 of the EEC Treaty constitutes the normative context for free movement. Article 30 prohibits the member states, after 31 December 1969, from maintaining 'quantitative restrictions [quotas] on imports' as well as 'all measures having equivalent effect'; article 33 empowers the Commission to adopt, on its own, secondary legislation to clarify and enforce article 30; and article 36 permits exceptions to the article 30 prohibition, on the grounds of public morality, public policy, public security, health, and cultural heritage. These provisions can be interpreted variously. What exactly are 'effects' that are equivalent to quotas, and what types of national measures produce them? What national measures, otherwise prohibited by article 30, could not be justified with reference to an article 36 exception? For that matter, what exactly is a 'public policy' exception? Pursuant to article 33, the Commission sought to resolve questions like these in a 1970 directive. The directive established a 'discrimination test': national rules that treat national goods differently than imported goods are considered to be measures prohibited under article 30. Almost immediately, however, the Court's jurisprudence rendered the Council's directive obsolete.

The leading decision is *Dassonville* (ECJ 1974c). In 1970, Mr Dassonville imported some Johnnie Walker Scotch Whiskey into Belgium, after having purchased it from a French supplier. When Dassonville put the whiskey on the market, he was prosecuted by Belgian authorities for having violated customs rules. The rules prohibited the importation from an EC country, in this case France, of spirits that originated in a third country, in this case Britain, unless French customs rules were substantially similar to those in place in Belgium. Dassonville was also sued by an Belgian importer who possessed, under Belgian law, an exclusive right to market Johnnie Walker in the country. Dassonville argued that, under the Treaty, goods that had entered France legally must be allowed to enter Belgium freely, and exclusive rights to import and market goods were not legally valid.

The case provided the Court with its first real opportunity to consider the meaning of article 30. Dismissing the objections of Britain and Belgium, both of which argued that such rules were not prohibited under article 30, the Court found for Dassonville, declaring the following:

[18] Based on Stone Sweet and Caporaso (1998).

All trading rules enacted by the Member States, which are capable of hindering, directly or indirectly, actually or potentially, intra-Community trade are to be considered as measures having an effect equivalent to quantitative restrictions.

Thus the Court replaced the Commission's discrimination test with a rigorous 'hindrance of trade' test (Gormley 1985: 22). National measures that negatively impact trade, even indirectly or potentially, are prohibited. If put to a vote, this Treaty interpretation—more expansively integrationist than any in circulation at the time—would not have been accepted by a majority, let alone all, of the member states.

The ruling posed a delicate policy problem for the Court. Ordering the wholesale removal of national regulations would strip away legal regimes serving otherwise legitimate public interests, such as the protection of public health, the environment, and the consumer. Further, given the Council's seeming inability to produce harmonized legislation in a timely fashion (partly a product of the Luxembourg compromise), this lack of protection could well become quasi-permanent. The ECJ resolved the problem by declaring that member states could, within reason, continue to regulate the production and sale of goods in the public's interest, pending harmonization by EC legislation. The Court stressed that: (1) the burden of proof rests with the member state to prove it has acted reasonably; (2) such regulations—as with national measures justified under article 36 grounds—could not 'constitute a disguised restriction on trade between member states'; and (3) the European judiciary would review the legality of these exceptions to article 30 on a case-by-case basis. The decision thus laid the foundations of what became an ongoing, normative discourse about the relationship of Treaty law, and its inherent purposes, and national regulatory regimes, and their purposes.

The 'Dassonville principles' have animated the Court's free movement jurisprudence to this day. They enabled the EC legal system, with the complicity of traders, to monitor member state behaviour, but also to shape national law by progressively elaborating the permissible exceptions to article 30 (Gormley 1985; Oliver 1988). More generally, virtually every important domain of negative integration is today governed by judicially constructed rules resembling, in their broad outline and logic, the Dassonville principles. That is, the Court works to remove barriers to the movement of persons, or to the provision of services, while requiring member states to justify such barriers on public interest grounds. The Court then controls the legality of these justifications with reference to proportionality doctrines.

The purely judicial construction of a common market on a case-by-case basis, although theoretically possible, would have been a slow and inefficient process. The (re-)construction of the Treaty law governing free movement, however, exerted a profound impact—a normative feedback effect—on the European polity as a whole. In 1979, the Court ruled, in *Cassis de Dijon*, that Germany could not prohibit the sale of a French liqueur merely because that liqueur did not conform to German standards (ECJ 1979). While a seemingly straightforward application of the *Dassonville* principles, the Court also declared that it could not divine:

[any] valid reason why, provided that they have been lawfully produced or marketed in one of the member states, alcoholic beverages should not be introduced into any other member states.

The Commission ran with the ruling. It immediately issued a communiqué abstracting from the decision a rule of general applicability, today called 'the principle of mutual recognition of national standards'. The Court had shown the Commission how member states might retain their own national rules, capable of being applied to the production and sale of domestic goods within the domestic market, while prohibiting member states from applying these same rules to goods originating elsewhere in order to hinder trade.

After *Dassonville* and *Cassis de Dijon*, levels of free movement litigation rose sharply, rulings of non-compliance proliferated, and national regulatory frameworks were placed in a creeping 'shadow of the law'. At the same time, the Commission, in alliance with transnational business coalitions, worked to convert member state governments to the idea that mutual recognition could constitute a general strategy for breaking intergovernmental deadlock. They were successful at doing so. The political science literature on the sources of the Single Act has sufficiently demonstrated the extent to which governments were dragged along in this process (Alter and Meunier-Aitshalia 1994; Dehousse 1994; Sandholtz and Zysman 1989; but Moravcsik 1995 disagrees). Governments acted, of course, in the form of a treaty that codified pro-integration solutions to their own collective action problems. But these solutions had already emerged, out of the structured interactions between traders, the Court, and the Commission; and they were given urgency by globalization and the failure of 'go it alone' policies to sustain economic growth.

Constitutional Rights and Negative Integration

In a development of enormous long-range importance, the ECJ has grafted
its (post-*Wachauf*) rights jurisdiction onto its case law relative to the
removal of barriers to exchange. Two cases, both decided in 1991, reveal the
potential of this new rights discourse to structure, but also to legitimize,
judicial control of national policies. In the *Commission* v. *the Netherlands*
(ECJ 1991*b*), the Court annulled a Dutch law requiring a fixed percentage
of all radio and television programmes broadcasted in Holland to be made
by a national production company. The Commission had attacked the law
as contrary to the freedom to provide services established by article 59
(EEC). The Dutch government justified the law as a permissible derogation
from article 59, on the grounds that the rule was designed to further a 'general good' and a 'fundamental right' that it called 'cultural pluralism': the
right of Dutch audiences to a Dutch point of view. The Court took the
opportunity to state (echoing national constitutional courts) that pluralism, 'connected [to] freedom of expression, as protected by article 10 of the
European Convention on Human Rights', indeed constituted one of the
'fundamental rights guaranteed by the Community legal order'. It found no
compelling link between the Dutch law and the protection of rights, however.

In the second case, *Grogan*, the European Court was asked to review
Irish abortion law (ECJ 1991*c*). Although abortion has never been legal in
Ireland, its status was constitutionalized in a 1983 amendment to the constitution which declares that 'the State acknowledges the right to life of the
unborn and . . . guarantees in its law to respect, to defend, and to vindicate
that right'. In a 1988 decision, the Irish Supreme Court read the amendment to prohibit family planning clinics and medical health professionals
from counselling women about alternatives to carrying their pregnancies
to term. In protest, student organizations in several Irish universities produced and distributed information on obtaining abortions outside of
Ireland, particularly in Britain, whereupon they were prosecuted. The students claimed that EC law established fundamental rights to obtain information about the availability of abortion services in the Community, as
well as to travel to obtain those services. Thus two fundamental rights were
potentially in conflict.

In its decision, the European Court ruled that the provision of abortions
did constitute a 'service' under EC law, and that fundamental rights guaranteed by the Community were at issue. None the less, the students lost.
The ECJ ruled that

the link between the activity of the students' associations . . . and medical termi-nations of pregnancies in another member state is too tenuous for the prohibition on the distribution of information to be capable of being regarded as a restriction within the meaning of art. 59.

The Court thus sidestepped a political landmine (although it implied that foreign abortion clinics could not be prohibited from advertising their ser-vices directly in Ireland).

As these two cases demonstrate, the Court has positioned itself as the balancer of constitutional rights guaranteed under the Community's con-stitution, against the general interest expressed in member state policy. Further, the Irish abortion case indicates that as constitutionalization deepens, potentially any national legal controversy can be transformed into a Community dispute, under the rubric of a conflict between Community rights and national rights.

The ECJ and Positive Integration

Whereas negative integration results in the removal of barriers to integra-tion, positive integration results in the construction of EC legal regimes that replace national ones. In positive integration processes, governments would seem to have enhanced means of controlling policy outcomes: a minority of Council members can veto secondary legislation; and, in con-sequence, lowest common denominator regulations and directives can be expected. If we restrict the empirical domain of positive integration to the process by which the Council of Ministers adopts secondary legislation, then governmental control of policy outcomes appears to be quite obvious. However, if we expand the empirical domain of positive integration to include judicial processes that have taken place both before and after the EC's legislative institutions adopt secondary legislation, then the Council's control of process and outcomes can only be an open empirical question. I argue here, again, that the legal system responds to and provokes the expansionary logic of judicialization. This dynamic undermines member state control and enhances the power of private actors, national judges, and the EC's supranational institutions within policy-making processes.

The ECJ's impact on positive integration (the elaboration of EC legisla-tion) can be studied exactly as we studied the legislative impact of national constitutional courts: as a constitutional politics of anticipatory reaction and corrective revision. As the Single Act example indicates, the European Court relies a great deal on the Commission—whereas national courts rely heavily on parliamentary oppositions—to give its case law dynamic agency.

There are dozens of instances of ECJ decisions effectively 'judicializing' European and national legislative processes (see Berlin 1992). In 1986, for example, the ECJ (1986b, *Nouvelles Frontières*) invalidated certain price-fixing policies of a national airline, widespread across the EC, ruling that such policies violated competition rules residing in the EEC treaty. The Court then all but ordered the EC to liberalize the airline transport regime by legislation. Within weeks, the Commission initiated legal actions against the practices of several nation states and, in 1987, the Council of Ministers approved a package of legislation, inspired by the ECJ's juris-prudence (O'Reilly and Stone Sweet 1998). Dramatic moves to liberalize national telecommunication systems, and to reregulate the regime at the European level, were also provoked by ECJ rulings and the consequent strengthening of the Commission's position within EC policy processes (Sandholtz 1998). In these cases, judicial policy-making and the threat of future censure prompted Community legislators, who had been dragging their feet, to act.

Such examples reveal only part of the story. Because the ECJ interacts simultaneously with both national and supranational legislators, the full impact of its rulings can only be understood by paying attention to policy-making processes and outcomes at both levels at once. At the member state level, ECJ rulings declaring laws incompatible with EC law routinely gen-erate corrective revision processes. As the ECJ interprets EC law, it gradu-ally rewrites it. An EC directive may have meant one thing to the Commission, to the governments that have adopted the directive in the Council, and to the national legislatures that transposed the directive into national law. As the directive is litigated and then interpreted by courts, however, it may come to mean something very different. Sometimes the Court's jurisprudence forces national parliaments to adapt, or to harmon-ize, the provisions of a censored statute with the Court's jurisprudence. This type of corrective revision takes place under the surveillance of poten-tial litigators and national judges.

Gender Equality 1975–95

An important example is the elaboration of EC law governing the equal treatment of men and women in the workplace (based on Stone Sweet and Caporaso 1998). The formal treaty basis for social provisions (articles 117–122) is thin: it establishes the competence of the Community's insti-tutions to develop social policy, without laying down content-based duties binding on the member states. The great exception is article 119, which obliges the member states to ensure that men and women receive 'equal pay for equal work'. The rationale for article 119 was related to market integration: labour is treated as a commodity and a factor of production; and member states should not be able to obtain productivity advantages by allowing wage discrimination.

In *Defrenne II* (ECJ 1976*b*), the Court ruled that article 119 was directly effective, and could therefore be invoked by women in litigation initiated in national courts. But the Court went further, declaring that the very principle of equal pay for equal work, and more broadly, non-discrimination, comprised 'part of the social objectives of the Community, which is not merely an economic union, but is at the same time intended . . . to ensure social progress and seek the constant improvement of the living standards and working conditions of [its] peoples'. Thus the Court, through the window of article 119, envisioned a social Community. Three pieces of secondary legislation served to focus this vision: the Equal Pay Directive (1975), the Equal Treatment Directive (1976), and the Social Security Directive (1979). Each was adopted under unanimity voting rules. I foreshadow what is to come by noting that article 177 references drove a process that converted article 119 and these three directives into expansive, judicially enforceable rights attaching to EC citizens, at a time when the concept of EC citizenship and EC rights was still in its infancy.

I now turn to law-making and litigation in the area. It is well known that the British government has constituted the crucial veto point in Council deliberations on the three major pieces of legislation that have been adopted (Pillinger 1992, 85–101). Generally, the British government has diligently vetoed Commission proposals that would have enshrined, in EC law, rules that were not already present in British statutes. A large body of scholarship exists on litigation of equal pay and non-discrimination on the impact of ECJ's case law on the British legal system (e.g. Ellis 1991; Kenney 1992, 1994, 1996; Prechal and Burrows 1990). This literature has shown that the ECJ has used its powers to expand the Community's jurisdiction over important areas of social policy, while shrinking member state control. British Conservative governments of the 1980s and 1990s, who have staunchly opposed the Court's interpretation of the law in this area, have been forced by national court decisions to ask parliament, on successive occasions over the past fifteen years, to amend British statutes to conform to the ECJ's evolving case law.

As these adjustments have been well documented, I will focus here on how British efforts to contain the development of EU law in this field have failed. Britain has pursued a clear and consistent strategy in the Council of

Ministers, one designed to anticipate and then seal off pathways that might lead to the pre-emption of national by supranational authority. Thus, it has refused to support any secondary legislation containing provisions that would innovate, when compared with the state of existing British law, in the area of equal pay and non-discrimination. And it has written into directives detailed 'exceptions'—derogations to the proposed rules—the purpose of which is to permit practices which, although lawful under British law, would be rendered, in the absence of the exception, unlawful under the proposed directive.

Despite these efforts, the Court has consistently interpreted the directives progressively, obliterating the containment devices erected by the British and other governments. A few examples will suffice. During Council negotiations on the Equal Pay Directive, Britain insisted on writing into the Council's minutes its understanding of the relationship between article 1 of the directive and British law, namely, that the latter already conforms to the obligations to be laid down by the former. Article 1.1 of the Equal Pay Directive of 1975 calls for the 'elimination of discrimination on grounds of sex' for 'the same work' or 'for work to which equal value is attributed'. The provision employs language that is not contained in article 119 of the Treaty, which speaks only of 'equal work', and not 'equal work of equal value'. The relevant British rules then in place defined 'equal work' restrictively, as 'like work', as when a man and a woman perform essentially the same job. Article 1.2 then goes on to state that job classification schemes may be used to determine when 'unlike work' might none the less be of equivalent value. British statutes on the matter recognized a woman's right to equal pay for work of 'equal value', but only after, first, her employer had commissioned a study of the sources and effects of how tasks in any workplace setting were organized along gender lines and, second, that this study had determined that women were being systematically routed into lower paying jobs. Under British law, however, women employees could not require their employers to commission such a study. In the Council, Britain thought they had preserved this situation.

In 1982, the Court ruled on the lawfulness of British rules (ECJ 1982). In its argument before the Court, Britain relied on a literal reading of the directive: according to article 1.1, 'equal value' must be 'attributed' by some means; the only means to attribute equal value that is recognized in the directive is that which is found in British practice—the evaluation of job classification practices; and, the directive does not confer a right on employees to demand—or an obligation on employers to commission—such an evaluation. Last, Britain argued that its support of the directive in the Council was contingent on the reading of the directive just given, and referenced the Council's minutes on the matter.

The Court rejected these arguments, stating that the situation under British law 'amount[ed] to a denial of the very existence of a right to equal pay for equal of equal value where no [evaluation of] classification has been made'. The judges then declared that, in national law, 'a worker must be entitled to claim . . . that his work has the same value as other work and, if that is the case, to have his rights under the Treaty and the Directive acknowledged by a binding decision'. In phrasing its ruling in this way, the Court had effectively: (1) conferred a judicially enforceable right on individuals (to have the value of their work evaluated for the purpose of determining the existence of discrimination in pay); *and* (2) anchored that right in the Treaty (although the Treaty says nothing about equal pay for work of equal value). Interpreting the provisions of a directive in terms of Treaty law is a common technique in this area of EC law. Among other things, this technique displaces the Council of Ministers as the site of reversal: to overturn this decision, and many others like it, member state governments would have to reassemble as a constituent assembly, and then revise the Treaty. In this case, the impact of the Court was swiftly registered: Britain amended its law to conform with the Court's ruling (Ellis 1991: 99–101).

The Court has also bypassed other containment devices built into directives, including those exceptions which reflect important, and unambiguously stated, national interests. Article 1.2 of the Equal Treatment Directive, which laid down the principles of non-discrimination on the basis of sex in employment, promotions, and working conditions, excluded from the purview of the directive all pension and retirement schemes. A series of decisions pursuant to article 177 references originating in Britain eroded the legal consequences of this exception. In *Marshall I* (ECJ 1986c, discussed further below), the Court was faced with an alleged violation of article 5 of the directive, which extends equal treatment to 'conditions governing dismissal'. Ms Marshall, a dietitian working for a British Health Authority, had been forced to retire at 60 years of age, whereas the mandatory retirement age for male employees was fixed at 65. The retirement deprived Marshall of certain pension benefits. In its decision, the Court announced that the provision excluding of 'social security matters from the scope of [the] directive, must be interpreted strictly [i.e. narrowly], in view of the fundamental importance of the principle of equal treatment', thus relegating article 1.2 to a position of inferior status. The ECJ then grounded its decision on article 5: 'the dismissal of a woman solely because she has attained the qualifying age for a state pension, which age is different under national legislation for men and women, constitutes discrimination on grounds of sex, contrary to [the] Directive'.

In its post-Marshall case law, the Court went on to pre-empt the Council as the Community's legislator in this field. In 1990, in *Barber* (ECJ 1990*b*) the Court enacted, as a matter of Treaty interpretation, the basic terms of a directive designed to extend non-discrimination to certain old-age pensions. First proposed by the Commission in 1987, France and Britain had blocked the directive's adoption in the Council (Curtin 1990). Ruling that certain types of pension benefits constituted pay, and that therefore the provision of these benefits must conform to the principle of non-discrimination proclaimed by article 119, the Court ordered the British government to compensate Mr Barber for pension payments lost due to discriminatory rules permitting women to retire earlier than men. In an extraordinary example of a court freely admitting the policy consequences of its own activism, the Court sought to mitigate what the member states had characterized, at oral argument, as the 'serious financial consequences' retrospective compensation for all victims of such policies would pose for national budgets. 'The member states and other parties concerned', the Court declared, 'were reasonably entitled to consider that article 119 did not apply to pensions' before its ruling, and that therefore only pending and future litigation would be subject to the new rules.

The pre-emption of the Council in *Barber* is not an isolated incident in the domain of equal pay and non-discrimination.[19] In *Dekker* (ECJ 1991*d*), the Court enacted, by judicial decision, the main elements of the pregnancy directive that had been opposed by Britain. The case, referred by a Dutch court, was brought by a woman who had been denied a teaching position at a youth training centre. The centre's hiring committee informed Ms. Dekker, three months pregnant at the time, that although she was the best candidate for the job, they could not hire her because its employment insurance did not cover sick leave for illnesses that (a) would occur during the first six months of employment, if (b) these illnesses could be anticipated at the time of hiring. At issue was the interpretation of article 2 of the Equal Treatment Directive prohibiting employment discrimination on the grounds of sex, marital, or family status. Dekker, supported by the Commission, argued that the centre's decision constituted sex discrimination, since women but not men can become pregnant. In its observation to

---

[19] I am aware of yet another example. In *Hertz* (ECJ 1990*c*), the Court enacted the main terms of the 'burden of proof' directive, proposed by the Commission, and designed to place the burden of proof on the member states in certain cases involving maternity and sex discrimination. The directive had been blocked by a British veto.

the Court, Britain argued that the directive requires only that men and women be treated equally when they 'become unable to work' for health reasons. The ECJ agreed with the Commission, and ordered national judges to apply national laws as if they distinguished pregnancy from 'illness'. In 1992, the Council adopted the pregnancy directive, catching up to the Court.

Finally, I illustrate one of the core arguments of the book, namely, that the progressive elaboration of constitutional rules generates an expansionary dynamic tending to recast policy processes and outcomes. Consider the combined impact of two very different sex discrimination cases on the work of British courts. As noted above, in the 1986 *Marshall I* case the Court declared that British law requiring women to retire earlier than men violated the Equal Treatment Directive, and ordered British judges not only to apply British law in conformity with the ECJ's equal treatment case law, but to compensate Marshall for her losses. Compensation, however, proved to be a difficult task. Although the British industrial tribunal assessed damages at £19,405 plus interest, the British sex discrimination act set a ceiling for such awards at £6,250, and excluded interest payments. On reference of the matter by the House of Lords, the Court ruled, in *Marshall II* (ECJ 1993), that EC law requires 'full and complete compensation' (including interest), and that national rules that did not meet this standard be set aside by national judges.

In the second case, *Webb* (ECJ 1994), the ECJ declared that provisions of Britain's Sex Discrimination Act of 1975 must be construed by British courts so that they would conform to *Dekker*. In 1987, Mrs Webb was hired by an air cargo company to replace a female clerk who was scheduled for maternity leave. During her training period, Webb discovered that she was pregnant. The company dismissed her, on the grounds that she was no longer able to do the job for which she was hired. Webb lost a succession of appeals, including a unanimous judgment of the high court in Britain, the House of Lords. British courts distinguished between *Dekker*, which prohibits the dismissal of a woman simply because she is pregnant, and Webb's dismissal, which was due to Webb's failure to fulfil her contract. Further, the Lords, backed in oral argument by the British government, had determined that discrimination was not at issue, since if a male employee had been hired to replace a pregnant woman and then requested an extended leave of absence, he too would have been dismissed. The Lords nevertheless agreed to refer the matter to the ECJ. The European Court, in a terse decision, found for Webb, strongly implying that the legal questions raised had already been decided by *Dekker*.

The *Dekker* and *Webb* line of cases, coupled with the *Marshall II* requirement for full compensation, opened a floodgate of claims from women discharged from the British armed forces. In the 1978–90 period, some 5,500
women were discharged on the grounds that pregnancy made them unable
to perform their duties. Before *Marshall,* following the government's
understanding of EC law on the matter,[20] the Defence Ministry began settling claims at £3,000 per woman. In settlements reached after *Marshall,*
courts awarded one woman £33,000 plus pension rights, and an air force
pilot £173,000. As of Spring 1994, 1,800 compensation claims were pending (Current Survey 1994: 221).

Principal–Agent Issues

The EC legal system operates according to a generalizeable dynamic, and
this dynamic is broadly congruent with theory of judicialization that
underlies this book. Individual litigants, pursuing their own or representing a group's interests, ask national judges to void national rules or practices in favour of EC rules within a particular domain of activity. The
interaction between national courts and the ECJ recasts the law governing
that domain of activity, and therefore recasts the policy-making environment. As new rules are generated and existing rules are reinterpreted,
member states, whose national rules are now out of step with EC rules, are
placed 'in the shadow of the law': they can expect to be the target of litigation until they act to comply with the dictates of the ECJ's case law. Further,
that case law enhances the capacity of individuals to initiate future litigation, by providing potential litigants with more precise information about
the content and scope of European law. In short, we find the dynamics of
judicialization that resemble those found in Chapters 3 and 4.

It is clear that the member states, as principals, have not been able to
control the activities of their agent very effectively. In the negotiations leading to the Single Act, governments adjusted their interests to the interests
of traders, and to the ECJ's jurisprudence on free movement. The governments did not reverse the *Dassonville* line of case law (ECJ 1974c), nor did
they succeed in maintaining the Luxembourg compromise. Instead,
increasingly cognizant of the costs associated with maintaining disparate
national regulatory regimes, they ratified the Court's moves, and reduced
the intergovernmental aspect of the Council of Ministers, and therefore of
the EC. In the social provisions field, policy outcomes, as fixed by directives

[20] In *Marshall I* (ECJ 1986c), the British government had argued that EC law required
only that compensation be possible under national law, not that it be full and complete.

adopted by the Council of Ministers and by national legal regimes controlled by member state governments and parliaments, have not remained. The ECJ has interpreted directives broadly, in terms of their effects on individuals, as bearers of rights guaranteed under EC constitutional—not just secondary—law. Member state interpretations of these directives, to the extent that they would reduce the effectiveness of individual rights, have been pushed aside. Further, the Court has supplanted the Council as the locus of law-making on more than one occasion, enacting legislative provisions that had stalled in the Council under unanimity voting. Lacking the unanimity necessary to reverse the Court in this area, the member state governments have been forced to adapt to the Court's case law, by ratifying the ECJ's policy choices in Council directives, and by revising national legal regimes.

This last point deserves more discussion. In response to the *Barber* decision (ECJ 1990*b*), the member states addressed themselves as a constituent assembly to a decision of the Court. In the so-called 'Barber Protocol', attached to the Maastricht Treaty on European Union, the member states declared that

the direct effect of article 119 may not be relied upon in order to claim entitlement to a pension with effect from a date prior to that of this judgment [the ruling in *Barber*, 17 May 1990], except in the case of workers . . . who have before that date initiated legal proceedings or raised an equivalent claim under the applicable national law.

The Protocol does not reverse the Court's ruling. On the contrary, the Protocol selects, from among several possible interpretations, one way to understand the temporal effects of its decision, and asserts that this is the correct interpretation. Simply stated, their preferred interpretation gives the member states the longest period possible to adjust to the dictates of article 119 (as interpreted by the Court in *Barber*). As principals, the member states have acted but, relative to the means at their disposal, only weakly. While a definitive evaluation of how effective the Protocol will be in constraining the Court is premature,[21] a recent study of post-Protocol judgments reveals that the member states have *not* induced the Court to abandon its pre-Protocol case law (Whiteford 1996). Thus, again, we find

---

[21] The legal status of the Barber Protocol is ambiguous. Even if we accept that the Protocol enjoys a rank equivalent to that of Treaty provision, the problem of how to resolve a potential conflict between the terms of the Protocol and conflicting Treaty provisions remains. The Court's ruling in *Barber* is based on an authoritative interpretation of art. 119 of the Treaty, and the Protocol may well have been meant to enshrine rules that are contrary to art. 119 (see Hervey 1994).

that intergovernmental capacity to control judicial outcomes is limited, even when governments—unanimously—try to do so.

In other areas as well, governments have ratified, rather than reversed, the Court's most important moves. They have done so implicitly, by not reversing the ECJ's case law on supremacy and direct effect, for example. But they have also done so explicitly, by giving formal treaty basis to some of the Court's most innovative doctrines. Thus, in negotiations on the Single European Act, the member states followed the Commission's lead on mutual recognition, not least, because the ECJ's free movement case law made it clear that mutual recognition had quickly become formal law anyway (see Dehousse 1994: 92–5). In 1977, after the Court had constructed a charter of rights and granted to itself jurisdiction over that charter, the European Parliament, the Commission, and the Council adopted a joint resolution approving the move. In the Treaty on European Union (chapter F),[22] the member states simply echoed the Court: 'the Union shall respect fundamental rights as guaranteed by the European Convention on Human Rights . . . and as they result from the constitutional traditions common to the member states as general principles of Community law'. Nor is this statement simply symbolic. Recent cases, such as *Commission* v. *Netherlands* (ECJ 1991*b*) provide important evidence that member states have begun to defend themselves, in cases involving Community fundamental rights, in the language of rights. Thus, they have legitimized the ECJ's construction of a rights discourse and, ultimately, the centrality of the Court's position as constitutional balancer of rights against the general interest. As I argued in Chapter 5, judicialization serves to legitimize the judge.

On the other hand, intergovernmental attempts to constrain the Court's impact have been weak and few. A declaration annexed to the Single Act, stating that the 31 December 1992 deadline for completion of the internal market did not 'create an automatic legal effect', was the first formal attempt. The member states sought to ensure, in the event of failure to meet the deadline, that 'the Court was not to assume responsibility for filling in the gaps' (Arnull 1994: 7). The intergovernmental negotiations leading to the adoption of the Treaty on European Union yielded several such restrictions. Article L of the Treaty of European Union excludes from the Court's jurisdiction foreign and security policy, and cooperation on justice and immigration, two 'pillars' of the new European Union. Two Protocols

---

[22] The Treaty of European Union also endorsed the ECJ's post-*Francovich* (ECJ 1991*a*) jurisprudence on governmental liability (art. 171), and on the certain powers of the EP (art. 173).

attached to the Treaty addressed recent ECJ jurisprudence. The failure of the first, the 'Barber Protocol', to control outcomes has been discussed. The second, the 'Grogan Protocol', demanded by the Irish government, declares that 'nothing in the Treaty of European Union shall effect that application in Ireland of [the prohibition on abortion contained] in the Constitution of Ireland'. Even adopting a broad definition of measures designed 'to reign in the Court', what measures that have been adopted can hardly be considered 'court curbing'. Rather, they constitute tepid efforts to constrain the *potential* impact of judicial policy-making, an acknowledgment on the part of the member states of the Court's demonstrated capacity to pre-empt the Council and national parliaments.

Like all European constitutional courts, the European Court of Justice has used its constitutional review powers to expand the relevance of constitutional law within policy-making processes, thereby altering the nature of the polity. The capacity of the principal (the member states) to constrain the behaviour of its agent (the ECJ), however, is conditioned by restrictive decision rules, and the fact that one of the agent's basic functions is to exercise control over the principals themselves. A constitutional court can be effectively reigned in, but only by revision of the constitution, requiring the unanimous vote of the member states. Thus, the factor that undergirds strong intergovernmental elements of the Community—the requirement of unanimity—also undermines the ability of the member state governments to control the Court once it has rendered a judgment.

CONCLUSION

European legal integration, provoked by the European Court and sustained by litigants and national judges, has gradually but inexorably transformed the nature of European governance. It has not only displaced the traditional, state-centric, 'international regime' of the diplomat and the international relations scholar (Stone 1994*b*). It altered, within a very wide zone in Western Europe, how individuals and companies pursue their interests, how judges resolve disputes, and how policy is made. By binding together the European and the national legal orders, in complex but highly structured ways, the constitutionalization of the treaty system has served to enhance the policy-making role of both the ECJ and ordinary judges. In today's multi-tiered European polity, the sovereignty of the legislature, and the primacy of national executives, are dead. In concert or in rivalry, European legislators govern with judges.

7

Theory of Constitutional Politics

I now present a theory of constitutional politics, and summarize some of the book's main findings. The theory is causal in that I specify the mechanisms—the connections among otherwise autonomous factors and processes—that serve to generate specific outcomes. Notwithstanding important differences among cases (the sources and consequences of which are identified in Chapters 2–5), this chapter focuses on those dynamics that are more or less generalizeable across cases. In particular, I wish to explain, first, how legislators are gradually placed under the tutelage of the constitutional court or, more precisely, the pedagogical authority of constitutional case law and, second, why the techniques of constitutional decision-making, as developed and employed by constitutional judges, tend to diffuse to other public authorities. Although I do not deal explicitly with European legal integration in this chapter, it should be apparent how the theoretical materials presented here can be adapted to help explain the construction of the EC legal system, and the attendant judicialization of EC policy-making (see Chapter 6 and Stone Sweet and Caporaso 1998).

THE JUDICIALIZATION OF LAW-MAKING

Figure 7.1 depicts a model of the process through which a particular mode of governance—characterized by the interdependence of legislating and constitutional adjudication—emerges and is institutionalized. The theory breaks down this process into four stages, each a chronological shift along a circular path, moving clockwise. I have labelled the right hemisphere of the model, stages 2 and 3, *depicts the politicization of constitutional justice.* By *politicization*, I mean (a) the move to activate constitutional review in order to alter legislative outcomes or the state of the constitutional law, and (b) the situation that constitutional judges find themselves as a results of this move. The left hemisphere, stages 4 and 1 of the model, *depicts the*

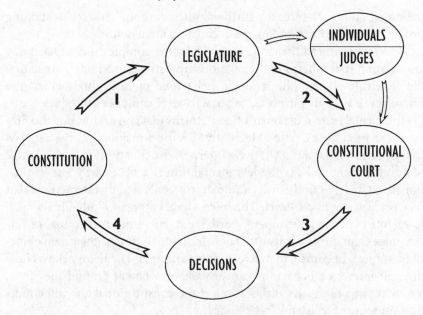

FIG. 7.1. *The evolution of constitutional politics*

judicialization of law-making. By *judicialization*, I mean (a) the production, by constitutional judges, of a formal normative discourse that serves to clarify, on an ongoing basis, the constitutional rules governing the exercise of legislative power, and (b) the reception of these rules, and of the terms of this discourse, by legislators.

Under certain conditions, politicization produces judicialization. We do not expect to find one without the other. Levels of judicialization vary—cross-nationally, and across policy sectors within the same polity—as a function of the relative intensity of the relationships between legislators and constitutional judges. This relationship depends, in the first place, on an institutional environment that enables and encourages delegation to the court. In the second place, it depends on developments internal to the law, that is, on how judges have resolved prior constitutional conflicts. Judicialization, the impact of constitutional decision-making on subsequent legislative processes and outcomes, constitutes a feedback effect. The sequence—constitutional conflict → delegation to the constitutional court → constitutional decision-making/rule-making → judicialization—has a tendency to regenerate itself. That is, each iteration of the sequence tends to expand the grounds for future politicization, for future interventions by the court and, therefore, for further judicialization. This self-sustaining property is at the heart of European constitutional politics.

Movement around the circle is driven by the complex mix of harmony and tension that inheres in the relationship between normative structure, the macro-level, and the strategic behaviour of individual actors, the micro-level. For our purposes, the macro-level comprises three elements: (1) the formal system of constitutional norms that constrains, but also creatively shapes, the exercise of legislative decision-making; (2) the case law of those courts that authoritatively interpret the constitution in the course of adjudication; and (3) the less formal, but not necessarily less institutionalized, behavioural norms and patterns generated by interactions that take place at the micro-level. The micro-level comprises individuals, such as members of the government, parliament, constitutional courts, ordinary judges, and private litigants. These individuals pursue their own objectives, subject, of course, to macro-level constraints. The theory shows how this self-interested behaviour can provoke movement around the circle, and why the progressive elaboration of the constitutional law will condition subsequent legislative behaviour.

Although what happens at any given stage partly depends on what has happened in previous stages, the discussion focuses on what is analytically distinct about each shift.

Shift 1: The Constitution and the Legislature

Although the ideology of parliamentary sovereignty (majority rule; the general will) retains a hold on the European legislator's self-identity, its grip has been steadily undermined by the rise of a counter ideology, that of modern constitutionalism. The constitution is a body of higher law norms that, among other things, governs the production of statute. It establishes the legislative institutions, fixes certain legislative procedures, and announces human rights, in the form of a long list of vaguely expressed, ideologically charged, but nevertheless formal constraints on the substantive content of statute. Due to the existence of an enforcement mechanism—constitutional review as exercised by the constitutional court—the normativity of the constitution, and therefore of rights provisions, is a brute fact of the legislator's world.

The spectre of constitutional censure hovers over the legislative process. Or, more precisely, it does so as long as law-makers believe that the court, in the exercise of its constitutional review authority, will invalidate statutes it judges to be in violation of the constitution. Given this simple condition—the expectation that constitutional judges will respectably do their jobs—the government and parliament have an interest in anticipating the court's likely response to a *future* claim that a legislative bill under discussion is unconstitutional. If, subsequent to such an exercise, legislators actually do constrain their behaviour in a manner that affects the terms of a future legislative act, then the court will have exercised a form of legislative power, the impact of which is indirect and deterrent. It is difficult, perhaps impossible, for legislators, in the beginning and in the absence of an existing case law relevant to the bill being debated, to know with precision the nature of the constitutional constraints that face them. At this point, then, governments and parliaments possess relatively more discretion, but exercise that discretion in the face of constitutional uncertainty.

Fear of constitutional censure alone is enough to lead legislators to treat the constitutional law as directly relevant, and immediately urgent, to their activity. But there are other reasons no less important. Legislators easily and naturally express their ideological differences as conflicts about the nature and content of rights. Indeed, the rights provisions we find in contemporary European constitutions reflect, rather than harmonize, the opposed visions of society held by the political parties at the time the constitution was negotiated. The existence of judicially enforceable rights ratchets up the political stakes of constitutional development, because it raises the possibility that rights provisions may be developed in one direction rather than another, thus privileging some policy routes and closing off others. We should not be surprised, therefore, to see political parties working, often fiercely, to implement their own version of a right, or of a proper balance between two rights, in legislation. When they do, legislators deliberate the constitutional law: they establish the context for how rights are understood; and they push the development of the constitution in specific directions.

Thus, the constitution has the capacity not only to constrain legislative behaviour, but to produce practice.

Shift 2: Politicization—The Move to Constitutional Review

The European constitutional court is not self-activating. Consequently, it can evolve into a political actor worthy of our attention only with the complicity of individuals who would initiate review processes. Individuals go to the court to alter legislative regimes already in place, and/or to revise the constitution rules governing in a specific policy domain, as long as the costs of activating the court do not outweigh these potential benefits.

Where abstract review exists, legislative and constitutional review processes are nested in one other. The normal legislative process looks like this: government (drafts bills) → parliament (deliberates, amends, and adopts bills). After promulgation, the legislative process gives way to administrative and judicial processes (entry into force, interpretation, application, enforcement, and litigation of statute). An abstract review referral adds another stage, that of constitutional review, wherein the court, in effect, undertakes a final 'reading' of a referred statute. The modified legislative process looks like this: government → parliament → constitutional court (review of constitutionality). Because abstract review is an efficacious mechanism of constitutional control—the court must review those statutes that are referred; statutory provisions deemed unconstitutional by the court are immediately voided; and no appeal of the court's decisions is possible—the procedure is an efficacious instrument of parliamentary opposition.

The rules governing the exercise of constitutional review differ radically from the rules governing parliamentary decision-making. This difference is exactly what attracts the opposition to the court, since under majority decision rules, the opposition always loses. Because the court is not a parliamentary chamber, but a judge of the constitution, the move to the constitutional review stage recasts the strategic environment in which legislators find themselves. (More will be said about the law-making consequences of this move later.) At this point, it is enough to note that the referral instantaneously redistributes political initiative in the opposition's favour, and reduces the influence of the government and the parliamentary majority over legislative outcomes. The government and its majority are placed on the defensive, forced to participate, as a co-equal party, in processes that they can neither block nor control.

For the opposition, the immediate costs of referral are virtually zero, while the potential gains are enormous. It bears the expense of drafting the referral, a legal argument, addressed to the court, stating why the law being referred is unconstitutional. Given the expansiveness of constitutional rights provisions, transforming a partisan struggle into a formal juridical conflict turns out to be a relatively simple exercise. If a legislative bill is important, it will usually generate a rights claim with partisan implications. The longer-term costs of going to the court are, however, potentially great. If and when a party of opposition becomes the party of government, it may find itself caught in the same web of constitutional constraints that it had helped to construct. In addition, the court could side with the government, and develop constitutional rules in a direction antithetical to the opposition's own programme. (In practice, the lure of short-run benefits have generally outweighed long-run concerns. When they are in power, political parties complain of the court's growing authority over the legislative process but, in opposition, they exploit, without apology, the capacity of constitutional review to obstruct majority rule.)

Although the legislator's law has traditionally been conceived as a corpus of sovereign commands absolutely binding upon the judiciary, concrete review jurisdiction formally undermines the sovereign status of statute, subjugating it to judicially initiated controls. Ordinary judges are responsible for detecting possible violations of the constitutional law by the legislator (and by those who administer statutory provisions), for sending these to the constitutional court for review, and for setting aside statutes that the constitutional court has declared unconstitutional. In addition, the direct, juridical, effect of the constitutional rights has expanded opportunities for judges to apply the constitution, as law, on their own, thus weakening further their subservience to the legislator. Private individuals, companies, and interest groups who want to provoke changes in statutes, and to build constraints on the exercise of legislative power in the future, have an interest in bringing litigation that raises constitutional objections. Of course, court actions can be costly, but these costs will be evaluated both with reference to potential benefits, and to the costs of alternative strategies, such as lobbying political parties and the government. The result is that judicial processes have become sites of policy-making that supplement, and at times rival, the legislature. In systems in which the individual complaint procedure exists, this outcome is reinforced, since litigants can appeal judicial decisions (denying standing or their constitutional claims) and statutes (under certain conditions) directly to the constitutional court.

Shift 3: The Crisis of Legitimacy

The politicization of constitutional review poses a potentially intractable dilemma for the constitutional judge. On the one hand, the political legitimacy of the constitutional court (as for adjudicatory bodies more generally), rests partly on the perception that it is neutral, both with respect to the specific disputants, and to the policy dispute that has erupted in parliament. On the other hand, in resolving the dispute, the court may compromise its reputation for neutrality by declaring one party, let us say the government, the loser. In any case, that is what the opposition (or litigating party) hopes will happen. We can express this dilemma as a fundamental, institutional interest: the interest of the constitutional court is to resolve legislative conflicts about constitutionality, while maintaining, or reinforcing, the political legitimacy of constitutional review into the future.

In pursuit of this objective, the court deploys two main tactics. First, it defends its behaviour normatively, as both enabled and constrained by constitutional rules. The judges commonly treat the relevant constitution provisions, and their own extant case law, as if both provide, in and of themselves, all of the necessary materials for the resolution of the dispute. They pretend to ignore the political context that generates conflicts, focusing all public attention on how they have reasoned through the constitution, and on how they have conceptualized the relationship between relevant constitutional norms and the work of the legislator (or other public authority). In doing so, the court seeks to demonstrate that the policy consequences of the decision are second order effects that are not of themselves desired by the judges, but rather are required by the law. Second, the court anticipates political reactions to its decisions. The tactic, entirely extralegal in nature, leads the judges to try to limit negative reactions by, for example, deferring to majority will, or fashioning settlements that avoid the declaration of a clear winner or loser. These tactics may be combined.

Anticipating analysis proper to stage 4, the following proposition is implied. The more politically controversial the policy conflict to be resolved, the more acute the court's dilemma and, therefore, the more we will expect the court to produce: a partial victory for both the opposition and the government; a complex constitutional justification for its decision; and a set of rules governing how such issues ought to be settled in the future. The court does so in order to secure or further enhance the centrality of constitutional decision-making as an essential element of parliamentary governance now and for the future.[1]

Shift 4: Constitutional Decision-making and Rule-making

By *constitutional decision-making*, I mean the process of determining the meaning of a given constitutional provision (or set of provisions) in order to resolve a dispute about the constitutionality of a public act, including

---

[1] Although constitutional judges both legislate and revise the constitution constantly, I neither assumed that judges wish for legislative powers, nor that they enjoy exercising legislative authority. And I do not rely on claims (which I find compelling) that individual judges will seek to impose their own policy preferences by way of their decisions. Instead, I assume that judges behave defensively, that is, that they struggle to expand the relevance (and therefore the legitimacy) of constitutional law and review.

statutes and the exercise of public authority pursuant to statute. In deciding, the constitutional court simultaneously resolves a legislative dispute *and* enacts the constitution. Although both constitute forms of rule-making, their effects are quite different.

First, the court disposes of a specific legislative (abstract review) or a judicial (concrete review) conflict by determining the legality of a statute. The court's impact on the legislative process is both retrospective and direct. It is retrospective, in the sense that the court has authoritatively settled an existing conflict about constitutionality, and direct, in that the court's decision attaches to the reviewed statute as an approbation, an amendment, or a veto. Second, in justifying its decision—in telling us why, normatively, a legislative provision is, or is not, constitutional—the court (re-)constructs the constitutional law. In doing so, the court clarifies or alters the rules governing law-making, and signals to legislators how similar disputes may be resolved in the future. The legislative impact of the decision will be indirect and prospective, to the extent that it affects future law-making activity (stage 1 of the model).

This second form of rule-making constitutes a predictable response to the court's dilemma (see first tactic, above). Yet it raises a delicate, second order legitimacy issue. From the point of view of the legislature, the progressive elaboration of the constitution makes evident that the rules governing a particular legislative dispute were not ascertainable at the time the dispute erupted. The perception of the court's neutrality erodes as its capacity to rewrite the constitution is revealed. Constitutional judges can mitigate, but can *never* permanently resolve, this problem.[2] Judges have a powerful interest in portraying constitutional decision-making as deliberation about the precise relationship of constitutional rules to legislating, and portraying the decision as a record of these deliberations. But in doing so, they assert pedagogical authority over future legislative processes.

Shift 1 (Again): The Judicialization of Policy-making

In moving through shifts 1–4, we see how the processes of law-making, constitutional decision-making, and the construction of the constitution, come to be knotted together. Consider what happens when oppositions go to the court on an ongoing basis. Thus: a partisan dispute about the constitutionality of a legislative bill has erupted in parliament; the opposition has referred the matter to the court; the governing majority responds to the

[2] If judges ceased to furnish constitutional justifications for their decisions, they would be even worse off.

referral with its own arguments; the court resolves the conflict, and in the process clarifies and revises (at least subtly) the constitutional rules governing law-making. In returning to shift 1, the impact of the constitution on law-making, we come full circle, to our initial starting point. But legislators find ourselves in a rather different world: they have learned something about the nature of their work (legislating), about the normative environment (the constitution) that enables and sustains that work, and about how the court has co-ordinated the relationship between the two binding them together. Although concrete review referrals and individual complaints originate outside of parliament, constitutional decision-making pursuant to both kinds of referrals regularly leads to the same result.

Given two conditions, constitutional rule-making will generate powerful pedagogical—or feedback—effects, to be registered on subsequent legislative processes, and on subsequent constitutional litigation. First, potential litigators must believe that activating constitutional review is worthwhile, and therefore continue to supply the court with a case load. Second, litigators must perceive that the court's case law possesses some authoritative (i.e. precedential) value. Put negatively, if self-interested individuals stop going to the court, or if the court renders capricious decisions that fail to provide potential litigators with any normative guidance, then the politicization–judicialization dynamic will be blocked; but, for reasons given, neither event is likely.

If the above conditions are met, law-making will inexorably be placed in the 'shadow' of constitutional review. As we move around the circle a second time, and then again and again, we can expect this shadow to deepen in those policy domains in which legislative–constitutional court interactions are most intensive, and to creep into those domains newly subject to such interactions. In this way, the constitutional uncertainty facing legislators (e.g. at point 1 in time, within a given policy area) is gradually replaced by constitutional obligation (e.g. at point 5 in time). In consequence, both the interest and the capacity of legislators to anticipate a subsequent constitutional decision of the court, in that policy area, is enhanced. To the extent that legislators adjust their behaviour as constitutional rules develop, the court's authority is consolidated (see the earlier discussion of shift 1, pp. 196–7).

This is, indeed, what has happened. Legislators today routinely take decisions that they would not have taken in the absence of review, and governing majorities anticipate likely decisions of the court and constrain their behaviour accordingly. In addition, governments and parliaments have developed new practices designed to accommodate the constitutional law, as it is progressively elaborated by the court. Judicialization provokes the emergence and institutionalization of a new kind of legislative politics. It serves to construct and then to perpetuate an expansive discourse about the relationship of constitutional rules to law-making. In this mode of governance, legislators define, express, and pursue their political interests by means of constitutional interpretation and deliberation. Considered in this way, judicialization is the process by which legislators absorb the behaviour norms of constitutional adjudication, and the grammar and vocabulary of constitutional law, into those repertoires of reasoning and action that constitute political agency. In judicialized politics, legal discourse mediates partisan debate and structures the exercise of legislative power.

CONSTITUTIONAL DECISION-MAKING AND GOVERNANCE

The notion of governance underlying this book is a straightforward one. Governance is the process through which the rules systems (the normative structure, the macro-level) in place in any community are adapted to the purposes of those who live under them (individuals, the micro-level). When parliament legislates, it adapts rules and therefore governs; when administrators take decisions pursuant to grants of statutory authority, they apply rules to situations and people, and thereby govern; and when judges resolve legal disputes by interpreting statutes in order to enforce them, they too are co-ordinating what is relatively abstract (legal norms) with what is relatively particular (litigation).

The constitutional law constitutes a set of meta-rules that authoritatively condition these activities; yet this law is also continuously being adapted. Constitutional judges co-ordinate what is abstract and normative (the constitution) with what is relatively more concrete and particular (a specific dispute about the legality of a particular act, in order to resolve that dispute). Although constitutional courts are the privileged sites of this form of governance, review does not take place in a vacuum. Instead, the terms of the referral, the arguments brought to the court by the parties to the dispute, embed review in a particular social context.

Context conditions the judges' work in powerful ways, all the more so if the judges hope to fashion a compelling judgment that both resolves the case at hand and provides normative guidance for the future. If they do, constitutional courts, in the course of their deliberations, will re-enact crucial aspects of decision-making of those they are asked to control.[3] In order to determine whether the legislature had violated the constitution in adopting a law, or whether a court has done so in dismissing a suit, constitutional judges will evaluate the decision-making processes of that legislature or that judge. They will put themselves in the latter's shoes, and walk through these processes, on a step-by-step basis. The judges will, in effect, expect those whose decision-making is being controlled to have reasoned through the constitutional norms as the constitutional court has, and to have acted in accordance with the dictates of the law. Because this kind of exercise regularly occurs, constitutional rule-making constitutes a relatively detailed record of how legislators, ordinary judges, and administrators should behave, if they wish to exercise their authority lawfully.

The techniques of constitutional adjudication will then tend to diffuse.[4] Sites of public governance are gradually saturated with models of action (rules, discursive tools, modes of reasoning) prescribing how officials ought to do their jobs. Officials will make use of these models to insulate their activities from future constitutional censure. They will also acquire the capacity to participate in the construction of the constitution, thereby conditioning how constitutional courts do *their* jobs.

In the end, governing with judges also means governing like judges.

[3] This observation would appear to apply to adjudication in all communities where courts effectively resolve disputes on an ongoing basis. To explain fully why this is so, we would need a more explicit theory of judicial interpretation. Although certain core elements of such a theory are implied here and in Chs 4 and 5, I do not specify or explain the paradigmatic ways in which judges resolve constitutional disputes. Instead, I have focused on the social logic and consequences of giving normative justifications for decision-making.
[4] As Shapiro (1988: ch. 5) has shown with respect to the growth of administrative law in the US, the more intensive the interaction of agencies with courts that control agency decision-making, the more agencies are led to behave like adjudicators.

BIBLIOGRAPHY

CONSTITUTIONAL COURT DECISIONS CITED

The European Court of Justice

ECJ decisions, which are numbered from the date of the reference (not the date of decision), are published in the *European Court Reports* (*ECR*), published annually.

ECJ 1994	*Webb*, case 32/93, *ECR* 1994, p. 3567
ECJ 1993	*Marshall II*, case 271/91, *ECR* 1993, p. 4367
ECJ 1991*a*	*Francovich*, case C–6 & 9/90, *ECR* 1991, vol. I, p. 5357
ECJ 1991*b*	*Commission* v. *The Netherlands*, case 353/89, *ECR* 1991, p. 4069
ECJ 1991*c*	*Grogan*, case 159/90, *ECR* 1991, p. 4685
ECJ 1991*d*	*Dekker*, case 177/88, *ECR* 1991, vol. I, p. 3941
ECJ 1990*a*	*Marleasing*, case C-106/89, *ECR* 1990, vol. I, p. 4135
ECJ 1990*b*	*Barber*, case 262/88, *ECR* 1990, vol. I, p. 1889
ECJ 1990*c*	*Hertz*, case 179/88, *ECR* 1991, vol. I, p. 3979
ECJ 1989	*Wachauf*, case 5/88, *ECR* 1989, p. 2609
ECJ 1987	*Foto Frost*, case 314/85, *ECR* 1987, p. 4199
ECJ 1986*a*	*Commission* v. *Germany*, case 249/86, *ECR* 1989, p. 1263
ECJ 1986*b*	*Nouvelles Frontières*, joined cases 209–213/84, *ECR* 1986, p. 1425
ECJ 1986*c*	*Marshall I*, case 152/84, *ECR* 1986, p. 723
ECJ 1984	*Von Colson*, case 14/83, *ECR* 1984, p. 1891
ECJ 1982	*Commission* v. *United Kingdom*, case 61/81, *ECR* 1982, p. 2601
ECJ 1979	*Cassis de Dijon*, case 120/78, *ECR* 1979, p. 649
ECJ 1978	*Simmenthal II*, case 92/78, *ECR* 1978, p. 629
ECJ 1976*a*	*Simmenthal I*, case 35/76, *ECR* 1976, p. 629
ECJ 1976*b*	*Defrenne II*, case 43/75, *ECR* 1976, p. 455
ECJ 1975	*Rutili*, case36/75, *ECR* 1975, p. 1219
ECJ 1974*a*	*Van Duyn*, case 41/74, *ECR* 1974, p. 1337
ECJ 1974*b*	*Nold*, case 4/73, *ECR* 1974, p. 491
ECJ 1974*c*	*Dassonville*, case 8/74, *ECR* 1974, p. 837
ECJ 1973	*Commission* v. *Italy*, case 39/72, *ECR* 1973, p. 103
ECJ 1970	*Internationale Handelsgesellschaft*, case 11/70, *ECR* 1970, p. 1125
ECJ 1969	*Stauder*, case 29/169, *ECR* 1969, p. 419
ECJ 1964	*Costa*, case 6/64, *ECR* 1964, p. 585
ECJ 1963	*Van Gend en Loos*, case 26/62, *ECR* 1963, p. 1
ECJ 1958	*Stork*, case 1/58, *ECR* 1959, p. 43

The French Constitutional Council

Council decisions are numbered consecutively with the case number following the date of referral (not the date of decision). The official source, *Recueil des Décisions du Conseil Constitutionnel* (*Recueil*), is published annually.

Council 1993   case 93–325, *Recueil* 1993, p. 224
Council 1986*a*   case 86–210, *Recueil* 1986, p. 110
Council 1986*b*   case 86–217, *Recueil* 1986, p. 141
Council 1984   case 84–181, *Recueil* 1984, p. 73
Council 1982*a*   case 81–132, *Recueil* 1982, p. 18
Council 1982*b*   case 82–146, *Recueil* 1982, p. 66
Council 1975   case 74–54, *Recueil* 1975, p. 19
Council 1971   case 71–44, *Recueil* 1971, p. 29
Council 1962   case 162–18L, *Recueil* 1962, p. 31

The German Federal Constitutional Court

GFCC decisions are reported in *Entscheidungen des Bundesverfassungsgerichts* (*BVerfGE*) by volume and page number. In this book, rulings are cited in the text by the year of decision, not year of publication.

GFCC 1993*a*   *BVerfGE* 1993, vol. 88, p. 203
GFCC 1993*b*   *BVerfGE* 1993, vol. 89, p. 155
GFCC 1992   *BVerfGE* 1992, vol. 85, p. 264
GFCC 1986*a*   *BVerfGE* 1987, vol. 73, p. 40
GFCC 1986*b*   *BVerfGE* 1987, vol. 73, p. 339
GFCC 1984   *BVerfGE* 1985, vol. 67, p. 26
GFCC 1979*a*   *BVerfGE* 1979, vol. 50, 290
GFCC 1979*b*   *BVerfGE* 1980, vol. 52, p. 63
GFCC 1977   *BVerfGE* 1978, vol. 45, 187
GFCC 1975   *BVerfGE* 1975, vol. 39, p. 1
GFCC 1973*a*   *BVerfGE* 1974, vol. 35, p. 79
GFCC 1973*b*   *BVerfGE* 1974, vol. 34, p. 269
GFCC 1973*c*   *BVerfGE* 1974, vol.37, p. 27
GFCC 1969   *BVerfGE* 1969, vol. 25, p. 256
GFCC 1968   *BVerfGE* 1969, vol. 24, p. 300
GFCC 1966   *BVerfGE* 1967, vol. 20, p. 56
GFCC 1958*a*   *BVerfGE* 1958, vol. 8, p. 51
GFCC 1958*b*   *BVerfGE* 1958, vol. 7, p. 198
GFCC 1957   *BVerfGE* 1959, vol. 6, p. 32
GFCC 1954   *BVerfGE* 1956, vol. 4, p. 7

The Italian Constitutional Court

ICC cases, which are numbered annually from the date of the decision, are published in *Giurisprudenza Costituzionale* (*G.C.*).

ICC 1993   case 243/1993: *G.C.* 1993, vol. 38 Parte II, p. 1756

ICC 1988*a*   case 220/1988, *G.C.* 1988, vol. 33 Parte I (1), p. 862

ICC 1988*b*   case 200/1988, *G.C.* 1988, vol. 33 Parte I (1), p. 753

ICC 1988*c*   case 1146/1988, *G.C.* 1988, vol. 33 Parte I (4), p. 5565

ICC 1988*d*   case 826/1988, *G.C.* 1988, vol. 33 Parte I (3), p. 3893

ICC 1986   case 35/1986: *G.C.* 1986, vol. 31 Parte I (1), p. 211

ICC 1985*a*   case 231/1985: *G.C.* 1985, vol. 30 Parte I (2), p. 1879

ICC 1985*b*   case 161/1985: *G.C.* 1985, vol. 30 Parte I (1), p. 1173

ICC 1984   case 133/1984: *G.C.* 1984, vol. 29 Parte I (2), p. 852

ICC 1981   case 148/1981: *G.C.* 1981, vol. 26 Parte I, p. 1379

ICC 1980   case 26/1980, *G.C.* 1980, vol. 25 Parte I, p. 206

ICC 1979   case 98/1979: *G.C.* 1979, vol. 24 Parte I, p. 719

ICC 1976   case 202/1976: *G.C.* 1976, vol. 21 Parte I, p. 1267

ICC 1975   case 232/91, *G.C.* 1975, III, p. 2211

ICC 1974*a*   case 225/1974, *G.C.* 1974, Parte II, p. 1775

ICC 1974*b*   case 226/1974, *G.C.* 1974, Parte II, p. 1791

ICC 1965*a*   case 11/1965, *G.C.* 1965, vol. 4, p. 57

ICC 1965*b*   case 52/1965, *G.C.* 1965, vol. 4, p. 228

ICC 1964   case 14/1964, *G.C.* 1964, p. 82

The Spanish Constitutional Tribunal

SCT cases, which are numbered annually from the date of the decision, are published in *Jurisprudencia Constitucional* (*J.C.*).

SCT 1994   case 337/1994, *J.C.* vol. XL, p. 917

SCT 1987*a*   case 160/1987, *J.C.* vol. XIX, p. 146

SCT 1987*b*   case 161/1987, *J.C.* vol. XIX, p. 185

SCT 1987*c*   case 159/1987, *J.C.* vol. XIX, p. 134

SCT 1986   case 104/1986, *J.C.* vol. XV, p. 559

SCT 1985*a*   case 53/1985, *J.C.* vol. XI, p. 546

SCT 1985*b*   case 20/1985, *J.C.* vol. XI, p. 190

SCT 1984   case 75/1984, *J.C.* vol. IX, p. 259

SCT 1983   case 87/1983, *J.C.* vol. VII, p. 97

SCT 1982*a*   case 15/1982, *J.C.* vol. III, p. 196

SCT 1982*b*   case 80/1982, *J.C.* vol. IV, p. 519

SCT 1982*c*   case 12/1982, *J.C.* vol. III, p. 160

REFERENCES

Ackerman, Bruce (1997). The Rise of World Constitutionalism. *Virginia Law Review*, 83: 771–97.

Agranoff, Robert (1996). Federal Evolution in Spain. *International Political Science Review*, 17: 385–401.

—— (1993). Inter-governmental Politics and Policy: Building Federal Arrangements in Spain. *Regional Politics and Society*, 3: 1–28.

Aguiar de Luque, Luís (1987). El Tribunal Constitucional y la Función Legislativa: El Control del Procedimiento Legislativo y de la Inconstiucionalidad por Omisión. *Revista de Derecho Político*, 24: 9–30.

Alter, Karen J. and Sophie Meunier-Aitshalia (1994). Judicial Politics in the European Community: European Integration and the Pathbreaking Cassis de Dijon Decision. *Comparative Political Studies*, 26: 535–61.

Aragón Reyes, Manuel (1987). Algunas Consideraciones sobre el Tribunal Constitucional. *Revista Jurídica de Castilla-La Mancha*, 1: 27–53.

Arce Janariz, Alberto (1989). Normas sobre Derecho Aplicable en la Jurisprudencia del Tribunal Constitucional. *Revista Española de Derecho Constitucional*, 9: 89–113.

Arechederra, Luis (1991). The Death of a Bullfighter: Spanish Law on Privacy and the Right to Name and Likeness. *International and Comparative Law Quarterly*, 40: 442–5.

Arnull, Anthony (1994). Judging the New Europe. *European Law Review*, 19: 3–15.

Barav, Ami (1985). Cour Constitutionnelle Italienne et Droit Communautaire: Le Fantôme de Simmenthal. *Revue Triméstérielle de Droit Européen*, 21: 313–41.

Barendt, Eric (1991). The Influence of the German and Italian Constitutional Courts on their National Broadcasting Systems. *Public Law*, 2: 93–115.

Beck, Anthony (1994). Is Law an Autopoietic System? *Oxford Journal of Legal Studies*, 14: 401–16.

Bell, John, Sophie Boyron, and Simon Whitaker (1998). *Principles of French Law.* Oxford University Press.

Berlin, D. 1992. Interactions between the Lawmaker and the Judiciary within the EC. *Legal Issues of European Integration*, 17: 17–48.

Beyme, Klaus von (1989). The Genesis of Constitutional Review in Parliamentary Systems. In C. Landfried (ed.), *Constitutional Review and Legislation: An International Comparison.* Baden-Baden: Nomos.

Blair, Philip M. (1981). *Federalism and Judicial Review in West Germany.* Oxford: Clarendon Press.

—— (1978). Law and Politics in West Germany. *Political Studies*, **26**: 348–62.

Blondel, Jean (1973). *Comparative Legislatures*. Englewood Cliffs, NJ: Prentice Hall.

Bognetti, Giovanni (1982). Direct Application and Indirect Impact of the Constitution in the Italian Legal System. In *Italian National Reports to the XIth International Congress of Comparative Law, Carcas*. Milano: Giuffrè.

Boland, Reed (1994). Abortion Law World-wide: A Survey of Recent Developments. In J. Bednaridova and F. Chapman (ed.), *Festschrift für Jan Stepan zum 80. Geburstag*. Zürich: Schulthess.

Bon, Pierre (1991). La Constitutionnalisation du Droit Espagnol. *Revue Française de Droit Constitutionnel*, **5**: 35–54.

—— (1988). Espagne: L'Interruption Volontaire de Grossesse dans la Jurisprudence du Tribunal Constitutionnel Espagnol. *Annuaire International de Justice Constitutionnelle 1986* II: 119–33.

Braunthal, Gerard (1983). *The West German Social Democrats: Profile of a Party in Power*. Boulder, CO: Westview.

Brennan, Geoffrey and James M. Buchanan (1985). *The Reason of Rules: Constitutional Political Economy*. Cambridge University Press.

Brewer-Carias, Allan R. (1989). *Judicial Review in Comparative Law*. Cambridge University Press.

Brünneck, Alexander von (1992). *Verfassungsgerichtsbarkeit in den Westlichen Demokratien: Ein systematischer Verfassungsvergleich*. Baden-Baden: Nomos.

—— (1990). Le Contrôle de Constitutionnalité et le Législateur dans les Démocraties. *Annuaire International de Justice Constitutionnelle 1988*, **IV**: 15–49.

Burgess, Susan R. (1993). Beyond Institutional Politics: The New Institutionalism, Legal Rhetoric, and Judicial Supremacy. *Polity*, **25**: 445–59.

Burley, Anne-Marie and Walter Mattli (1993). Europe before the Court: A Political Theory of Legal Integration. *International Organization*, **47**: 41–76.

Cappelletti, Mauro (1989). *The Judicial Process in Comparative Perspective*. New York, Clarendon Press.

Carter, Lief (1991). *Introduction to Constitutional Interpretation*. White Plains, NY: Longman.

Cartier, Marie-Elisabeth (1995). La Cour de Cassation et l'Application de la Déclaration des Droits de 1789. In *La Cour de Cassation et la Constitution de La République*. Aix-en-Provence: Presses Universitaire d' Aix-en-Provence.

del Castillo Vera, Pilar (1987). Notas Para el Estudio del Comportamiento Judicial: El Caso del Tribunal Constitucional. *Revista Española de Derecho Constitucional*, **7**: 177–91.

Certoma, G. Leroy (1985). *The Italian Legal System*. London: Butterworths.

Claes, Monica and Bruno deWitte (1998). Report on the Netherlands. In A-M. Slaughter, J. H. H. Weiler, and A. Stone Sweet (eds.), *The European Courts and National Courts: Doctrine and Jurisprudence*. Oxford: Hart.

Clark, Robert P. (1989). Spanish Democracy and Regional Autonomy: The Autonomous Community System and Self-government for the Ethnic Homelands. In J. Rudolph and R. Thompson (ed.), *Ethnoterritorial Politics, Policy, and the Western World*. Boulder, CO: Lynne Rienner.

Coppel, Jason and Aidan O'Neill (1992). The European Court of Justice: Taking Rights Seriously? *Legal Studies*, 12: 227–45.

Craig, Barbara Hinkson and David O'Brien (1993). *Abortion and American Politics*. Chatham, NJ: Chatham House.

Craig, P. P. (1998). Report on the United Kingdom. In A-M. Slaughter, J. H. H. Weiler, and A. Stone Sweet (ed.), *The European Courts and National Courts: Doctrine and Jurisprudence*. Oxford: Hart.

—— (1991). Sovereignty of the UK Parliament After Factortame. *Yearbook of European Law*, 221–56.

Currie, David P. (1993). Separation of Powers in the Federal Republic of Germany. *American Journal of Comparative Law*, 41: 201–60.

Current Survey (1994). *European Law Review*, 19: 221.

Curtin, Deirdre (1990). The Province of Government: Delimiting the Direct Effect of Directives. *European Law Review*, 15: 195–223.

Dadomo, Christian and Susan Farran (1993). *The French Legal System*. London: Sweet & Maxwell.

Dahl, Robert (1957). The Concept of Power. *Behavioral Science*, 2: 201–15.

D'Amico, Marilisa (1991). Juge Constitutionnel, Juges du Fond et Justiciables dans l'Évolution de la Justice Constitutionnelle. *Annuaire International de Justice Constitutionnelle 1989*, V: 79–96.

Davis, Michael (1987). A Government of Judges: An Historical Re-View. *American Journal of Comparative Law*, 35: 559–80.

Deakin, Simon, Christel Lane, and Frank Wilkinson (1994). Trust or Law? Towards an Integrated Theory of Contractual Relations Between Firms. *Journal of Law and Society*, 21: 329–49.

Dehousse, Renaud (1994). *La Cour de Justice des Communautés Européennes*. Paris: Montchrestien.

Díez Moreno, Fernando (1986). El Equilibrio de Poderes en las Relaciones entre las Cortes Generales y el Tribunal Constitucional. *Jornadas de Derecho Parlamentario, Cortes Generales, Madrid*, II: 27–45.

Díez Picazo, Luis María (1994a). Dificultades Practicas y Significado Constitucional del Recurso de Amparo. *Revista Española de Derecho Constitucional*, 40: 9–37.

—— (1994b). Sources of Law in Spain: An Outline. *European University Institute*, Law Working Paper No. 94/10. Florence, Italy.

Di Manno, Thierry (1998). *Le Juge Constitutionnel et la Technique des 'Décisions Interprétatives' en France et en Italie*. Aix-Marseille: Economica-Presses Universitaires d'Aix-Marseille.

—— (1992). Italie: L'Activité Contentieuse de la Cour Constitutionnelle en 1990:

Éléments Statistiques et Techniques de Jugement. *Annuaire International de Justice Constitutionnelle 1990*, VI: 769–96.

Eckstein, Harry (1988). A Culturalist Theory of Political Change. *American Political Science Review*, 82: 789–804.

Eighth Conference of Constitutional Courts (1992). La Hiérarchie des Normes Constitutionnelles et sa Fonction dans la Protection des Droits Fondamentaux. *Annuaire International de Justice Constitutionnelle 1990*, VI: 15–215.

Ellis, Evelyn (1991). *European Community Sex Equality Law*. Oxford University Press.

El Pais, 18 April 1985.

——, 13 April 1985.

——, 12 April 1985.

Elster, Jon (1989). *The Cement of Society: A Study of Social Order*. Cambridge University Press.

Ely, John H. (1982). *Democracy and Distrust: A Theory of Judicial Review*. Cambridge, MA: Harvard University Press.

Errera, Roger (1998). Recent Decisions of the French Conseil d'État. *Public Law*, 2: 152–4.

Escarras, J. C. (1987). Italie: Éléments de Référence. *Annuaire International de Justice Constitutionnelle 1985*, I: 475–550.

Ezquiaga Ganuzas, Francisco Javier (1991). Diez Años de Fallos Constitucionales, Sentencias Interpretativas y Poder Normativo del Tribunal Constitucional. *Revista Vasca de Administración Pública*, 31: 117–41.

Fabri, Marco (1994). Theory Versus Practice of Italian Criminal Justice Reform. *Judicature*, 4: 211–16.

Fassler, Lawrence (1991). The Italian Penal Procedure Code: An Adversarial System of Criminal Procedure in Continental Europe. *Columbia Journal of Transnational Law*, 29: 243–78.

Favoreu, Louis (1996). La Notion de Cour Constitutionnelle. In P. Zen-Ruffinen and A. Auer (ed.), *De la Constitution: Études en L'Honneur de Jean-François Aubert*. Basel: Helbing & Lichtenhan.

—— (1994). La Légitimité du Juge Constitutionnel. *Revue Internationale de Droit Comparé*, 2: 557–81.

—— (1990). Le Droit Constitutionnel, Droit de la Constitution et Constitution du Droit. *Revue Française de Droit Constitutionnel*, 1: 71–89.

—— (1988). *La Politique Saisie par le Droit*. Paris: Economica.

—— (1986). Europe Occidentale. In L. Favoreu and J-A. Jolowicz (ed.), *Le Contrôle Juridictionnel des Lois*. Paris: Economica.

—— (1982). Décentralisation et Constitution. *Revue du Droit Public*, 98: 1259–95.

—— and Loïc Philip (1997). *Les Grandes Décisions du Conseil Constitutionnel*. Paris: Dalloz.

Foster, Nigel G. (1993). *German Law and Legal System*. London: Blackstone.

Friedrich, C. J. (1946). *Constitutional Government and Democracy*. Boston, MA: Ginn.

Furlong, Paul (1988). The Constitutional Court in Italian Politics. *West European Politics*, **11**: 7–23.

García de Enterría, Eduardo (1993). La Constitución y Las Autonomías Territoriales. In Gomez, Ubaldo (ed.), *Estudios de Derecho Público en Homenaje a Ignacio de Otto*. Oviedo: Universidad de Oviedo Servico de Publicaciones.

—— (1991). *La Constitución Como Norma Juridica y el Tribunal Constitucional*. Madrid: Civitas.

—— (1989). La Constitución y las Autonomías Territoriales. *Revista Española de Derecho Constitucional*, **9**: 17–34.

Garrett, Geoffrey (1992). International Cooperation and Institutional Choice: The EC's Internal Market. *International Organization*, **46**: 533–60.

Gascón Abellan, Marina (1994). La Justicia Constitucional: Entre Legislación y Jurisdicción. *Revista Española de Derecho Constitucional*, **41**: 63–87.

George, Robert P. (ed.) (1996). *The Autonomy of Law: Essays on Legal Positivism*. Oxford: Clarendon Press.

Giddens, Anthony (1984). *The Constitution of Society: Outline of the Theory of Structuration*. Berkeley, CA: University of California Press.

Giorgis, Andrea, Enrico Grosso, and Jörg Luther (1995). Á Propos de Quelques Nouveautés dans la Jurisprudence de la Cour Constitutionnelle Italienne en 1993. *Annuaire International de Justice Constitutionnelle 1993*, **IX**: 531–43.

Golay, John Ford (1958). *The Founding of the Federal Republic of Germany*. Chicago, IL: University of Chicago Press.

Gordon, Robert (1984). Critical Legal Histories. *Stanford Law Review*, **36**: 57–135.

Gormley, Laurence (1985). *Prohibiting Restrictions on Trade within the EEC*. Amsterdam: Elsevier/TMC Asser Instituut.

Greer, Steven (1994). Police Powers in Spain: The 'Corcuera Law.' *International and Comparative Law Quarterly*, **43**: 405–16.

Greif, Avner (1989). Reputation and Coalitions in Medieval Trade: Evidence on the Maghribi Traders. *Journal of Economic History*, **49**: 857–82.

Grossi, Pierfrancesco (1972). *Introduzione ad uno Studio sui Diritti Inviolabili nella Costituzione Italiana*. Padova: CEDAM.

Guanter, Salvador del Rey (1995). Employee Privacy in Spanish Labor Relations. *Comparative Labor Law Journal*, **17**: 122–38.

Guasch, Jacques (1994). La Mise en Cause de la Constitutionnalité des Lois à Travers le Recours d'*amparo* en Espagne. *Annuaire International de Justice Constitutionnelle 1992*, **VIII**: 25–109.

Guastini, Riccardo (1991). Réflexion sur les Garanties des Droits Constitutionnels et la Théorie de l'Interprétation. *Revue du Droit Public et de la Science Politique*, **2**: 1079–87.

Haas, Ernst B. (1961). International Integration: The European and the Universal Process. *International Organization*, **15**: 366–92.

—— (1958). *The Uniting of Europe: Political, Social, and Economic Forces, 1950–57.* Stanford, CA: Stanford University Press.

Habermas, Jürgen (1992). *Faktizität und Geltung: Beiträge zur Diskurstheorie des Rechts und des Demokratischen Rechtsstaats.* Frankfurt: Suhrkamp.

—— (1986). Law as Medium and Law as Institution. In G. Teubner (ed.), *Dilemmas of Law in the Welfare State.* Berlin: de Gruyter.

Hechter, Michael (1987). *Principles of Group Solidarity.* Berkeley, CA: University of California Press.

Hervey, Tamara K. (1994). Legal Issues Concerning the Barber Protocol. In D. O'Keefe and P. M. Twomey (ed.), *Legal Issues of the Maastricht Treaty.* London: Chancery Law.

Herzog, Roman (1992). The Hierarchy of Constitutional Norms and its Function in the Protection of Basic Rights. *Human Rights Law Journal,* 13: 90–3.

Heyde, Wolfgang (1994). *Justice and the Law in the Federal Republic of Germany.* Heidelberg: C.F. Müller Juristicher Verlag.

Il Sole 24 Ore, 24 October 1994.

Jackson, Donald J. and C. Neal Tate (ed.) (1990). Symposium: Judicial Review and Public Policy in Comparative Perspective. *Policy Studies Journal,* 19.

Jepperson, Ronald L. (1991). Institution, Institutional Effects, and Institutionalism. In W. M. Powell and P. J. Dimaggio (ed)., *The New Institutionalism in Organizational Analysis.* Chicago, IL: University of Chicago Press.

Jounjan, Olivier (1995). Révision de la Constitution et Justice Constitutionnelle: République Fédérale d'Allemagne. *Annuaire International de Justice Constitutionnelle 1994,* X: 229–44.

Kasha, Jeremy R. (1996). Education Under Catalonia's Law of Linguistic Normalization: Spanish Constitutionalism and International Human Rights Law. *Columbia Journal of Transnational Law,* 34: 621–76.

Katzenstein, Peter (1987). *Politics and Policy in West Germany: The Growth of a Semi-Sovereign State.* Philadelphia, PA: Temple University.

Kelsen, Hans (1942). Judicial Review of Legislation: A Comparative Study of the Austrian and the American Constitution. *The Journal of Politics,* 4: 183–200.

—— (1928). La Garantie Juridictionnelle de la Constitution. *Revue du Droit Public,* 44: 197–257.

Kenney, Sally J. (1996). Pregnancy Discrimination: Toward Substantive Equality. *Wisconsin Women's Law Journal,* 10: 351–402.

—— (1994). Pregnancy and Disability: Comparing the United States and the European Community. *The Disability Law Reporter Service,* 3: 8–17.

—— (1992). *For Whose Protection? Reproductive Hazards and Exclusionary Policies in the United States and Britain.* Ann Arbor, MI: University of Michigan Press.

Keohane, Robert (1984). *After Hegemony: Cooperation and Discord in the World Political Economy.* Princeton, NJ: Princeton University Press.

Kilroy, Bernadette A. (1996). Member State Control or Judicial Independence? The Integrative Role of the European Court of Justice, 1958–1994. (Unpublished manuscript.)

King, Michael (1993). The 'Truth' about Autopoiesis. *Journal of Law and Society*, 20: 218–36.

Kommers, Donald P. (1997). *The Constitutional Jurisprudence of the Federal Republic of Germany* (2nd edn). Durham, NC: Duke University Press.

—— (1994). The Federal Constitutional Court in the German Political System. *Comparative Political Studies*, 26: 470–91.

—— (1989). *The Constitutional Jurisprudence of the Federal Republic of Germany*. Durham, NC: Duke University Press.

Krasner, Stephen (ed.) (1983). *International Regimes*. Ithaca, NY: Cornell University Press.

Kratochwil, Friedrich (1994). The Limits of Contract. *European Journal of International Law*, 2: 465–91.

Lambert, E. (1921). *Le Gouvernement des Juges et la Lutte contre la Législation Sociale aux États-unis*. Paris: Giard.

Lamprecht, Rolf (1992). *Richter contra Richter: Abweichende Meinungen und ihre Bedeutung für die Rechtskultur*. Baden-Baden: Nomos.

Landfried, Christine (1992). Judicial Policymaking in Germany. The Federal Constitutional Court. *West European Politics*, 15: 50–67.

—— (ed.) (1989*a*). *Constitutional Review and Legislation: An International Comparison*. Baden-Baden: Nomos.

—— (1989*b*). Legislation and Judicial Review in the Federal Republic of Germany. In C. Landfried (ed.), *Constitutional Review and Legislation: An International Comparison*. Baden-Baden: Nomos.

—— (1984). *Bundesverfassungsgericht und Gesetzgeber*. Baden-Baden: Nomos.

Laufer, Heinz (1991). *Das föderative System der Bundesrepublik Deutschland*. München: Landeszentrale für Politische Bildungsarbeit.

Le Monde, 9 August 1993.

Lenaerts, Koen (1990). Constitutionalism and the Many Faces of Federalism. *American Journal of Comparative Law*, 38: 205–64.

Levi, Margaret (1988). *Of Rule and Revenue*. Berkeley, CA: University of California Press.

Levitsky, Jonathan E. (1994). The Europeanization of the British Style. *American Journal of Comparative Law*, 42: 347–80.

McCubbins, Matthew, R. Noll, and Barry Weingast (1987). Administrative Procedures as Instruments of Political Control. *Journal of Law, Economics, and Organization*, 3: 243–77.

McGee, Henry W. (1987). Counsel for the Accused: Metamorphosis in Spanish Constitutional Rights. *Columbia Journal of Transnational Law*, 25: 253–99.

Majone, Giandomenico (1996). Temporal Consistency and Policy Credibility:

Why Democracies need Non-majoritarian Institutions. *European University Institute RSC*, Working Paper No. 96/57. Florence, Italy.

Mancini, Federico G. (1991). The Making of a Constitution for Europe. In R. Keohane and S. Hoffman (ed.), *The New European Community*. Boulder, CO: Westview.

—— and David T. Keeling (1994). Democracy and the European Court of Justice. *Modern Law Review*, 57: 175–90.

March, James G. and Johann P. Olsen (1989). *Rediscovering Institutions*. New York: Free Press.

Markovits, Andrei S. (1986). *The Politics of the West German Trade Unions*. Cambridge University Press.

Merino-Blanco, Elena (1996). *The Spanish Legal System*. London: Sweet & Maxwell.

Merryman, John Henry (1985). *The Civil Law Tradition*. Stanford, CA: Stanford University Press.

—— and Vicenzo Vigoriti (1967). When Courts Collide: Constitution and Cassation in Italy. *American Journal of Comparative Law*, 15: 665–86.

Milgrom, Paul and John Roberts (ed.) (1992). *Economics, Organization and Management*. Englewood Cliffs, NJ: Prentice Hall.

Moe, Terry (1987). An Assessment of the Positive Theory of Congressional Dominance. *Legislative Studies Quarterly*, 12: 475–520.

Moravscik, Andrew (1995). Liberal Intergovernmentalism and Integration: A Rejoinder. *Journal of Common Market Studies*, 33: 611–28.

—— (1993). Preferences and Power in the European Community: A Liberal Inter-governmentalist Approach. *Journal of Common Market Studies*, 31: 473–524.

—— (1991). Negotiating the Single European Act: National Interests and Conventional Statecraft in the European Community. *International Organization*, 45: 19–56.

Neuman, Gerald L. (1995). *Casey* in the Mirror: Abortion, Abuse and the Right to Protection in the United States and Germany. *American Journal of Comparative Law*, 43: 273–314.

Neumann, F. (1964). *The Democratic and the Authoritarian State*. NewYork, NY: Free Press.

North, Douglas (1990). *Institutions, Institutional Change, and Economic Performance*. Cambridge University Press.

Oliver, Peter (1988). *Free Movement of Goods in the EEC*. London: European Law Centre.

Onuf, Nicholas (1989). *World of our Making: Rules and Rule in Social Theory and International Relations*. Columbia, SC: University of South Carolina Press.

O'Reilly, Dolores and Alec Stone Sweet (1998). The Liberalization and European Reregulation of Air Transport. In W. Sandholtz and A. Stone Sweet (ed.), *European Integration and Supranational Governance*. Oxford University Press.

Pace, Alessandro (1990). Constitutional Protection of Freedom of Expression in Italy. *Revue Européennee de Droit Public*, 2: 71–113.

Panza, Salvatore C. and Reposo, Antonio (1981). Corte Costituzionale. *Quaderni Costituzionali*, 2: 595–600.

Perez Royo, Javier (1986). Crónica de un Error: El Recurso Previo de Inconstitucionalidad Contra Leyes Orgánicas. *Revista Española de Derecho Constitucional*, 17: 137–70.

Perry, Michael J. (1982). *The Constitution, the Courts, and Human Rights.* New Haven, CT: Yale University Press.

Philip, Loïc (1985). La Constitutionalisation du Droit Pénal Français. *Revue de Science Criminelle et de Droit Pénal Comparé*, 4: 711–54.

Pierson, Paul (1998). The Path to European Integration: A Historical–Institutionalist Analysis. In W. Sandholtz and A. Stone Sweet (ed.), *European Integration and Supranational Governance.* Oxford University Press.

Pillinger, Jane (1992). *Feminising the Market.* London: Macmillan.

Pizzorusso, Alessandro (1990). Italian and American Models of the Judiciary and of Judicial Review of Legislation: A Comparison of Recent Tendencies. *American Journal of Comparative Law*, 38: 373–86.

—— (1989). Constitutional Review and Legislation in Italy. In C. Landfried (ed.), *Constitutional Review and Legislation: An International Comparison.* Baden-Baden: Nomos.

—— (1985). The Italian Constitution: Implementation and Reform. *Jahrbuch des Öffentlichen Rechts der Gegenwart*, 34: 105–21.

—— and Emanuele Rossi (1995). Révision de la Constitution et Justice Constitutionnelle: Italie. *Annuaire International de Justice Constitutionnelle 1994*, X: 133–43.

——, Vigoriti,V. and Certoma, G. Leroy (1984). The Constitutional Review of Legislation in Italy. *Civil Justice Quarterly*, 3: 311–38.

Plötner, Jens (1998). Report on France. In A-M. Slaughter, J. H. H. Weiler, and A. Stone Sweet (ed.), *The European Courts and National Courts: Doctrine and Jurisprudence.* Oxford: Hart.

Pollack, Mark (1998). The Engines of Integration? Supranational Autonomy and Influence in the European Union. In W. Sandholtz and A. Stone Sweet (ed.), *European Integration and Supranational Governance.* Oxford University Press.

Polsby, Nelson (1975). Legislatures. In N. Polsby and F. I. Greenstein (ed.), *Handbook of Political Science.* Reading, MA: Addison Wesley.

Ponthoreau, Marie-Claire (1991). L'Article 2 de la Constitution Italienne et la Concrétisation de Droits Non-Écrits. *Annuaire International de Justice Constitutionnelle 1989*, V: 97–13.

Powell, Walter M. and Paul J. Dimaggio (ed.) (1991). *The New Institutionalism in Organizational Analysis.* Chicago, IL: University of Chicago Press.

Prechal, Sacha and Noreen Burrows (1990). *Gender Discrimination Law of the European Community.* Aldershot, UK: Gower–Dartmouth.

Prützel-Thomas, Monika (1993). The Abortion Issue and the Federal Constitutional Court. *German Politics*, 2: 467–84.

Quint, Peter E. (1989). Free Speech and Private Law in German Constitutional Theory. *Maryland Law Review*, 48: 247–347.

Renoux, Thierry S. (1994). Le Conseil Constitutionnel et le Pouvoir Judiciare en France et dans le Modèle Européen de Contrôle de Constitutionnalité des Lois: De la Diversité des Institutions à l'Unité du Droit. *Revue Internationale de Droit Comparé*, 3: 891–9.

—— and Michel de Villiers (1994). *Code Constitutionnel.* Paris: Litec.

Ress, Georg (1995). République Fédérale d'Allemagne. *Annuaire International de Justice Constitutionnelle 1993*, IX: 205–32.

Rivers, Julian (1994). Stemming the Flood of Constitutional Complaints in Germany. *Public Law:* 553–63.

Rohde, David W. and Harold J. Spaeth (1976). *Supreme Court Decision Making.* San Francisco, CA: Freeman.

Rosenberg, Shawn W. (1995). Against Neoclassical Political Economy: A Political Psychological Critique. *Political Psychology*, 16: 95–136.

Roselli, Orlando (1994). Corte Costituzionale: Verso la 'Dissenting Opinion?' *Quaderni Costituzionali*, 3: 513–24.

Rubio Llorente, Francisco (1995). Révision de la Constitution et Justice Constitutionnelle: Espagne. *Annuaire International de Justice Constitutionnelle 1994*, X: 75–81.

—— (1991). La Igualdad en la Jurisprudencial de Tribunal Constitucional: Introducción. *Revista Española de Derecho Constitucional*, 11: 9–36.

—— (1988a). Constitutional Jurisdiction as Law-making. In A. Pizzorusso (ed.), *Law in the Making.* Berlin: Springer.

—— (1988b). La Jurisdicción Constitucional como Forma de Creación de Derecho. *Revista Española de Derecho Constitucional*, 22: 9–51.

Sala Sanchez, Pascual (1994). La Delimitación de Funciones Entre las Jurisdicciones Constitucional y Ordinaria en la Protección de Derechos Fundamentales. *Actualidad Jurídica Aranzadi*, IV, 12 September.

Sánchez Morón, Miguel (1986). Le Système de Protection des Droits Fondamentaux et Libertés Publiques en Espagne. *Jahrbuch des Öffentlichen Rechts der Gegenwart*, 35: 143–68.

Sandholtz, Wayne (1998). The Emergence of a Supranational Telecommunications Regime. In W. Sandholtz and A. Stone Sweet (ed.), *European Integration and Supranational Governance.* Oxford University Press.

—— (1996). Membership Matters: Limits to the Functional Approach to European Institutions. *Journal of Common Market Studies*, 34: 403–30.

—— (1993). Choosing Union: Monetary Politics and Maastricht. *International Organization*, 47: 1–39.

—— and Alec Stone Sweet (ed.) (1998). *European Integration and Supranational Governance.* Oxford University Press.

Sandholtz, Wayne and John Zysman (1989). 1992: Recasting the European Bargain. *World Politics*, 42: 95–128.

Schenke, Wolf-Rüdiger (1986). Die Subsidiarität der Verfassungsbeschwerde gegen Gesetze. *Neue Juristische Wochenschrift,* **39**: 1451–1514.

Schlink, Bernhard (1993). German Constitutional Culture in Transition. *Cardozo Law Review,* **14**: 711–36.

Schmitt, Carl (1958). Das Reichsgericht als Hüter der Verfassung. *Verfassungsrechliche Aufsätze.* Berlin: Duncker & Humboldt.

Segal, Jeffrey A. and Harold J. Spaeth (1993). *The Supreme Court and the Attitudinal Model.* New York: Cambridge University Press.

Seventh Conference of Constitutional Courts (1989). La Justice Constitutionnelle dans le Cadre des Pouvoirs de l'État. *Annuaire International de Justice Constitutionnelle 1987,* **III**: 15–221.

Shapiro, Martin, J. (1992). The European Court of Justice. In A. M. Sbragia (ed.), *Euro-politics.* Washington, DC: Brookings Institution.

—— (1991). The Conseil Constitutionnel and the Capacity for Constitutional Deliberation of Legislatures. *Tocqueville Review,* **12**: 3–20.

—— (1988). *Who Guards the Guardians: Judicial Control of Administration.* Athens, GA: University of Georgia.

—— (1980). *Courts: A Comparative and Political Analysis.* Chicago, IL: University of Chicago Press.

—— (1965). *Law and Politics of the Supreme Court: New Approaches in Political Jurisprudence.* London: Free Press.

—— and Alec Stone (ed.) (1994*a*). Special Issue: The New Constitutional Politics of Europe. *Comparative Political Studies,* **26**.

—— and Alec Stone (1994*b*). Introduction: The New Constitutional Politics. *Comparative Political Studies,* **26**: 397–420.

Singer, Michael (1982). The Constitutional Court of the German Federal Republic: Jurisdiction over Individual Complaints. *International and Comparative Law Quarterly,* **31**: 331–56.

Slaughter, Anne-Marie, Alec Stone Sweet, and Joseph Weiler (ed.) (1998). *The European Courts and National Courts: Doctrine and Jurisprudence.* Oxford: Hart.

Smith, Rogers (1988). Political Jurisprudence, the 'New Institutionalism', and the Future of Public Law. *American Political Science Review,* **82**: 89–109.

Spanish Report (1992). Eighth Conference of Constitutional Courts. La Hiérarchie des Normes Constitutionnelles et sa Fonction dans la Protection des Droits Fondamentaux. *Annuaire International de Justice Constitutionnelle 1990,* **XIII**: 99–130.

Stein, Eric (1981). Lawyers, Judges, and the Making of a Transnational Constitution. *American Journal of International Law,* **75**: 1–27.

Stith, Richard (1987). New Constitutional and Penal Theory in Spanish Abortion Law. *American Journal of Comparative Law,* **35**: 513–58.

Stone, Alec (1996). The Constitutional Council, Constitutional Politics and Malaise. In J. T. S. Keeler and M. Schain (ed.), *New Patterns of Public Policy in*

France: State Responses to Social Change and European Integration. New York: St. Martins.

—— (1994*a*). Judging Socialist Reform: The Politics of Coordinate Construction in France and Germany. *Comparative Political Studies*, 26: 443–69.

—— (1994*b*). What is a Supranational Constitution? An Essay in International Relations Theory. *Review of Politics*, 56: 441–74.

—— (1992*a*). *The Birth of Judicial Politics in France.* New York: Oxford University Press.

—— (1992*b*). Where Judicial Politics are Legislative Politics: The French Constitutional Council. *West European Politics*, 15: 29–49.

—— (1990). The Birth and Development of Abstract Review in Western Europe: Constitutional Courts and Policy-making in Western Europe. *Policy Studies Journal*, 19: 81–95.

—— (1989). In the Shadow of the Constitutional Council: The 'Juridicisation' of the Legislative Process in France. *West European Politics*, 12: 12–34.

Stone Sweet, Alec (1999). Judicialization and the Construction of Governance. *Comparative Political Studies*, 32: 147–84.

—— (1998*a*). Rules, Dispute Resolution, and Strategic Behavior: Reply to Vanberg. *Journal of Theoretical Politics*, 10: 327–38.

—— (1998*b*). Constitutional Dialogues in the European Community. In A-M. Slaughter, J. H. H. Weiler, and A. Stone Sweet (ed.), *The European Courts and National Courts: Doctrine and Jurisprudence.* Oxford: Hart.

—— (1997). The New GATT: Dispute Resolution and the Judicialization of the Trade Regime. In M. Volcansek (ed.), *Supranational Courts in a Political Context.* Gainesville, FL: University of Florida Press.

—— and Thomas Brunell (1998*a*). Constructing a Supranational Constitution: Dispute Resolution and Governance in the European Community. *American Political Science Review*, 92: 63–81.

—— —— (1998*b*). The European Court and the National Courts: A Statistical Analysis of Preliminary References, 1961–95. *Journal of European Public Policy*, 5: 66–97.

—— and James Caporaso (1998). From Free Trade to Supranational Polity: The European Court and Integration. In W. Sandholtz and A. Stone Sweet (ed.), *European Integration and Supranational Governance.* Oxford University Press.

—— and Wayne Sandholtz (1997). European Integration and Supranational Governance. *Journal of European Public Policy*, 4: 297–317.

Stumph, Harry P., Martin J. Shapiro, David J. Danelski, Austin Sarat, and David M. O'Brien (1983). Whither Political Jurisprudence? A Symposium. *Western Political Quarterly*, 36: 533–70.

Summers, Robert S. and Michele Taruffo (1991). Interpretation and Comparative Analysis. In D. N. MacCormick and R. S. Summers (ed.), *Interpreting Statutes: A Comparative Study.* Brookfield, VT: Dartmouth.

220 References

Table Ronde (1995). Révision de la Constitution et Justice Constitutionnelle. *Annuaire International de Justice Constitutionnelle 1994*, X: 27–282.

—— (1994). Les Méthodes de Travail des Juridictions Constitutionnelles. *Annuaire International de Justice Constitutionnelle 1992*, VIII: 163–311.

—— (1990). Les Juges Constitutionnels. *Annuaire International de Justice Constitutionnelle 1988*, IV: 80–227.

Tate, C. N. and T. Vallinder (ed.) (1995). *The Global Expansion of Judicial Power*. New York: New York University Press.

Teubner, Gunther (1987). Juridification: Concepts, Aspects, Limits, Solutions. In G. Teubner (ed.), *Juridification of Social Spheres: A Comparative Analysis in the Areas of Labor, Corporate, Antitrust and Social Welfare Law*. Berlin: de Gruyter.

—— and Alberto Febbrajo (ed.) (1992). Special Issue: State, Law and Economy as Autopoietic Systems. *European Yearbook of the Sociology of Law*. Milano: Giuffrè.

Thwaite, Gregory J. and Wolfgang Brehm (1994). German Privacy and Defamation Law: The Right to Publish in the Shadow of the Right to Human Dignity. *European Intellectual Property Review*, 8: 336–51.

Tilford, Roger (1981). The State, University Reform and the *Berufsverbot*. *West European Politics*, 4: 149–65.

Tomás y Valiente, Francisco (1994). Juzgar, Arbitrar, Legislar. *El Pais*, 11 February 1994.

Tribe, Laurence H. (1988). *American Constitutional Law*. Mineola, NY: Foundation Press.

—— (1985). *Constitutional Choices*. Cambridge, MA: Harvard University Press.

Troper, Michel (1995). Constitutional Justice and Democracy. *Cardozo Law Review*, 17: 273–97.

—— (1994). *Pour une Théorie Juridique de l'État*. Paris: Leviathan.

Tsebelis, George (1990). *Nested Games: Rational Choice in Comparative Politics*. Berkeley, CA: University of California Press.

Tushnet, Mark (1988). *Red, White and Blue: A Critical Analysis of Constitutional Law*. Cambridge, MA: Harvard University Press.

—— (1986). Critical Legal Studies: An Introduction to its Origins and Underpinnings. *Journal of Legal Education*, 36: 505–17.

United Nations (1995). Spain. In *Abortion Policies: A Global Review, 1992–1995*. New York: United Nations.

Vanberg, Georg (1998a). Abstract Judicial Review, Legislative Bargaining, and Policy Compromise. *Journal of Theoretical Politics*, 3: 299–326.

—— (1998b). Reply to Stone Sweet. *Journal of Theoretical Politics*, 3: 339–46

van Zyl Smit, Dirk (1992). Is Life Imprisonment Constitutional? The German Experience. *Public Law*, 2: 263–78.

Vedel, Georges (1992). Schengen et Maastricht: À Propos de la Décision no. 91-294 DC du Conseil Constitutionnel du 25 Juillet 1991. *Revue Française de Droit Administratif*, 8: 173–84.

—— (1988). Le Conseil Constitutionnel, Gardien du Droit Positif ou Défenseur de la Transcendance des Droits de l'homme. *Pouvoirs*, 45: 149–59.

Velázquez Vidal, Christina (1994). The Spanish Constitutional Tribunal and the State of the Autonomies. (Unpublished manuscript)

Volcansek, Mary L. (in press). *Constitutional Politics in Italy*. London: Macmillan.

—— (1994). Political Power and Judicial Review in Italy. *Comparative Political Studies*, 26: 492–509.

—— (ed.) (1992). Special Issue on Judicial Politics in Western Europe. *West European Politics*, 15.

—— (1990). Decision-making Italian Style: The New Code of Criminal Procedure. *West European Politics*, 13: 33–45.

Watkin, Thomas G. (1997). *The Italian Legal Tradition*. Aldershot, UK: Ashgate.

Weber, A. (1987). Le Contrôle Juridicitionnel de la Constitutionnalité des Lois dans les Pays d'Europe Occidentale. *Annuaire International de Justice Constitutionnelle 1985*, I: 39–74.

Weiler, Hans N. (1985). Equal Protection, Legitimacy, and the Legalization of Education: The Role of the Federal Constitutional Court in West Germany. *The Review of Politics*, 47: 66–91.

Weiler, Joseph H. H. (1995). The State 'über alles': Demos, Telos and the German Maastricht Decision. In O. Due, M. Lutter, and J. Schwarze (ed.), *Festschrift für Ulrich Everling*. Baden-Baden: Nomos.

—— (1994). A Quiet Revolution: The European Court and Its Interlocutors. *Comparative Political Studies*, 26: 510–34.

—— (1991). The Transformation of Europe. *Yale Law Journal*, 100: 2403–83.

—— (1986). Eurocracy and Distrust. *Washington Law Review*, 61: 1103–42.

—— (1981). The Community System: The Dual Character of Supranationalism. *Yearbook of European Law*, 1: 268–306.

—— and Nicolas J. S. Lockhart (1995a). 'Taking Rights Seriously' Seriously: The European Court and its Fundamental Rights Jurisprudence—Part I. *Common Market Law Review*, 31: 579–98.

—— —— (1995b). 'Taking Rights Seriously' Seriously: The European Court and its Fundamental Rights Jurisprudence—Part II. *Common Market Law Review*, 32: 579–627.

Whiteford, Elaine A. (1996). Occupational Pensions and European Law: Clarity at Last? In T. K. Hervey and D. O'Keefe (ed.), *Sex Equality Law in the European Union*. New York: Wiley.

Wildavsky, Aaron (1987). Choosing Preferences by Constructing Institutions: A Cultural Theory of Preference Formation. *American Political Science Review*, 81: 3–21.

Youngs, Raymond (1996). Freedom of Speech and the Protection of Democracy: The German Approach. *Public Law*, 225–34.

Zagrebelsky, Gustavo (1988). La Doctrine du 'Droit Vivant.' *Annuaire International de Justice Constitutionnelle 1986*, II: 169–75.

—— (1981). Objet et Portée de la Protection des Droits Fondamentaux: Cour Constitutionnelle italienne. *Revue Internationale de Droit Comparé*, 33: 511–77.

Zanon, Nicoló (1991). La Polémique entre Hans Kelsen et Carl Schmitt sur la Justice Consitutionnelle. *Annuaire International de Justice Constitutionnelle 1989*, V: 177–89.

Zeidler, Wolfgang (1987). The Federal Constitutional Court of the Federal Republic of Germany: Decisions on the Constitutionality of Legal Norms. *Notre Dame Law Review*, 62: 504–25.

INDEX